MONITORING THE  NEWS

The Christian Science Center's 11-acre campus in Boston's Back Bay. Clockwise from upper left corner of the campus: The Publishing Society; the long, low Broadcast Center (Colonnade Building); the 25-story Church Administration Building; the 110 foot reflecting pool; the Sunday School Building at the bottom; the Mother Church domed annex and original Church at the center. Photograph courtesy First Church of Christ, Scientist.

MONITORING THE  NEWS

The Brilliant Launch and Sudden Collapse of The Monitor Channel

Susan Bridge

M.E. Sharpe
Armonk, New York
London, England

Library of Congress Cataloging-in-Publication Data

Bridge, Susan, 1939
Monitoring the news : the brilliant launch and sudden collapse of The Monitor Channel /
Susan Bridge
p. cm.
Includes bibliographical references and index.
ISBN 0–7656–0315–2 (hardcover : alk. paper)
1. Monitor Channel (Television network)   2. Television broadcasting of news—United
States.   I. Title.
PN4888.T4B75   1998
070.1′95—dc21   98–10021
CIP

Printed in the United States of America

The paper used in this publication meets the minimum requirements of
American National Standard for Information Sciences—
Permanence of Paper for Printed Library Materials,
ANSI Z 39.48-1984.

∞

BM (c)   10   9   8   7   6   5   4   3   2   1

To the memory of

John Gardiner Bridge Jr.
1940–1997

A Wonderful Brother

Table of Contents

List of Figures

Foreword

Sue Bridge has responded to an increasingly urgent voice heard by more and more "journalistic patriots." And she has responded in the form of a very interesting, at times even suspenseful, drama, a drama begun by seismic changes in competition and technology and often troubling changes in the media.

This is a story of a relatively quick beginning and a very quick and sad end to The Monitor Channel, the television offspring and new media extension of the *Christian Science Monitor* begun in the late 1980s. The *Monitor* was responding to a fact: TV is the dominant news source. But most importantly, it was a TV test of the *Monitor*'s journalistic credo first articulated in 1908: "To injure no man, but bless all mankind."

"To injure no man, but bless all mankind"; few journalists today would even recognize those eight words as representing a journalistic ideal. This obsolescence has given rise to that "urgent voice." This book, against a background of ideals, human strengths and weaknesses, and "attack journalism," concentrates our mind both on the questions we must face and on some possible answers.

My first concentrated thought about today's journalism and its implications came while I was Chairman of the FCC from 1988 to 1993. I was often asked to intervene where the First Amendment to our Constitution said I was not to do so. Some thought "if TV networks need to get straightened out, that must be the job of the FCC."

While generally complaints about TV news were quite personal, an overriding issue began to haunt me: now that TV news was the principal source of news, and easily the most dramatic source, should its leaders feel a new responsibility? Shall they spend more of their efforts on what people need to know at the risk of spending less time on what they want to know? The importance of this issue to the nation is clear: in a broadly representative form of government, the leadership will ultimately be no better than those it represents.

ix

Ironically, I was in a position from which I might make some difference, but I was quite specifically restrained. The First Amendment to our Constitution did not contemplate, in fact it expressly prohibits, government efforts to alter speech. In the final analysis, the First Amendment is what makes this book such an important contribution. For you see, it is not unusual to read a book with various prescriptions requiring government action (generally rationalized on the basis of the government owning the airwaves); while the authors of such books are undoubtedly well-meaning, their prescriptions could be easily challenged by a first-year law student.

Sue Bridge refuses to be drawn into the sophomoric. Her analysis is free of cant and myth. She is that rarest of writers, an excellent social critic who both understands and approves of business. While she is reluctant to conclude that there is a good business in vigorous day-to-day TV journalism, her analysis is thoughtful and, at times, even supplies a bit of hope.

I am also hopeful, but that's my nature. I just can't see this grand experiment in self-government and self-regulation failing. I think I see in our nation the vision, the adaptability, and maybe even the technologies that will respond to an increasingly widespread view that much of "today's TV journalism" ill-serves a representative democracy.

At some level, however, business attitude and public aptitude also need to be considered. Big companies don't aspire to keep people uninformed on the issues of a public policy; companies do strive, however, to earn a return on investment. The public's aptitude is quite important.

What does the U.S. public want? Has Hollywood's fetish with "visual energy" destroyed the public's appetite for complicated stories that are long on "citizenship" and short on "entertainment?" Does today's TV viewer's visual orientation mean that pictures are always trump? Or, with the miniaturization of public issues has the public simply "changed channels"?

Regardless of the oscillation of important news and the frequent trivialization of the news genre with "tabloid journalism," an independent and thoughtful fourth estate must somehow survive and remain healthy. What we need are at least some widely available news sources that strive daily to honor journalism's first principles: truth, fairness, balance, and depth. And these sources must not be bland; good journalism can have an edge. The edge, however, should come from good writing and production, not from personal bias or pandering. Bland doesn't sell, and if it doesn't sell, it will fail. In a healthy democracy, an informed elite, while important, cannot function as a surrogate for the masses. The more people understand how the world works, the more likely it is that human effort will result in accomplishment.

In the author's "Perspective" chapter, she talks about the "risk" of good journalism. She discusses the tension between "quality and profits." She observes that "An interesting common thread runs though many of these stories, does it not? Many of the important sources of news and public information in the United States today, some of which are also commercial successes as mature businesses and some not, would not exist at all, if the market as commonly used to gauge investment and risk were the only arbiter of events." She goes on to comment on the importance of a strong-willed visionary with considerable autonomy and a lot of money, whose motives push him/her toward the "first principles of journalism."

The United States, when measured by the standards of an historian, is an incubator for visionaries. Freedom and capitalism are its progenitors. The latter produces fortunes, while the former frequently enables and ennobles. TV journalism that is true to "first principles" will require patient capital and will be a noble undertaking. It will, as tabloid journalism, honor a human impulse, but it will be the opposite one.

It could also be a part of a very interesting strategic marketing plan. How are General Electric, CBS, Disney, News Corporation, and Time-Warner going to differentiate themselves? Jack Welch, Michael Eisner, and Ted Turner, in particular, just might have the cash and viscera to try something ennobling. And I should add that in this case, ennoblement will come not from personal views of how the world should work, but from a commitment to the "first principles."

There might also be a new role for the Associated Press. The AP should consider developing a service that strives to present news in an historical context. One of today's problems is that many TV journalists cannot put news in more than a several-year context.

As I look further to the future, I am a bit more sanguine than the author about the potential for successive generations of the Internet's World Wide Web.

Today's Web is basically flat. While it is an extraordinarily fertile place to find information about almost anything and from everywhere, technical limitations do not allow animating the news and information as TV does. It is also available principally by computer, giving it limited reach beyond an information elite. These circumstances will, however, change rather quickly.

In the next several years, we are going to see the development of a sensory-led new interactive medium. Text, graphics, still images, animations, video, and sound will be blended by a new artistry which will serve up compelling news packages. Any of these news packages will be drawn from an ever-wider universe of sources.

Computer software will allow us to assemble personalized news shows. In this new medium, arbiters of good journalism could themselves develop a software metric for those who wanted "first principles" honored, a sort of "seal of approval." The software would then assemble informative news packages drawn from recommended sources and blend these reports with local news and information.

Sue Bridge, ever the realist, warns against such hopeful theories. She quite bluntly states: "To assert that the loss of a Monitor Channel will somehow be compensated for in some vaguely automatic way through the evolution of new technologies for delivery or through the actions of the market alone, is to indulge in magical thinking."

I agree. Whatever happens, if it is a discernible step toward "first principles," it will not be automatic. It will be informed by vision and courage. It will succeed or fail based on keen market insight, tenacity, and sound economics. And, in the final analysis, it will succeed or fail if painful events alter the public's appetite. I am confident of the latter and I am vaguely hopeful of the former. I am, however, certain, that *Monitoring the News* will have contributed to the cause.

Alfred C. Sikes
President, Hearst New Media and Technology

Introduction

All life forms depend for survival on getting appropriate information. Without relevant, intelligible, widely disseminated information to guide individual and collective action, even human society cannot hope to survive and thrive.

In today's complex world, however, quality news and public information is so expensive to compile, update, and deliver, that if it is well done, the news component in mass communications is unlikely to be robustly profitable on its own. Gathering and sorting a cacophony of facts, subjecting the facts to skillful in-depth analysis, then moving on to wise, broad understanding is a long process, and a costly one. This is true whether the medium is print, radio, television, or the Internet. And it is most true—paradoxically and perniciously—for video-based vehicles such as television, the medium that, for three decades now and counting, the general public has found most compelling.

Plainly put, given the present mass communications market, resources can almost always be more gainfully invested elsewhere, such as in sports or entertainment programming or, for that matter, in energy futures. But if news and public information is almost prohibitively expensive to compile, update, and deliver, who will pay? At the turn of the century, the news business is heading at top speed into a dangerously narrow pass with the rest of society following close behind.

What kinds of motives can prompt responsible corporate decision-makers to produce quality news and public information in a business environment this unreliable? Because the stakes for society are so high, it behooves us to examine carefully both the economics of television news (and, by implication, any video-based news service) and the wellsprings of non-economic behavior—whether they be government regulation, individual ego, glamour, altruism, or something else.

If what follows were only the story of how one of the twentieth century's most respected news organizations, divided within and under assault from a local competitor, was brought summarily to its knees, it would still be of genuine interest. But the Monitor story is also a prism through which to examine the complicated tangle of forces, from personal to structural, that determine what we will know—and what we will really understand—as we struggle collectively to adapt in the post-modern world of tomorrow.

The Arena

The Monitor Channel, a high-concept twenty-four-hour-a-day cable television network of global news and in-depth public information, was programmed and distributed by Monitor Television, Inc., a wholly-owned for-profit subsidiary of the First Church of Christ, Scientist in Boston. Launched in May 1991 after two years in development, The Monitor Channel was widely praised and closely watched throughout the public communications industry. Thirteen months later, in June 1992, following considerable public controversy and ten weeks of automated re-runs, The Monitor Channel went dark.

The human drama that follows was played out against a background of institutions and markets shifting in bewildering ways with gathering speed, pushed from one side by changing technology, pushed from another by changing public preferences. For those men and women most directly involved, much was at stake: conflicting visions of what journalistic excellence would mean in such a setting, as well as considerable personal pride and large potential material loss and gain.

Until the 1980s, the Christian Science Publishing Society's franchise in the world of journalism rested on the strong reputation of its internationally distributed daily newspaper, the *Christian Science Monitor*. By then, though—like much of the newspaper industry—the old *Monitor* had been in gradual decline for years and was little by little losing its public and its advertising base to electronic media.

In the late 1980s, a group of bold reformers at the Publishing Society, backed by the Church Board, resolved to reenergize the *Monitor*'s fading franchise for thoughtful global journalism by diversifying into the new media that the public now favored including, at greatest expense, television. To do so, this visionary leadership brought together an eclectic, high-energy team of dedicated television professionals and old *Monitor* hands under the banner of excellence, to execute a plan that looked at the time to be eminently realistic: to modernize and reposition Monitor journalism for the new information age.

The Role of Participant-Observer

This writer was one of several hundred outside professionals attracted by Monitor television's promise of adventure and the quest for excellence. I was there for two and a half years, eventually heading Monitor MultiMedia, a small division organized with an aggressively for-profit mandate to re-shape print and broadcast materials both for educational use and for the general market, including dissemination on the Internet. Like most of the newcomers, I was not a member of the Church that provides the philosophical underpinning for Monitor journalism's high standards. First trained and employed for many years as a social scientist, in the mid-1980s I cofounded and helped run a small regional cable television network for five years. With the benefit of this background, and with direct access, at least potentially, to all the major players in the Monitor drama, I found myself uniquely well placed to attempt to answer the many questions that hung over the rubble of the collapsed enterprise.

The Monitor Channel's sudden collapse was a loss for the American public. I am not a partisan of any individual or group in this story, but I am a passionate champion of the broad dissemination of quality public communications. My purpose here is to use the Monitor story to illustrate some important truths about the business of public communications, truths vital to our common well-being, as we carom into the next century.

Focusing the Big Question

Today's world is changing in unplanned and unanticipated ways at break-neck speed, and the rate of change seems to be accelerating. But is the gathering, analysis, and redistribution of information in our society working well enough to permit us, individually and collectively, to adapt to rapidly changing surroundings? Who will assign meaning to facts? Who will build wisdom and foresight into the global information infrastructure?

In the two short generations following World War II, the American public turned rapidly from print and radio to a video-based medium—tele-vision—for news and public information. As early as 1962, most of the public received more of its news and public information from television than from any other source. But what might constitute quality in the new medium was elusive, and from a strictly business perspective, even in the early years quality news and public affairs programming on television was never in and of itself an especially good investment.

A sudden turnover in corporate ownership in the mid-1980s at ABC, CBS, and NBC and continuing changes in information markets began systematically to debase such quality of information in television as existed. There were no villains. It was nobody's fault that entertainment made such fantastic money for a variety of reasons intrinsic to the product, and that for similar reasons high-quality public information did not and apparently could not make much, if any, money at all. By then, only Turner's CNN specializing in around-the-clock breaking news seemed likely to be a strong stand-alone business, and even there, investment had run into hundreds of millions of dollars, with break-even not—yet—a reality.

The Monitor Channel's several professionally prepared business plans showed break-even in five or six years following a net investment of about $100 million. If the Monitor's brand of in-depth journalism could be offered in a compelling and accessible television format that made money, like CNN's specialty in breaking news, this would be a watershed event for the electronic communications industry—and for society.

What Happened?

In the aftermath of The Monitor Channel's collapse, a *Rashomon*-like grab-bag of competing explanations were offered: perhaps the problem had been naiveté about the cable fraternity, or wild overspending, or a fatal confusion about corporate mission, or enemies within and without, or bad timing with respect to the economy. Most disheartening were the pronouncements from some sophisticated observers that, given the structure of information markets, the undertaking had been impossible from the outset.

The large question providing the impetus for a close look at the fate of The Monitor Channel is, thus:

> Can high-quality, global news and public information for television (or for other video-based media) be produced and distributed as a viable for-profit business proposition in today's information marketplace?

Holding the Focus

Strong, intelligent, charismatic individuals such as Jack Hoagland, Netty Douglass, Harvey Wood, and Kay Fanning who stood at center stage in the Monitor tragedy represented powerful social and economic forces, just as surely as if they had been sent by central casting to do so. These larger-than-life actors embodied the long-term, irreversible displacement of traditional print media by new print and electronic media and the indispensable roles of entrepreneurial vision, of authority to act, and of willingness to accept risk in meeting the future.

A dense nexus of other events surrounded the central drama of the launch and collapse of The Monitor Channel. While these are of legitimate interest to many participants and to some readers, they are not included prominently as part of the narrative. The most important omission is the story of the Publishing Society's other media enterprises: the weakened newspaper; MonitoRadio; the international shortwave network; and the handsome, cosmopolitan *World Monitor Magazine.* Several ancillary themes, such as the nature of the bitter divisions within the Christian Science community, the complexities of the Church's internal borrowings, or an accounting of Jack Hoagland's years of government service, are at least covered in extended notes.

Also lying beyond the scope of the present study is any full understanding of the *Boston Globe*'s protracted attack on the Monitor's media enterprise in the winter and spring of 1992. Here, I have concentrated on the public record only: what was published, what effect it had at the Publishing Society and elsewhere, and a brief description of what was known publicly about the *Globe*'s own formidable business challenges at the time.

Access and Acknowledgments

Despite my proximity to the action and familiarity with many of the principals, getting the access I needed to tell this story was hardly a foregone conclusion.

When the project was first broached in late March 1992, The Monitor Channel's top executives, Jack Hoagland and Netty Douglass, suggested that the proposed book be an "as told to" story from their perspective. Within twenty-four hours, they stepped aside and, subsequently, gave me full access to literally rooms full of their own unsorted business records, memos, chronologies, and correspondence covering the decade from 1982 to 1992. They also endured a dozen or so open-ended interviews over a two-and-a-half-year period, as well as numerous shorter queries about specific matters. I was often moved by their grace and fortitude in dealing with my questions: my need to know was of necessity intrusive, a bit like having an uninvited auditor in residence.

The man who acted as venture capitalist to the entrepreneurial team, Harvey Wood, Church Director from 1977 to 1992, also made himself available for several long, wide-ranging interviews and has remained available by phone throughout.

Additionally, among those deeply invested in the revolution at the Monitor who talked to me at length about their experiences were Paul Beckelheimer, Marilyn Berryman, Lincoln Bloomfield, Tim Burditt, Lyn Chamberlin, Peggy Charren, David Cook, William Bruce Dredge, Earl Foell, Pete Gatseos, Scott Goodfellow, Gail Harris, Gordon Imrie, Harry King, Frank McGill, Shepley Metcalf, Richard A. Nenneman, Malcolm Netburn, Mary O'Neill, Sandi Padnos, John Parrott, Willis Peligian, Gail Pierson, Schuyler Sackett, Mort Sahl, Barbara Bellafiore Sanden, Sandy Socolow, Florence Tambone, Peter Tonge, Judy Umlas, and Danny Wilson. John Parrott shared his six-year chronicle of events. Sandi Padnos sent me a number of useful documents, including the original detailed media strategy for The Monitor Channel, and Barbara Bellafiore Sanden sent half a dozen cartons of her meticulously organized records to Boston for my use.

Although Sid Topol, former Vice Chairman of the board of Monitor Television and, after Jack Hoagland's resignation, in charge of the last few weeks of the desperate search for outside investors, never consented to an interview, he was helpful in three separate informal conversations. *World Monitor News* anchor John Hart, an articulate in-house critic who resigned over what he felt were matters of principle, flatly refused to talk. Bill Chesleigh, Hart's executive producer, did not return calls.

For the better part of a year, the incumbent Church directors, who reluctantly moved to close down The Monitor Channel in the spring of 1992, ignored my letter telling them a book was in progress, then communicated that it was their intention not to cooperate. As the project moved forward, however, the Directors changed to a constructive, albeit meticulously arms-length, posture.

The late Don Bowersock, then Managing Treasurer, permitted two long interviews, and Board Chairman Virginia Harris made it easy for me to talk at length to key current employees, notably former Broadcast Editor David Cook. The Directors also verified expenditures I had compiled using other sources and, on one occasion, supplied an important confidential document that the *Globe* had obtained, but I had not. Virginia Harris and long-time Church director John Selover answered some questions informally at a brief breakfast meeting. When I felt I needed to follow up information obtained at the offices of the Massachusetts Attorney General on the Church's controversial internal borrowings, Church counsel Gary Jones arranged for me to meet with the Church's outside counsel in these matters, and he later also responded to a further written inquiry from me.

Those in the cable television industry who consented to be interviewed included Discovery Channel executives Ruth Otte and Greg Moyer, the *Providence Journal*'s Steve Hamblett and Trygvie Myhren, and cable company TCI's Jedd Palmer.

Executives at CNN, including Kitsy Bassett Riggell, gave me access to

previously unpublished data on CNN's early years that were essential to
establishing whether The Monitor Channel's start-up costs were reasonable
or, as some critics claimed, badly out of control. These detailed data from
CNN form the book's empirical foundation, the baseline against which the
costs incurred in launching The Monitor Channel are evaluated.

Others who were especially helpful include Dennis Liebowitz, Senior
Vice President at Donaldson, Lufkin, Jenrette, and the late David Glickstein
of Tendrel Associates. Bill Clark, Jack Hoagland's son-in-law and a Senior
Vice President at Fleet Financial, answered questions at length and supplied
a number of important documents pertaining to Monitor Television's search
for equity participation from other cable players. Happy Sprague Rowe of
Tucker Anthony supplied key background information on various media
companies at several points. When I was looking for data from the news
divisions of the three broadcast networks, the *New Yorker*'s Ken Auletta
provided me with contacts. Professor Robert Hilliard of Emerson College,
formerly a member of the Carter Administration's Federal Communications
Commission (FCC), commented extensively on Chapter 1.

A speech given by FCC Chair Alfred C. Sikes in March 1992, and
summarized in *Broadcasting Magazine* a few weeks later, gave voice to
what I knew: that some high up in the industry shared the general concerns
for quality in news and public information that were prompting me to
undertake a book on The Monitor Channel. Al Sikes has since given me
important encouragement as the project moved toward completion.

Several active opponents of The Monitor Channel were personally gracious, as well as generous with their time. They were also sources of important information, including extensive written records documenting the
events in question and explaining their opposition. These include David
Anable, Katherine Fanning, Stephen Gottschalk, Judge Thomas P. Griesa,
and Sara Terry. Attorney Carol Swenson, former general counsel for Stanford University, shared her views on the University's decision in the fall of
1991 to dispute a large bequest whose trustees had named the Church as
beneficiary.

Several good people have allowed me to impose on them as readers.
Early on, I asked long-time Monitor insiders Earl Foell and Dick Nenneman
to read each chapter in draft for fairness and accuracy. Six good friends who
represent the general public I hope to reach gave important encouragement
and stylistic advice along the way: Phyllis Miriam, Lawrence Locke, David
and Kitty Rush, and Stephen and Barbara Roop.

Abundant thanks are also due to the second-floor staff at the Kirstein
Business Branch of the Boston Public Library, to Trevor Johnson in the
Boston Athenaeum's reference division, and to Polly McGee and Joyce

McMillan at the Publishing Society's reference library, for their unstinting professional assistance. Carol Douglass in the Church Directors' office was an efficient and cheerful liaison with her employers and others.

Nor would thanks be complete without mentioning my former colleague Geoff Barss's expert professional assistance in preparing the manuscript for publication.

Finally, M.E. Sharpe's Peter Coveney proved the sort of editor most authors can only dream of in today's publishing world. Peter brought an intense, sophisticated, long-term interest in the business of communications to this project, then took time from a demanding schedule for that crucial old-fashioned close read. His suggestions for edits were substantive and stylistic, big and small, and did much to help make the sometimes difficult subject matter more accessible to a general readership.

This project would have foundered at several points, without moral and material support from friends and family members. Such debts are probably best discharged, as they were incurred, with private expressions of my gratitude. .

MONITORING
THE  NEWS

Chapter 1

The Changing Business of News

1920–1985: The tilt of the field in the era of broadcast news

> I believe television is going to test the modern world, and that
> in this new opportunity to see beyond the range of our vision
> we shall discover either a new and unbearable disturbance of
> the general peace or a saving radiance in the sky. We shall
> stand or fall by television—of that I am quite sure.
>
> —*E.B. White, 1938*[1]

The Tilt of the Playing Field in the Television News Business

In 1982, visionary, reform-minded Jack Hoagland accepted the position of Manager of the Christian Science Publishing Society. By early 1985, when, under Hoagland's leadership, the Publishing Society began to make its first serious moves into radio and television, electronic media had dominated public communications in the United States for four decades. American adults overwhelmingly preferred to get news and public information from radio and TV—especially TV. For the past twenty-five years, the general public had been telling pollsters that for them television news was more credible than all other media. In 1985, after nearly eighty years of service to the public in the United States and abroad through a distinguished daily newspaper, top management and the publishers of the *Christian Science Monitor* had begun in earnest to confront the realities of this historic shift in the communications marketplace.[2]

The Monitor was not alone in its dilemma. By 1985, many traditional publishers and print journalists lived in quiet desperation or in denial. Beginning with public acclaim for radio's gripping coverage of World War II, broadcast live daily from Europe and the Pacific, the once-familiar playing field for those in the news business had gradually heaved up to a sharp tilt. The *Christian Science Monitor*—and many other newspapers and news magazines—found themselves facing uphill.

By 1985, the First Church of Christ, Scientist in Boston, the newspaper's owner, had made quality journalism its distinctive vocation for nearly eighty years. Neither merger with another newspaper nor buy-out was an option—nor, for reasons of deeply held principle, was any editorial shift away from the Monitor's balanced, humanitarian emphasis on global news. Shutting down the news operation entirely could not be entertained either, yet the status quo was becoming intolerable. By 1985, the Pulitzer-winning newspaper had been losing circulation for years and, as staffers put it, was clearly "more respected than read." Annual deficits had grown to nearly $20 million a year, with no end in sight.[3]

After extensive analysis of the print market and considerable soul-searching, key members of the Monitor's management team resolved—at first cautiously, then more and more boldly—to diversify their journalistic mission into electronic media. Eventually, the Monitor's venture into electronic journalism would lead them to invest heavily in a highly controversial, big-ticket item, a full twenty-four-hour television channel. The Monitor Channel won the respect of a skeptical cable industry faster than any knowledgeable observer had predicted and seemed to be building an audience. It broadcast nationally only a little more than a year, however, from April 1991 to June 1992, when it was shut down in an atmosphere charged with innuendoes of fiscal mismanagement, or worse.

Ten years of bold experiment came to an abrupt end. No man or woman who entered the fray escaped without sustaining serious injuries. Yet from the beginning, the Monitor story was less a struggle among strong-willed individuals than one of institutional bias, technological change, and shifting power in the communications business. The bitter conflicts over the Monitor's attempt to become a significant player in television news between 1985 and 1992 took many forms, some of which may remain forever cloaked in mystery, but at one level or another, every personal rivalry resonated with institutional conflicts of interest, disagreements about news values, and the imperatives of broad historic change.

The Monitor had entered a market for television news shaped by decades of changing technology, a communications industry born and bred in hardball competition; dramatic shifts in the public's preferences from print to electronic media, never to be reversed; and ambivalent government over-sight of the quality of broadcast content. That fraction of the typical broad-cast day known as "the news" moved from its early status as an all-but-legally mandated public service into thirty years and more of charmed existence as a high-prestige loss leader. Then times changed: by the 1980s, the news was increasingly required to compete as a commodity with other communications products, and so, increasingly, news and public information became available to viewers only in such quantities and quali-ties as were most profitable (or least unprofitable) in the very short run.

To understand fully the collapse of The Monitor Channel in 1992, it is essential to place events in historical context. A brief look back—both at the evolution of the electronic news business and at the history of Monitor journalism—will help measure the tilt of the playing field and will illustrate such rules as exist in this very rough game.

The Original Bargain: Public Airwaves in Exchange for Public Service

By the mid-1920s, radio—historically television's training camp—had al-ready become a mass communications medium, with a free-for-all of entre-preneurs, technology buffs and evangelists competing with each others' signals for audiences. Under presidents Coolidge, Hoover, and Roosevelt, there was broad consensus in Congress and within the executive branch that industry players should, to some extent, be required to serve the public as a condition for doing business. Proposals to dedicate as much as 25 percent of the radio spectrum to noncommercial educational uses were given serious consideration, then put aside.[4]

The Federal Radio Act of 1927 set forth a system for allocating frequen-cies, creating some badly needed order in the unruly new industry. Under Roosevelt, the Communications Act of 1934 gathered federal oversight of the new communications technologies into a single, permanent Federal Communications Commission. These early government initiatives were key to stimulating growth: with a specific bandwidth assigned to each broad-caster, with clear procedures for maintaining technical standards and for granting licenses and license renewals in place, the necessary conditions were created for a rapidly expanding and highly lucrative new electronic communications market. The understanding reached in 1934 has remained in force, with periodic amendments, for more than six decades—through radio's distinguished service during World War II, on through broadcast television's meteoric ascendancy in the 1950s and 1960s, and right into the late 1980s, when cable became king.[5]

Who Should Communicate What, to Whom, and Why?

The premise underlying this early legislation, a premise upon which all subsequent rules were posited, was simple and ethically clear. Commercial broadcasters could make money using a scarce good that belonged to the public—the airwaves—and in return the young industry would deliver an unspecified mix of programs serving the "public interest, convenience, or necessity." Beyond providing communications in times of crisis, it was understood that local and national news and public affairs as well as educational programs would meet the public interest requirement intended under the law, even though in the final text this was nowhere spelled out.

Established news organizations saw the development of radio as a vehicle for news and public affairs communications as an intolerable competitive threat. The American Newspaper Publishers Association immediately sensed a challenge to its franchise, and from the mid-1920s they worked openly and behind the scenes to block radio from gaining a foothold in the news business or from having a legal right to accept advertising. When one of the new industry's young founding fathers, CBS owner William Paley, moved aggressively to add a news component to the line-up of his shaky network, the newspapers acted directly and in concert to derail his operation.[6]

Paley had made plans to broadcast election night results in 1932, but the newspapers forced the wire services to cancel their agreement to feed CBS the results as they came in—only to have the wire services make results available surreptitiously. In 1933, Paley put together a news service for broadcasters only, with bureaus and stringers around the country. The counterattack from the print media threatened to be devastating: first, the newspapers declared they would drop free listings of all commercially sponsored radio programs from their pages. Then, again using their leverage with the wire services, which depended on newspapers for most of their business, the publishers exacted terms intended to cripple radio's ability to deliver the news forever.

Known as the Biltmore Agreement, the 1934 "compromise" among the newspaper publishers, the radio networks, and the wire services placed drastic limits on how much a specially created news service would release to network newsrooms (bulletins of no more that thirty words) and on how much and when radio was free to broadcast the news (two five-minute newscasts daily, timed to appear well after the papers' morning and evening editions, respectively). Radio networks could not engage in independent newsgathering and could not accept advertisements for newscasts. CBS and NBC both acquiesced to these terms, resolving to concentrate on entertainment. Local affiliates and independent stations, however, were not bound by the Biltmore Agreement, and within two years, the sheer force of radio's expanding market rendered the newspaper publishers' attempt to block radio's growth as a news medium moot. The national radio networks moved back into the news business.[7]

Radio journalism came of age in a blaze of patriotic glory during World War II. Newsmen from CBS and NBC broadcast back to the United States live from around the globe—improvising, unself-consciously setting precedents, and, like their print colleagues, risking their lives and sometimes dying to get the job done. Martin Agronsky, Bill Dunn, Eric Sevareid, Charles Collingwood, Howard K. Smith, William Shirer, and Ed Murrow—authentic glamor attached to the courageous men whose voices became an immediate human link between the soldiers in Europe, North Africa, and the Pacific, and the citizens at home.[8]

Radio was a compelling medium in wartime, and those heady years changed the news business in the United States forever. By 1945, 88 percent of American households owned a radio, and a majority of the public already depended on the new medium for some or all of its news. Broadcast industry profits, robust in 1939, were boosted by a 90–percent exemption of advertising expenses from a wartime excess profits tax. Newspaper ad revenues were held down by wartime shortages of newsprint, and in 1943, radio's advertising dollars surpassed those of the newspaper industry nationally. By the end of the war, radio revenues had more than tripled. World War II abruptly thrust radio technology into the center of the country's public communications system and left radio broadcasting a powerful, prestigious, and very profitable industry.[9]

Neither radio's profitability nor its reputation as a public-spirited industry made it through the 1940s intact. As peace was restored and the troops came home, radio news lost some audience, and the overall quality of radio's public interest programming deteriorated precipitously, particularly at the local level. In 1946, the FCC published a careful empirical study of radio broadcasting, which came to be known as the *Blue Book*. Many local radio operators were flagrantly disregarding their promises to do public affairs programming, promises made in petitions to the Commission for broadcast licenses or renewals. Such high-minded statements of intent were routinely ignored once a license was secured. Too often, the study found, the actual programming amounted to paid program-length infomercials for assorted religious denominations and local foreign-language groups, interspersed with runs of a half-dozen or more spot commercials, back to back. Thoughtful public affairs programming provided by the two existing networks, CBS and NBC, was frequently ignored by their affiliates around the country, in favor of more profitable fare. What the report found, in sum, was rampant commercialism.[10]

The FCC report sought no punitive measures, nor even any specific remedial actions, but rather spelled out what would be required in future license hearings as evidence of adequate attention to public interest, convenience, or necessity, under the terms of the 1934 Act. The industry counterattack was direct, vitriolic, and on occasion highly personal. President Harry Truman did not see fit to come to the defense of the astonished commissioners, nor did they muster the political will on their own to stand behind their findings and modest plans for reform.

The report became a dead letter, and a pattern was established: Broadcasters would thenceforth remain virtually self-regulating with respect to what constituted public service programming.

For the broadcast industry there would be a dark side to this victory. Precisely because the terms of their mandatory public service were so vague, there was no sure way to prove compliance. The First Amendment to the Constitution notwithstanding, particularly in presenting news and public information, broadcasters could never afford to ignore the possibility that a sitting president or well-placed Congressman, if sufficiently displeased, might exact a price in matters of far greater consequence for overall corporate strategy than the news—such as the specifications required of a new technology, permissible concentrations of ownership, or the terms on which rival communications media could do business.

In the absence of any clear standards for public service content either at the FCC or elsewhere, the independence of broadcast news and public affairs programming was easier to trade off, in return for a freer hand on the business side.

1950–1985: Television News as a High-Prestige Loss Leader

The pioneering entrepreneurs of radio mastered television technology early on: NBC's David Sarnoff wrote colleagues enthusiastically in the 1920s about television's mass medium potential. Under his leadership, RCA—NBC's parent—began television transmission on an experimental basis from atop the Empire State Building in 1930. Determined to keep pace, CBS initiated trial television broadcasts in 1931.[11]

RCA dominated the industry, making large amounts of money selling radio receivers and simultaneously developing popular programming for radio to help drive demand. So as not to compete against itself in the lucrative consumer electronics market it was creating, RCA decided to hold television back until every middle class American household had bought at least one radio. By the late 1930s, when the time to move television into the market seemed ripe, RCA created a carefully promoted sensation with the first public demonstration of television technology at the 1939 World's Fair. Television broadcast licenses began to be issued in 1940, but when the United States entered the war, a freeze in the commercial development of television was immediately imposed, to ensure that electronic components would be available for the Allied war effort.[12]

Television programming started in earnest by the mid-1940s. The same enterprising network owners and radio journalists who had covered themselves in glory during the war began to broadcast television news as well. CBS led in developing a television news operation, with NBC not far behind, building an aggressive team around its own respected radio correspondents. ABC, until 1946 a small radio network owned by RCA and dedicated to cultural programming, began a feisty, underfunded television news operation in 1949. In 1950, although a mere 3.8 million television sets had been sold, television's clear appeal was already pushing radio advertising rates into decline. In 1951, when ten million households nationwide were equipped with the newfangled audio-visual receivers, Edward R. Murrow's news magazine *Hear It Now* left the radio waves to become *See It Now* on television. Two years later, the number of households with television stood at 23 million, well over half the total.[13]

History and technology combined to make television news, compelling as it was from the viewers' side of the set, an unattractive business proposition from its inception. Radio news had been costly to produce in wartime, but the public was gratefully enthusiastic and war was war, so no expense had been spared. Television news cost twelve to fifteen times more.[14] In addition, as a legacy of wartime coverage, television news operations inherited large staffs around the world. Basic in-studio television productions in those days required hundreds of pounds of elaborate equipment plus a team of specialized personnel, and taking cameras into the field was costlier still. Then it required a great deal more money to shoot, transport, develop, and edit film.

To cover these costs, astounding concessions were made to advertisers—there were *The Camel News Caravan* and *The Esso Newsreel,* for instance, and sponsors typically expected veto power over the on-camera talent. Some expectations dated from the long-standing radio practice of allowing ad agencies themselves to produce popular shows for their clients and simply hand them over to the networks for broadcast. In the late 1950s, as the cost of advertising on television went up and up, program sponsorships gave way to spot ads spread across many programs. The direct control that large advertisers had exercised over the programming became a thing of the past, but one harsh fact remained: when it came to news and public affairs programming more complex than a roundtable of unpaid experts, ad revenues not only did not turn a profit, they never even reliably covered basic production costs.[15]

Early television news operations were protected by the air of adventure and elevated mission inherited from radio's glory days during the war. This, combined with the need to forestall any grumbling about the broadcasters' commitments to public service, more or less freed network news divisions from the grubby business of balancing their budgets. At the same time, though, the economic value of the news to the networks began to decline. By the late 1950s, national life was far more settled, and television news, while still enjoying considerable prestige, was not an especially high priority for most viewers—nor, as a consequence, for advertisers or for owners. Television news was a money loser and would remain so well into the 1980s.

Other uncomfortable realities tested the dedication of the network owners and their employees to hard-hitting news and public affairs programming in the 1950s. The patriotic consensus of World War II gave way to a more confusing national agenda—the Korean War, the Eisenhower years, and, above all, the hunt led by Senator Joseph McCarthy for communist sympathizers in the communications industry and elsewhere. Behind the scenes at CBS, NBC, and ABC, a secret blacklist governed key personnel decisions during the 1950s and the 1960s, stifling controversy and creativity, demoralizing all concerned, and robbing TV journalists of the chance to develop a robust tradition of political independence.[16]

Television finished McCarthy—not TV journalists, but the unmediated eye of the camera, showing the junior senator from Wisconsin, as the printed record had not, for the disturbed and dangerous individual he was. In rare instances when heroes of yesteryear like Ed Murrow did find the courage to condemn the anti-communist hysteria on air, even though they never mentioned the devastation within their own ranks, they came to be seen as liabilities by their employers.[17]

Except for news, the business picture was sunny indeed: television quickly found programming formulas that made money, and lots of it. The big movie studios had refused to supply feature-length films to broadcasters, fearing that television might empty out their highly profitable chains of movie houses. Therefore, building on the foundations laid by radio, television developed its own genres: situation comedies, variety shows, low-budget serials, and quiz shows.[18]

A calculated public plea by Ed Murrow in 1957 for more resources for the news was rebuffed by his employer; yet months later, the news division (but not Murrow himself) would be called upon to help preserve CBS's

Figure 1.1 **The American Public's Sources for Daily News, 1959–1986.**

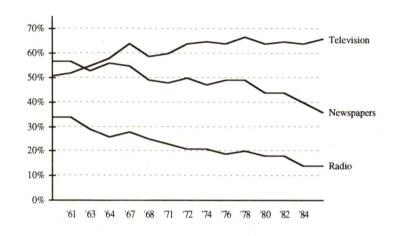

Source: The Roper Organization.

business image and save it from calls for regulation. A wildly profitable CBS quiz show, *The $64,000 Question,* had been rigged to make it more exciting and thus increase audience ratings and ad revenues—with the knowledge, many suspected, of those at or near the top. Corporate decision makers instinctively fought to limit damages to the core business—entertainment—by invoking the prestige of their news department and launching a highly publicized, well-financed series of news documentaries.[19]

Nineteen sixty-two was a watershed year. By then, 90 percent of all households in the United States owned a television, and in the same year television edged past the daily papers to become the most important source of news for the majority of the adult population in the United States. Not coincidentally, 1962 was also the last year that the *Christian Science Monitor* ever broke even.

If the shared sacrifices of World War II had unified the country in the 1940s and the politics of the 1950s left the population intensely ambivalent, the 1960s were out-and-out divisive, visually dramatic, and sometimes violent. It is nearly impossible to imagine what the impact of public events would have been without television—the civil rights marches, the Cuban Missile Crisis, the assassination and burial of handsome young President John F. Kennedy, the exhilaration of the space program, the violent deaths of Dr. Martin Luther King Jr. and Robert Kennedy, the war in Vietnam, the protest marches, the riots outside the Democratic National Convention in Chicago. National television news was not a reliably profitable business, but it shaped the nation's changing image of itself nonetheless.

Television News and the Federal Government in the Vietnam Era

If newscasters' relations to their audiences became increasingly complex, their relations with the federal government lost all semblance of innocence. Broadcast journalists, still holding the example of media patriotism during World War II and the deep chill of the McCarthy era in their memories, did not customarily make fine distinctions between presentations of the world as their news staffs saw it versus that of the government in power. Sarnoff's RCA was also a major Defense Department contractor before, during, and after World War II. During the war, as middle-aged captains of the broadcast industry, both Sarnoff and Paley were pleased to accept officers' commissions, don uniforms, and join high-profile intelligence and propaganda operations overseas as their contribution to the defense of freedom abroad. Their networks engaged in extensive voluntary self-censorship to support the war effort, and all concerned were unself-consciously proud of it.[20]

This cozy relationship continued through the 1960s. After the war, Frank Stanton—then newly appointed president of CBS—had written the occasional speech for President Truman with his employer's blessing, and ten years later, Ed Murrow quietly coached presidential candidate Adlai Stevenson. In the Kennedy administration, Murrow would cross over to head the country's newly established department for overseas propaganda, the United States Information Agency, with Stanton sitting on the board—"a clear conflict of interest" in the words of media chronicler David Halberstam. NBC's John Chancellor, who was to become that network's news anchor in 1971, did a stint as head of the Voice of America in 1965 and 1966.[21]

All this seemed natural and benign to the men involved, but where to draw the line? As the Vietnam War was heating up, reporters from all media at first accepted the need for self-censorship of the sort routinely exercised in World War II and Korea. When Lyndon Johnson became President, the ties between the U.S. government and CBS, arguably the most powerful purveyor of public information in postwar America, became even stronger, for Stanton had been personally responsible for making Johnson's family-owned radio station in Dallas a CBS affiliate in 1939. By the mid-1960s, this and related media properties were the cornucopia from which the president's personal fortune flowed.[22]

The two men had remained close associates over the years, and as the undeclared war in Vietnam escalated, Stanton stepped in personally from time to time at Johnson's bidding to manage sensitive news. When the president gave interviews to CBS correspondents, he flaunted his connection with their boss. In 1966, CBS's coverage of the Senate Foreign Rela-

Figure 1.2. **Television Advertising Revenues, 1950–1985.** (Dollar figures are in millions.)

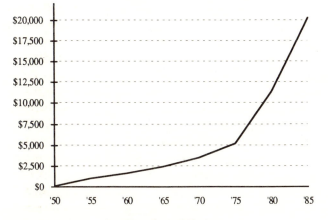

Source: Sterling and Kittross, *Stay Tuned*, pp. 640–41.

tions Committee hearings questioning the wisdom of Johnson's escalation of the war in Asia was preempted by *I Love Lucy*. Murrow's old producer, Fred Friendly, resigning from the industry altogether in protest, set a standard few would follow in years to come.[23]

Lyndon Johnson was a compulsive television viewer who liked to monitor the three networks simultaneously, and CBS put in two complete state-of-the-art installations at the White House, as a courtesy. Johnson is also known to have called Walter Cronkite directly on a regular basis as soon as the evening news ended, to give the anchor his own opinion of what had just been broadcast. The president also saw to it that military brass in Vietnam had copies of all domestic television coverage of the war flown in daily, and the commanders in the field could mete out privileged access to the correspondents responsible for the next week's coverage, or withhold it, accordingly. Even *Variety,* show-biz chronicle of record, referred scathingly to television's coverage of the war in Vietnam as "no-guts journalism."[24]

Such fine points, disturbing in terms of television's public service mandate, were only marginalia to the overriding business story: thanks to their highly profitable entertainment schedules, by the mid-1960s, the networks and their affiliates were, in the words of broadcast historian Erik Barnouw, "in a state of almost delirious prosperity." It only got better: network advertising revenues doubled in constant dollars between 1960 and 1970. The public had no idea that the news divisions were unprofitable, and their on-air personalities were seen as winners and trustworthy sources. By the 1970s, CBS's Paley could lure a trophy like Bill Moyers away from PBS for a handsome sum, but then he could not bring himself to depress profits enough to allow Moyers to host a regular show in prime time.[25]

Attempts to curb broadcasters' freedom to compete for the public's attention by whatever means they saw fit, short of certifiable pornography, failed. Senator Estes Kefauver repeatedly marshaled evidence in the 1950s that television violence might be contributing to antisocial behavior among youth, and the findings were roundly denounced by the National Association of Broadcasters (NAB). The upshot was that business continued as usual. Senate staff studies in 1961 and 1964 linking violent television programs with violent behavior in children and young people likewise came to naught. In 1964, when the chairman of the FCC suggested that the NAB's own standards on commercialization be adopted by the Commission as well, he was met with howls of outrage, and in a replay of the FCC's rout in 1946, the matter was dropped. In 1968, a presidential commission on violence in society headed by Milton Eisenhower included a book-length study of media violence, but no further action resulted.[26]

The single important exception to the pattern of successful industry defiance of oversight of broadcast content was the 1970 congressional ban on cigarette advertising, endorsed by both the FCC and the Federal Trade Commission (FTC). Broadcasters were deprived of a full 10 percent of their annual billings as a result. But when, between 1972 and 1976, the FTC proposed that broadcasters provide time for "counter-advertising" to balance the messages put forward in commercials, the FCC withheld its support and the matter died.[27]

In 1976, television writers went to court and successfully resisted an effort to create a "family time" in the evening without explicit sex or excessive violence. The Fairness Doctrine requiring that a forum be given to both sides of any important issue remained a thorn in the side of the industry, but hardly constituted a significant constraint. Television broadcasters were as jealous of their power to defy broad social and political oversight, as they were conscious of their narrow vulnerability to the displeasure of the president, whoever he might be.

Public Television, No!

Much of the rest of the English-speaking world has enjoyed some buffer against the conflicts of interest that naturally arise from the unrestrained, for-profit operation of the broadcast industry. Broadcast news and public information in Britain, Ireland, Canada, and Australia has traditionally been disseminated through publicly supported institutions protected from business imperatives and from direct pressure on the part of political incumbents. Some hoped to create a similar alternative to commercially supported broadcast communications in the United States. In 1967 the Carnegie Commission, with major support from the Ford Foundation headed by ex-CBS producer Fred Friendly, recommended creation of the Corporation for Public Broadcasting. Congress set up the CPB, which in turn created a Public Broadcasting Service, including both radio and television divisions.[28]

The Carnegie Commission's vision was significant, for purposes of this survey, for what it was not. PBS was not created as a national network, nor, as conceived, would it even produce television programming itself. The new entity was little more than a loose membership organization of local educational radio and TV stations around the country—an impoverished lot of institutions, if there ever was one—and its function was to facilitate the distribution of programming and federal funds to these stations. These crucial federal funds were appropriated annually by Congress and funneled through the CPB, whose chairman served at the pleasure of the president. Then-President Lyndon Johnson, for whom all issues had unhappily been reduced to one—namely, the escalating war in Southeast Asia—saw to it that the enabling legislation moved briskly through Congress, then appointed a Vietnam hawk to head the CPB.[29]

PBS's carefully decentralized structure and highly politicized funding procedures guaranteed that American citizens would have few significant noncommercial sources of televised news and public affairs programming. In any given year, should PBS member stations separately or in concert broadcast programming offensive either to the president or to powerful members of Congress, they would find the next year's funding in jeopardy. Richard Nixon's veto of the entire PBS budget in 1972 is legendary, because of the irony that, so soon afterward, PBS would broadcast the impeachment hearings against that same president and would chronicle his resignation in disgrace. But the fact is that funding as a weapon has been wielded against PBS—blatantly or subtly—by virtually every sitting president since, with the apparent exceptions of Gerald Ford and Bill Clinton.[30]

Beyond government support, to the extent that PBS stations and would-be producers seek public donations and corporate sponsorships, the system's powerful built-in incentives to avoid offending anyone are further reinforced. The *MacNeil–Lehrer News Hour*, specializing in that fragment of the world that can be communicated via in-studio conversations among Washington, D.C. insiders, might seem an exception of sorts, but it has been owned until very recently, not by PBS, nor by member stations, but by the on-air hosts themselves.

The Reagan Administration's assault on PBS in the 1980s, devastating as it was, was at least arguably based in part on principle. That principle was, of course, that the market—the market operating as unfettered by regulation as possible—was the ultimate good. Thus, public television should live or die in the marketplace like any other purveyor of goods and services. The process itself rather than any particular outcome, the Administration held, was the core value to salute, the only rule in the book really worth preserving.

Cable, 1975–1985: From Mavericks to Monarchs of the Public Information Industry

PBS never had a chance to compete with the networks, and cable had to struggle for many long years for its turn. As early as the 1950s, broadcasters began to use strong-arm tactics against the cable industry reminiscent of those once used against them by the newspaper publishers. The NAB's hue and cry against the upstart industry was often couched as an argument made in the public interest, that television should be free of charge for all viewers and thus universally accessible to all.[31]

By 1966, the FCC made common cause with broadcasters and ruled that cable operators could not import distant signals via microwave, nor refuse to carry any local stations, nor accept advertising—rulings that stood until the late 1970s. A tangle of further ad hoc regulations followed, all essentially intended to protect the perceived interests of either movie producers or broadcasters. Laboring under these handicaps and severely encumbered by the red tape, political headaches, and enormous capital costs of wiring large cities, cable television remained, until 1975, little more than a highly decentralized hardware and retransmission business. Operators made money in those days by getting local television signals to households willing to pay for better reception, and cable grew slowly but steadily across the country on a municipality by municipality basis.[32]

New technology abruptly changed all that in 1975, when Time Inc's Home Box Office leased space on RCA's new communications satellite and distributed movies to the handful of cable operators nationwide equipped to receive the signal. Satellite relays positioned cable to compete directly with the networks, although—with one prominent exception—it would be years before most of those in the communications industry fully grasped the implications of this change.[33]

The exception was Ted Turner. The renegade entrepreneur from Atlanta seems to have understood immediately that a whole new range of possibilities now existed, and in 1977 Turner began several years of canny maneuvers that permanently changed the delivery of television news and public information in the United States. First, he put his tiny UHF station up on RCA's satellite too, letting himself in for much ridicule from other broadcasters when he called this a "superstation." By 1979, WTBS—a distant last place in its own modest home market—was selling national ads for dirt-cheap entertainment and sports programming, and not only that, it was beginning to make a healthy profit, which Turner used to start Cable Network News, the cable-only service that would revolutionize the news business worldwide within a decade. CNN specialized in around-the-clock, no-frills, on-location coverage of breaking news, and Turner's team was under strict orders from the beginning to communicate its eccentric owner's global perspective.[34]

The big three networks were sure Turner would fail. NBC did market research that confirmed what to them had been obvious—that the public, mostly people who, except in times of crisis, were not heavy viewers of the news that was already available, certainly did not want news around the clock. Trade publications and the general press, accustomed to network news divisions that by the late 1970s spent upward of $100 million a year to produce a half hour of news nightly, assumed Turner's pockets would not be deep enough—and they very nearly were not. Leaving nothing to chance, however, ABC, CBS, and NBC tried to block CNN's attempt to use the AT&T land lines at their own heavily discounted rates for video feeds to Atlanta, and they tried to keep CNN out of pool reporting arrangements at the White House and elsewhere. Turner filed lawsuits left and right. To the general astonishment of the rest of the industry, CNN struggled on through 1980 and 1981. A little over a year after CNN's launch, ABC with Group W belatedly mounted, and then dropped, a rival service.

The networks waited for what they assumed would be Turner's inevitable collapse. They put money instead into fine arts channels for cable intended to rival PBS, every one of them destined to be a stunningly expensive failure. They dabbled amateurishly in cable programming for a year or less each and lost an estimated combined total of about $150 million.

The networks' early forays into cable programming were only an aside; their competitive focus was elsewhere. The broadcasters knew what they feared, and it was not the likes of a PBS or some playboy from Atlanta: it was AT&T. It was widely believed in the communications industry in the early 1980s that the giant telephone company, if unrestrained, would very likely fund upgrades of its own ubiquitous wires and acquire the ability to deliver text and video direct to the American home before many more years had gone by. Broadcasters joined forces with their oldest adversary—the newspaper publishers—to see to it that neither industry would suffer competition for ad revenues from that formidable rival, and the break-up of AT&T was the upshot.

Meanwhile, CNN's distinctly awkward on-air look was the butt of many jokes at the big three's Manhattan headquarters. Turner's do-or-die challenge in 1980 was to secure distribution: most of the country's 4,000–odd cable operators were techies, construction engineers, or technically sophisticated investors; they were mainly in the business of selling customers the benefits of improved reception, certainly not anything as esoteric as all-news programming. In the end, Turner's success hung on his ability to persuade the clannish cable industry to carry his product and that, although he came from broadcast, he was indeed, as he proclaimed at every opportunity, "a cable guy now!"[35]

1985 and Beyond: Television News as a Commodity

"Television is just a toaster with pictures," Ronald Reagan's flamboyant FCC chairman, Mark Fowler, was fond of saying. Reagan's revolutionaries proposed that public communications, including news and public affairs information as well as arts programming, are best thought of as commodities and that—the 1934 Communications Act and subsequent legal tradition notwithstanding—the federal government needed no broad fiduciary oversight of the industry. The value fundamental to all other values, the only public trust that is important to defend in the world of business, is the free market itself.

The spread of cable technology reinforced the Reagan team's position. After all, the 1934 compact between the government and the broadcasters had been based on a quid pro quo that cable television, by then the fastest-growing sector of the communications industry, seemed to make irrelevant. Not only did cable not broadcast over publicly owned, government-allocated frequencies, but with cable, the number of channels available for either radio or television transmission became, at least theoretically, unlimited.

The Cable Communications Policy Act of 1984, incorporated as a massive addendum to the Communications Act of 1934, released cable operators from virtually all the competitive constraints that the FCC, with prompting from broadcasters and movie producers, had put in place. By making the renewal of cable franchises all but automatic, the Cable Act also stripped states and cities of any significant ability to regulate the operation of local cable franchises on their own. By 1985, it was clear that, sooner or later, cable would be king of the TV mountain, but the sudden shift in the balance of power between cable and broadcast television that unfolded in the next five years took all concerned by surprise.[36]

Cash rich and no longer aggressively managed, the big three networks were natural take-over targets for the 1980s, and in the course of eighteen months in 1985 and 1986, corporate ownership that had long been in place—in two of three instances, since the 1920s—was swept aside. When the wake-up call came to the urbane, free-spending world of network television, few immediately understood what it meant. To the astonishment of its corporate officers, when ABC merged with Capital Cities—a trim and thrifty outfit built on small radio and TV stations and consumer publications scattered across America's communications hinterland—ABC became the junior partner. William Paley's CBS was taken over by real estate baron Lawrence Tisch, an unpolished multimillionaire wielding a notoriously sharp pencil. Then David Sarnoff's mighty RCA was bought by General Electric, a diversified international electronics colossus counting the U.S. defense industry among its customers and was run by men known to focus like lasers on the bottom line.[37]

When the new generation of owners at ABC, CBS, and NBC began to analyze their acquisitions for ways to improve profitability, the news divisions, with their sprawling, highly paid staffs, lavish operating budgets, meager and perishable product, and audience ratings that would prevent ad sales from ever reliably covering costs, presented them with an obvious target. The vision of the news as heroic mission, a remnant of corporate cultures crystallized in World War II, was no longer the sure protection it had been for over forty years.

Senior employees who (however imperfectly) embodied the old news ethic were inevitably vulnerable, as staffs were slashed. Producers and on-camera talent were pressured to make the news more enjoyable for the average citizen to watch on the average day, and "infotainment" was born. Television news magazines sought to extend the amount of inexpensive programming the news staffs, with their fixed overhead costs and capital equipment, could put out; in-your-face reality TV would soon seek truly low-budget, audience-grabbing, competitive solutions. Costly overseas bureaus were reduced in size or closed, and footage began to be bought from video services abroad and re-packaged for broadcast.

National television news, stripped of its old glamor and unprotected by government, was indeed becoming a commodity and, as such, was judged to be not much of a paying proposition to make and sell. The gathering crisis in the news business extended across media. Television journalism especially was being rapidly de-professionalized, but a new breed of owners—surviving newspapers included—had begun to see themselves as less in the news and public information business and more as simply in the business of business.

By the late 1980s, a system of public information that had served the American public tolerably well for the better part of a century was in slow-motion collapse, as new technologies and market forces gradually began to separate the best daily information providers from those loosely related operations that had traditionally supported them. Beginning in the early 1960s, daily newspapers lost national advertisers to television, and by the late 1970s, few regional economies could support more than one important print voice. In the 1980s, when network television news divisions themselves began to be reviewed carefully, they were found to be inferior investments compared to entertainment and sports, and were downgraded accordingly. All this went underreported and little analyzed, for the industry in question was precisely the very one that the media have traditionally been reluctant to discuss openly in a candid, hardheaded way: their own.

General entropy in the national television news business was the rule, but there was one outstanding exception. In 1985, after years of hardscrabble competition and an investment in excess of $500 million, Ted Turner's CNN finally moved into the black. The reasons were several. CNN was non-union and run with notorious parsimony, and the parent company absorbed satellite transponder, ad sales, and marketing costs. Most importantly, the costs of gathering a day's news were spread over a full twenty-four-hour schedule into which ads could be sold. True, audiences were small: *but for 365 days of the broadcast year, Cable Network News had forty-eight times more ad space for sale than did the network news divisions.* It would take years for the industry to grasp this reality, but a brand-new business model for television news—a profitable one—had just been born.

Chapter 2

Tradition Is Not Enough

1908–1982: A tradition of excellence leads to denial and despair

[It is intended that the *Christian Science Monitor*] will appeal to good men and women everywhere who are interested in the betterment of all human conditions and the moral and spiritual advancement of the race.

—*Colonel Archibald McLellan,*
editor of the forthcoming Christian Science Monitor, 1908[1]

A Tradition of Excellence Leads to Denial and Despair

The Christian Science Monitor's journalistic tradition was steeped in excellence and rife with anomaly. Founded in 1908 under the personal direction of Mary Baker Eddy, a charismatic mystic in her late eighties, year by year for the better part of the twentieth century, the *Monitor* built an unequaled reputation for even-handed, in-depth reporting based on pragmatic, humanitarian, internationalist values. This honorable history did not exempt the newspaper from the ravages of changing technology, demographics, and information markets. The past had much to do, though, with how the Monitor's entrepreneurial leadership went about attempting to reposition and reenergize that staid enterprise in the 1980s, and the nature of the bitter opposition their ambitious reforms provoked.

To 1908: How Christian Scientists Got into Journalism

Journalism was a cutthroat business around the turn of the last century, one of many. Although civic architecture, upper-class interiors, and ladies' fashions imitated the genteel tastes of the English gentry as they evolved from Victorian reserve to Edwardian playfulness, the public temper of the times in the new world remained a no-nonsense matter of survival of the fittest.

A powerful nation was being forged from sharp-eyed Yankee ingenuity; from the spoils of the subjugated South; from wave after wave of South and East European immigration; from the dislocations and hardships of industrialization in Pittsburgh, Pennsylvania, in Lynn, Massachusetts, in Akron, Ohio; from homesteading, land grabs, Indian-killing, vigilantism, desperate hard times, and courage in the march westward; from the joining of the continent by rail; and from gold fever and coolie labor on the Pacific Coast. The robber barons—men who had figured out how to turn the opportunities of the historical moment into massive personal fortunes—stood unapologetically astride the era. Teddy Roosevelt, a president who styled himself a "rough rider" (and later a "bull moose"!) laid the military and ideological groundwork for a U.S. overseas empire in Latin America and the Philippines. One Protestant revival after another swept the countryside, as the spiritually inclined tried to make sense of it all.

The W. Randolph Hearsts and the Joseph Pulitzers were the titans of the newspaper world, enjoying a degree of personal influence and a license for mischief unmatched in the news business of the late twentieth century. They set the pace for the competition, and their particular formula for success was to turn the daily paper into a highly profitable mass medium through a steady diet of violence, sensationalism, and eye-catching inks—hence the moniker "yellow journalism." These pioneers of the modern mass communications industry, working out the alchemy that would transform wood pulp day after day into gold, discovered that strict truthfulness was an optional ingredient.

Mary Baker Eddy and her followers were good copy, and in the course of that remarkable woman's long ministry—from 1870 to 1910—Christian Scientists found themselves slandered and ridiculed in the press, as well as occasionally the objects of more welcome attention. Mrs. Eddy's radical movement, begun among the factory workers of Lynn, Massachusetts, then drawn increasingly from the middle class, sought to return to the unadorned principles of earliest Christianity. The specific goal was to revive Jesus' practice as reported in the New Testament of healing the sick in mind and body through spiritual intervention. The Boston headquarters was known as The Mother Church and the deity was called the Father–Mother God, a liberated sense of the sacred not unknown among progressive New England Protestants of that day.[2]

By 1900, the core membership of those who had undertaken formal instruction was probably about 25,000 and growing, with followers numbering in the hundreds of thousands. Christian Scientists were said to be opening churches across the United States at the rate of one every four days.

From time to time sensationalist publications of the day turned what might arguably have been fair game into a nasty blood sport. In 1878, for example, the *Boston Globe* announced to the world that the body of a close Eddy associate—who had had a rancorous falling-out over his claim to own the copyrights to her works—was at the morgue, a victim of foul play. When the corpse was discovered not to be at the morgue after all, but the fellow in question was indeed among the missing, murder charges were pressed against Mrs. Eddy's husband and another close colleague. There was pandemonium in the movement and two weeks of field days for the Boston press before the "murdered" man turned up alive and well, saying he had been in hiding on the advice of the person who had brought his absence to the police's attention.

The mysterious accuser was unknown to church members, no motive for the bizarre deception was ever firmly established, and no apology for the affair was ever forthcoming from the *Boston Globe,* the newspaper that had sent forth the drumbeat of scandal in the first place.[3]

Mark Twain indulged over a period of many years in an intense ambivalence toward Mary Baker Eddy and her teachings. Beginning in 1899 when the founder of Christian Science was nearly eighty, Twain unleashed an attack in *Cosmopolitan Magazine,* in one breath calling Eddy "easily the most interesting person on the planet, and in several ways as easily the most extraordinary woman that was ever born upon it," and in the next breath branding her a charlatan.[4]

Hundreds of members left the movement as a result of Twain's widely distributed accusations, and the original article was eventually expanded into a book. At several points Twain noted, perhaps with a twinge of envy, how popular Eddy's main work, *Science and Health with Key to the Scriptures* was, and how very lucrative was the copyright enjoyed by its author. And yet he later confided to his biographer—surely knowing his remark would be recorded—that he believed Mrs. Eddy had "organized and made available a healing principle that for two thousand years has never been employed. . . . She is the benefactor of the age."

The most elaborate attack on the movement from the press establishment, and the most clearly culpable, came in 1906. In that year, representatives of Pulitzer's *New York World* and *McClure's Magazine* tracked down Mrs. Eddy's son in South Dakota and informed him that his mother—then eighty-five and for some years not in close contact with him—was mentally incompetent and under the influence of unscrupulous advisers. The newspaper proposed that the son and a nephew bring suit to gain control of her considerable fortune and offered to pay the legal bills if they did. Other estranged relatives joined in, and legal action known as the "Next Friends' Suit" was initiated. Eventually, Mrs. Eddy was examined by a judge and found competent, a conclusion supported by the transcripts of that long and lively interview, and the complaint was dismissed. The scheme concocted and bankrolled by the *New York World* to get control of the Eddy fortune was unsuccessful in itself. For the year that the suit had dragged on, though, it was a genuine media circus, and not at all bad for the newspaper business.[5]

Off and on for decades, Mrs. Eddy—a self-taught student of public affairs and international relations—had considered founding a newspaper herself. Very likely she was motivated by a wish to provide the public at large with what she and her followers would consider a balanced view of their own movement. Just as importantly, Mrs. Eddy must have wanted a publication that would reflect her own deeply felt, largely progressive concerns for social justice and personal freedom in those turbulent times. She had begun to include fairly extensive analyses of national and international affairs regularly in some of her religious periodicals as early as the 1890s.

Established Protestant, Catholic, and Jewish communities of the day were hardly indifferent to the human suffering that was such a distinctive by-product of the era. Many congregations responded with pragmatic compassion, leaving honorable monuments to conscience that still survive: soup kitchens, shelters, orphanages, hospitals, and educational institutions.

Perhaps it is not surprising that rather than addressing the physical needs of a suffering world, the Christian Science movement eventually chose to found a newspaper as their distinctive public service. It was not just that Mary Baker Eddy herself had followed current events worldwide all her life, nor just that she had been disturbed by the yellow press's treatment of her own teachings, nor even that the movement was organized without a formal clergy to put current events into perspective for the faithful from the pulpit.

At its most fundamental, Mrs. Eddy's metaphysics rests on a belief in the vast, God-given power of human consciousness and its primacy over the material dimension of creation—if only it could be freed of untruth and illusion. In her view, the yellow press, poisoning the public mind dollop by dollop, day by day with exaggerated depictions of a world of violence, unexplained suffering, random disaster, and images that degraded fellow human beings, caused mankind much anguish and illness in the all-important mental dimension. In the lexicon of the movement, Mind is a synonym for God and the traditional opposites referred to as good and evil were— and still are—referred to as truth and error.

For many years, Mrs. Eddy assumed her revival of the New Testament approach to healing would be reincorporated into Christian practice generally, rather than form the basis for a separate and distinct denomination. Consistent with this, she was long reluctant to allow her followers to build a physical church of their own. Once begun, however, the original Mother Church—a rough-hewn granite building of modest dimensions—was erected in fifteen months in 1883 and 1884 in a section of Boston created only a few years earlier by a mammoth landfill project known to this day as Back Bay. By 1906, a stately extension, far grander than the original church, was complete.[6]

In 1898, a few yards from the original church, another modest building had been erected to house the Christian Science Publishing Society. The Publishing Society, whose trustees were self-perpetuating but could be removed by the Church Board, was charged with putting out a number of religious periodicals specifically for the Church's members and followers. A somewhat larger edifice for the Publishing Society was added in 1907, and both projects, like the building of the original church, were executed with great speed. Mrs. Eddy nevertheless continued to live in Concord, New Hampshire, as she had since 1889, and kept her personal involvement in the Boston-based headquarters to a minimum.

Until January 1908, that is—months after the Next Friends Suit was thrown out of court—Mrs. Eddy and her large household decamped without explanation from their New Hampshire base and moved to a suburb of Boston. She was eighty-six. In the six months that followed, Mrs. Eddy began to draft—but did not send—short notes to trusted associates about her intention to start a daily newspaper and the name she had chosen for it. Then in mid-August of that year she finally informed the Church directors and the Publishing Society trustees of the formidable task she had set for them.[7]

Mary Baker Eddy's management style was intentional: she advocated secrecy in maturing a plan and speed in the implementation. She would turn an important matter over in her own mind carefully for however long she felt necessary, then move swiftly and purposefully without much discussion. Once she had decided on a course of action, she expected and for the most part got immediate action from those in her trusted inner circle, with no words wasted. So it went in 1908, when Mrs. Eddy resolved to establish a daily newspaper.

1908–1914: The Entrepreneurial Start-up

In 1908 not one of the three Trustees of the Publishing Society nor any of the five Directors of the Mother Church had had professional newspaper experience, and at first some tried to dodge the assignment. Others promptly rolled up their sleeves, and two days after Mrs. Eddy sent her

terse instruction to start a daily newspaper, these intrepid supporters sent
back a detailed plan complete with cost estimates. It was her turn to express
surprise at the size and scope of the newspaper they described and at the
level of expenditure necessary, but she approved the plan as submitted. She
also firmly instructed the Directors and Trustees not to consult her further
on details, including the size of the investment, but rather to move forward
without delay, using their own best judgment.

In the words of Erwin D. Canham, the *Monitor*'s long-time Editor and
chronicler of the paper's first fifty years, in his genial insider's account,
Commitment to Freedom:

> They started from scratch. The job was gigantic. They had to secure professional
> assistance and make a plan. It would be necessary to demolish a block of three-
> story brick apartment buildings which stood on the spot where the Publishing
> House had to be extended. Tenants of these dwellings, many of them away on
> summer holiday, must be interviewed and cared for. The Publishing House
> enlargement must be designed and erected. Machinery also must be designed,
> ordered, constructed, and set up. A skillful professional staff must be recruited
> and organized. News services must be acquired, at home and abroad. Above all,
> the policies and methods of operation of a completely new and very challenging
> venture must be worked out. A unique task of newspaper pioneering must be
> thought through from the very ground up.[8]

Doubts set aside or held quietly in abeyance, all concerned fell in behind "Colonel" Archibald McLellan—lawyer, businessman, already for six
years editor of the religious periodicals, Church Director and trusted Eddy
associate. The core team proceeded with entrepreneurial dispatch and flair
for improvisation to accomplish the impossible. A sample edition with a
front-page picture of the Wright brothers airplane—emblematic of Mrs.
Eddy's own keen interest in technology—was printed in secret by September 15.

Nothing could have been more natural: The accomplishments of the
Monitor's founders became a guiding mythology for succeeding generations. There is the story that Mrs. Eddy turned up the pressure even further,
letting it be known that publication should begin the day before Thanksgiv-
ing, scarcely 100 days after her first instruction to the Trustees and the
Directors in August. And of how essential composing room equipment,
ordered with no time to spare, went to the bottom in stormy seas between
New Jersey and Boston, yet against all odds was somehow replaced. And
how Western Union suddenly informed the *Monitor* that ticker service and
financial news bulletins would not be extended to the Publishing House as
agreed in time for the start of operations, because the city required that a

block and a half of deep trench be dug to bury the wires; yet well-placed Church members found it possible to reach a working compromise through Western Union's New York headquarters.

Between August and November of 1908, Mrs. Eddy involved herself in the details of launching the newspaper more intensely than she had initially intended. The general look, including the layout and typeface and the logo (a sheaf of wheat) were her choices, and she commented in detail on the approach and the tone of the articles in the sample editions. Above all, and in the face of some stiff internal opposition, she insisted that the newspaper be named the *Christian Science Monitor,* even though its goals were to be nonsectarian and nondenominational. She contributed the first lead editorial and, in a one-time gesture, signed it.

Archibald McLellan, named Editor of the new daily, understood very well what Mrs. Eddy had in mind: a "real" newspaper—operating in the open market; supported largely by advertising; designed, as he put it, to "appeal to good men and women everywhere who are interested in the betterment of human conditions and the moral and spiritual advancement of the race." The *Monitor* would inform this broad public of all news of "intrinsic merit and permanent value," in the words of another associate, placing local, national, and international news in perspective. A single religious article, clearly marked, appeared each day on an inside page, as it still does. Ads for tobacco, alcohol, caffeinated substances, drugs, or medical products—all deemed to contribute to the enslavement of the human mind—were not accepted.

As described in Mrs. Eddy's lead editorial on the first day of official publication, the *Monitor*'s mission was "to injure no man, but to bless all mankind." The "blessing" intended was to heal fear, mistrust, misunderstanding, and a sense of helplessness by applying "truth." "Truth" in this context meant truth in the ordinary sense: facts set forth in a calm tone, when possible with historical background and informed, nonpartisan analysis. The editorial purpose was to make the world a more familiar, more predictable, less terrifying place than that depicted in the yellow press.

A central directive quoted frequently down the years—and with special emphasis in the 1980s—was that the *Monitor* and all other Church publications be kept "abreast of the times."

The universal brotherhood of man was a given, and it was taken seriously. There would be no personal slander, no narrow nationalism, and all religions were to be treated with great respect. Armaments and armed action were deemed acceptable if they were defensive. Much hope was invested in man's progressive mastery of the material world through technology and human resourcefulness, and frequent criticism appeared in the *Monitor*'s pages of "industrial slavery," monopolistic practices, imperialism, and any abridgement of personal freedom or of competitive markets. A conscious effort was made to point to positive developments and pragmatic solutions whenever the facts warranted.

The unadorned history is impressive: it was a competent, high-energy start-up organized by intelligent generalists rather than professional newspaper people, and it was successfully executed at breakneck speed. Not surprisingly, with the passage of time, rich mythologies based on this history came to hold very different lessons for different kinds of people. This would become painfully evident in the tragic events that unfolded three generations later on that same spot, when Jack Hoagland, Harvey Wood, and their allies tried to take the Publishing Society first into radio, then into TV.

1915–1921: Dissent, Legal Challenge, and Consolidation of Authority

Few seasoned newsmen of the day expected the *Christian Science Monitor* to be around for long. Their rough and ready start-up notwithstanding, there followed six years of solid growth, as McLellan and his colleagues taught themselves the business side of newspapering and in effect set out to invent a new kind of journalism in the service of their humanitarian, internationalist ideals. In the first six months of the *Monitor*'s publication, Mrs. Eddy actively oversaw the editorial page, and—significantly—during that period explicit religious references were gradually eliminated.

After her death in late 1910, writers and Directors were less bold in taking positions on current affairs, yet in many ways, coverage continued to become more professional. By trial and error and through long staff deliberations, a collective sense began to evolve for deciding how and when to report sickness, death, and human disaster, how to distinguish between the important and the trivial, which social policies and national goals to endorse, how to remain nonpartisan, yet ethically engaged on a daily basis. Or, as one participant expressed it, the trick was to get beyond solutions by "sweetness and light" and put a professional edge on the *Monitor*'s stories.

Under McLellan and his capable young managing editor, the *Monitor*'s business side got off to a good start. Circulation was at 43,000 in the first year and had increased to about 60,000 by the time McLellan left in 1914. For several years as a public service during hard times, the *Monitor* ran "positions wanted" ads free of charge for all who submitted them, but paid linage also grew. No Church subsidy had been envisaged beyond the initial investment in plant, equipment, and early operations, and before long, apparently, no regular subsidy was needed.

In 1914, the Publishing Society's Trustees replaced the redoubtable

Archibald McLellan as Editor with one Frederick Dixon, and there began a gradually escalating seven-year struggle that shook the flourishing new institutions in Boston's Back Bay to their foundations. McLellan and his team had not consented to be replaced, and the transition was not a particularly smooth and happy one.

The new man was a cosmopolitan, exceptionally well connected Britisher who had been running the *Monitor*'s London bureau—and much of the paper's coverage of the rest of the world—since 1909. Dixon was imperious, learned, and on personal terms with many prominent statesmen, presidents, and other notables of the day. It is said that he raised eyebrows at the *Monitor* from time to time with vivid and detailed accounts of the sort one would expect from an eyewitness, when he had in fact been nowhere near the scene. His wife, Clementia Dixon, was his able right hand, working with him in his office at the Publishing Society, though not as an official employee. Both Dixons had been early students of Mrs. Eddy and over the years had been teachers of many new converts in their own right. Canham complained that, under Dixon, the paper's style became dry and even a bit pretentious, the content became overly focused on diplomatic maneuverings, and that the *Monitor*'s stand became too pro-British on international matters. And yet, Canham acknowledged, it was under Dixon that the technique of making current events more intelligible and thus less frightening by supplying thorough historical background became a basic tenet of Monitor journalism.

Dixon's presence was unsettling, but the power struggle that nearly brought the *Monitor* down at the beginning of its second decade entailed a gradual falling out between the Church Directors and the Publishing Society Trustees. Neither editorial standards nor religious principle as such were at stake. At the heart of the issue were whether control of the copyrights of much of Mrs. Eddy's work was vested in the Church Directors or in the Publishing Society Trustees. After several years of testing their muscle on operational and fiscal matters, the Publishing Society Trustees asserted their legal independence from the Church Board of Directors, and their right to control all of the Publishing Society's assets. At first a neutral intermediary, in time Dixon cast his lot with the Trustees. The issue of ownership and control of the Christian Science Publishing Society landed in the Massachusetts Supreme Judicial Court in 1919, and the Court eventually ruled in favor of the Church.[9]

Mary Baker Eddy herself was the author of the key documents in the case, principally *The Manual of the Mother Church* (1895) and two Deeds of Trust (1892, 1898). The *Manual* is a constitution for the whole movement, with by-laws that transfer the responsibilities of the aging first members to a self-perpetuating Board of Directors. No one knows why the astute Mrs. Eddy chose not to revise these documents to make them wholly unambiguous with respect to the Publishing Society in general and the *Monitor* in particular, for she certainly had ample time and more than sufficient intellect.

Whatever her reservations, the Church owns the Publishing Society's land, buildings, and business activities, including the newspaper. While the Church Directors do not actually appoint the three Trustees of the Publishing Society who oversee the business side of the publishing operations, they can remove them. Moreover, the Church Directors appoint a Manager of the Publishing Society who is charged with daily business operations. They also appoint the newspaper's Editor, who discusses overall editorial direction with them on an ongoing basis.

1921–1938: Monitor Journalism Matures

A "newspaperman's newspaperman" became Editor of the *Christian Science Monitor* in 1922, when control was returned to the Church Directors by the courts. Willis J. Abbot's lighthearted account of his first day as a young reporter in New Orleans in 1884, fresh out of college, is a classic: as he sat waiting to be told what to do, there was a loud cursing outside in the street, and a local political boss burst in and ran over to put his limp and bloody hand under the cold water tap at one side of the room. The damage had been done by the editor of the rival paper, who took exception when the politician, armed and accompanied by an armed sidekick, cornered him in his office to give him a piece of his mind. The sidekick now lay dead at the other newspaper. Abbot notes that his own respected editor began work every day by placing a loaded pistol at the ready on his desk.[10]

Abbot went on to work on papers in New York, Chicago, Kansas City, Washington, and London. His wife was a Christian Scientist, and he eventually tried her method on a persistent ailment of his own. Finding it worked, he had converted. Over the years he took leaves of absence from time to time to work on various political campaigns, acting as press chief for William Jennings Bryan in 1900 and again in 1908—such professional flexibility among journalists was routine in those days. In 1915, as war approached, Abbot felt compelled to resign from the Hearst papers, where by then he had worked for many years, in opposition to their pronounced pro-German position.[11]

Without the appointment of a mainstream professional like Abbot as Editor in 1922, the *Monitor* might never have become the distinguished publication it was at its fiftieth anniversary in 1958. By the time he arrived, the original staff was decimated, morale was at rock-bottom, and circulation had fallen to 17,500. Moreover, as Abbot notes, "A very articulate, though not numerous body of Christian Scientists who sympathized with the faction defeated in the courts, stood ready with biting criticism of every new step taken."[12]

In his years as Editor, Abbot rebuilt the professional staff (putting a woman in charge of the Washington bureau), reasserted the paper's nonreligious orientation, exacted the highest standards of fairness on even the slightest matters, and strengthened the force of early directives requiring that every piece of reporting have some lasting social meaning. Abbot oversaw the training of two future editors, Roscoe Drummond and Drummond's close friend, Erwin Canham, whose tenures, taken together, would span thirty years.

Under Abbot, the *Monitor* became more evenhanded in its treatment of Japan, kept a level head during the Red Scares of the 1920s, supported a fairer peace settlement for Germany as well as peaceful U.S. engagement worldwide, and published an approving editorial in support of the political methods and goals of an upstart Indian reformer, Mohandas Gandhi. The young Winston Churchill was among the paper's occasional contributors. The *Monitor* submitted a peace plan in the form of an amendment to the U.S. Constitution, intended to help prevent war by making it impossible for private business to profit from it.[13]

Circulation soon built back to 1918 levels and beyond, and advertising revenues multiplied accordingly. Zoned editions that allowed advertisers to target readerships in regional markets were begun in 1923. A collective editorship, including Abbot, two other editors, and the Manager of the Publishing Society, was established in 1927, as emphasis shifted to professionalizing the business side. As the *Monitor*'s twenty-fifth anniversary approached, the Church authorized construction of the majestic nine-story Publishing Society building, still in use today.

The *Monitor*'s circulation beyond Church membership remained disappointing and the Trustees formed a fact-finding committee of top employees and knowledgeable outsiders to address the matter. Among the committee's suggestions were that more vernacular English be used and that the notion be laid to rest once and for all that there were topics the *Monitor* could not cover. Innovative attempts of two sorts were made to ease the built-in tension between the *Monitor*'s worldwide circulation and its commitment to publish a daily paper delivered in many places days late by railroad and by boat. First, the number of daily Boston editions was increased to meet demands for immediacy in that market at least. Second, for the benefit of areas such as California and Great Britain where the *Monitor* had many readers, there would be a weekly magazine. The magazine, "a deluxe job" in Canham's words, would be edited by a woman and would depend heavily on contributed articles by respected figures from all walks of public life.[14]

Under Abbot, the *Monitor* began to make its distinctive mark on mainstream journalism throughout the English-speaking world in the late 1920s. The campaigns for "clean journalism"—a constant editorial theme since the paper's first year—grew more sophisticated. The *Monitor*'s advertising manager, a pillar of the Advertising Federation of America from its inception in 1911 until his retirement in 1935, was one of the most active organizers of that group's standards for truth in advertising. Abbot himself was a founding member of the American Society of Newspaper Editors.

During Roscoe Drummond's years as Editor from 1933 to 1939, with Roland R. Harrison as Manager of the Publishing Society, the *Monitor*'s tradition of editorial excellence continued to mature. By the mid-1930s, a generation of highly competent journalists, not all of them Church members, had been trained to *Monitor* standards. But the right business equation remained frustratingly elusive: while circulation had crept back up to 1929 levels as the worst hardships of the Depression years eased, profitability was not consistent and an estimated 90 percent of the *Monitor*'s subscriptions still went to Church members.[15]

1939–1964: The Golden Age of the Christian Science Monitor

In 1939, Drummond switched jobs with his friend and intellectual twin, Erwin Canham, the *Monitor*'s Washington correspondent. Canham was a quiet professional, a man of considerable intellectual scope held in high esteem by his colleagues, his peers at other publications, and by national and international political leaders of the day. He first became Managing Editor, then Editor—the greatest Editor that the *Monitor* has enjoyed in its long years of publication. He would hold the jobs of Managing Editor or Editor longer than anyone before or since.[16]

During most of the Canham era, the Manager of the Publishing Society was John H. Hoagland Sr., and he, too, would hold his post longer than any Manager before or since. His son Jack was a teenager in 1944, when the elder Hoagland relocated to Boston from Louisville, where he had worked for many years on the business side at the *Courier Journal*. Hoagland Sr. was also a highly regarded practitioner and teacher of Christian Science, with a large following of students. Summoned to Boston to fill a high position in the Church administration, he found himself within a week of his arrival appointed Manager of the Publishing Society, a job he held until his sudden death in early 1962.[17]

Together Canham and Hoagland, the one a cautious and reflective journalist, the other a more direct presence and a more analytical business mind, presided over what, in retrospect, must be considered the golden age of the *Christian Science Monitor*. In 1944 another task force had a go at the vexing problem of timely delivery to far-flung subscribers and sensibly articulated as policy what had by then been the practice for decades: give readers value beyond the merely topical in the form of historical background, thoughtful analysis, ethical insight, and pragmatic actions that might lead to a betterment of the human condition around the world. In 1947, expensive state-of-the-art presses were installed, and the debts for that and for the extension of the publishing building were paid off from revenues. Circulation continued to rise, slowly and steadily, from roughly 150,000 at the end of World War II to 180,000 in 1965.

But the years of growth and fiscal health that the *Monitor* enjoyed under the guidance of the senior Hoagland were deceptive. Advertising seemed to come in almost effortlessly over the transom, and the paper's bread-and-butter national accounts were for such prestigious items in the ad sales business as packaged goods and cars. Many loyal reps worked tirelessly part-time or on commission at local sales, and their efforts had symbolic importance for the prized we-are-all-neighbors touch that small ads from the four corners of the earth gave the paper. But local ads, especially classified ads—the platinum mine that in the mid-1990s local and regional newspapers still have virtually exclusive claim to—were not and could not be a major revenue stream, given that the *Monitor*'s circulation was spread thinly throughout the United States and, except for England, even more thinly abroad.

By 1953 and 1954, two historic developments that would completely change the economics of public communications in the United States in one swift decade had, because of its peculiar circulation and distribution patterns, already begun to hit the *Monitor*. First, television was quietly taking bigger and bigger bites out of national advertising accounts. On top of that, more and more national businesses began to place ads exclusively through agencies, rendering useless the personal ties the *Monitor*'s top ad executives had patiently cultivated in corporation after corporation over the decades to overcome the handicap of representing a church-connected publication. The paper's numbers did not add up in terms of the new demographic measures either, and *Monitor* salesmen began to find it hard to get appointments at the new agencies handling the big national accounts, let alone to make sales.

Hoagland Sr. agonized over what to do. Over 90 percent of the *Monitor*'s circulation in the mid-1950s consisted of subscriptions delivered by surface mail outside the Boston market, and readership surveys consistently

Figure 2.1 **The *Christian Science Monitor's* Circulation, 1908–1985**

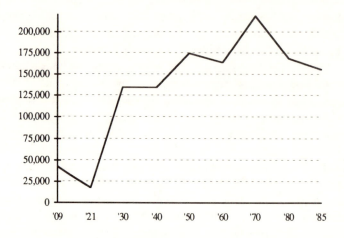

Source: Canham, *Commitment to Freedom*

brought in pleas for faster delivery. The Church Directors in particular hoped that if speedier distribution translated into increased circulation beyond the Boston market, stronger ad revenues would follow.

The key policy document of the elder Hoagland's tenure was "The *Christian Science Monitor:* Faster Delivery to Its Readers Everywhere"; this thirty-page, double-spaced report was presented to the two boards to which he reported in October 1955. Distribution of the only two newspapers with comparable challenges, the *New York Times* and the *Wall Street Journal,* is analyzed, using costs and other key information supplied as a professional courtesy by those publications. Five possible strategies are described, and the one Hoagland felt most appropriate is presented with detailed cost estimates. While extremely deferential in tone, the report provides a literal-minded snapshot of reality: the *Monitor* is an honorable but mature business, he plainly states. Faster delivery would raise costs by 14 percent a year, but based on evidence from the Boston market where delivery time was competitive with that of rival newspapers, such changes could be expected to increase circulation little, if at all. In truth, there was precious little flexibility, and he said so.[18]

In 1958, the *Christian Science Monitor*'s fiftieth year was celebrated in quietly triumphal style, with a large anniversary edition of the newspaper and publication of Canham's book describing the paper's first half-century. A well-made short film titled *Assignment: Mankind* emphasized the paper's use of the most advanced production and delivery systems available and the paper's by-then well-known dedication to even-handedness and objectivity. Erwin Canham is prominently featured, as are many of the *Monitor*'s stable of top-notch young stars—such as intense and manly John Hughes, shown in South Africa talking with black and white, high and low; the pleasant and ironic Takashi Oka, who would cover Asia for Monitor Television in the 1980s and the 1990s; or the dashing, eccentric Ed Stevens, winner of the *Monitor*'s first Pulitzer, standing in front of the onion-top domes of Moscow.[19]

Canham himself was much in demand on the lecture circuit at universities and at professional dinners that year, giving a popular talk titled "How to Publish a *Christian Science Monitor*," based on the last chapter of his book. His upbeat message was that quality journalism could and would prevail as a business proposition: if he understood the serious problems his paper was beginning to face, he chose to pass them over in silence. In all likelihood Canham, like most journalists and publishers then, had no notion of what the electronic communications revolution would mean. Probably he trusted, as did virtually all other newspapermen of the day, that incremental adjustments on the business side would allow them to adapt to the changing business environment in the future, as they had in the past.[20]

The elder Hoagland was instructed to proceed with faster delivery and promotions to boost circulation. Jet aircraft began commercial flights in 1958. By 1960, new presses were unveiled and contracts for printing the *Monitor* in London, Chicago, and Los Angeles in addition to Boston were announced: negatives were flown by jet to these remote plants daily, and delivery time was in fact significantly improved.

Nineteen sixty-two was a turning point at the *Monitor*. After each dramatic improvement in delivery time, circulation rose a bit, only to drop back a few months later. All-important national accounts continued to shift their advertising to TV, and the elder Hoagland could "see the deficit coming like an express train." In January 1962, Hoagland Sr. died on the job of a heart attack at age sixty-two, and on May 1, at the end of that fiscal year, the *Monitor,* heavily marketed and often heavily discounted under his policies, slipped decisively into the red, whence it has never returned.

By 1962, however, Monitor journalism was paying significant dividends in those most prized currencies of all: influence in the world of public affairs and respect from professional peers. The first of the *Monitor*'s five Pulitzer's had been awarded in 1950 to Canham's colorful Soviet correspondent Ed Stevens for his long series, "This Is Russia Uncensored." By the 1960s, the paper was "must" reading for heads of state, congressmen, a certain kind of traditional intellectual, and, most especially, for other journalists. In 1962, Nelson Mandela's long incarceration began: he would emerge in 1990, saying that the *Monitor* had been a treasured companion throughout the decades of enforced isolation. Fully 90 percent of the *Monitor*'s subscribers around the world remained Church members, however, a pattern that was a sore point for those in Boston who remembered the founder's instruction that the *Monitor* was intended for a general readership and that its mission was "to bless all mankind."[21]

Nineteen sixty-two was a turning point in the history of public communications in the United States as well. Television—even though still received for the most part in black and white, with poor signals in many markets—nevertheless overtook newspapers as the primary source of news and public affairs information across the United States. The change was like an invisible continental divide that one can hike across without noticing, yet everything on the other side flows toward a different ocean. Because, in contrast to most U.S. newspapers, the lion's share of the *Monitor*'s ad revenues were national, that paper came into direct competition with television early on. As the television industry developed local ad sales, other newspapers felt the inexorable squeeze—except, of course, in the all-important classifieds.

As Jack Hoagland came to see twenty years later, in this respect the future came first to the *Monitor*.[22]

1964–1978: Coasting Gently Downhill

In 1964, at age sixty, Erwin Canham was removed as Editor and shown upstairs to the ceremonial post of Editor-in-Chief, specially created for the occasion. Influential and politically conservative Church members based in Boston and in Texas had long campaigned for his removal, so the story goes, believing he (and the *Monitor*) were too far to the left politically. After the death of his first wife, Canham put further distance between himself and conservatives at the Publishing Society and in the Church by marrying the paper's book editor, much younger than he, and his outstanding tenure ended on a muffled note of discord. Canham eventually accepted a post as governor-general of the U.S. Trust Territory of the Northern Marianas in the middle of the Western Pacific and moved to Saipan, an island 1,500 miles south of Japan and 1,500 miles north of New Guinea.[23]

The next Editor, a trusted insider with little experience as a journalist and a political conservative by nature, served from 1964 to 1970, during which time the *Monitor* received three more Pulitzers. More and more expensive newsprint, rising postal rates, and inflation took their toll. By then Church membership was slowly declining, and with it, full-rate subscriptions. In 1968, the first of three computer conversions disrupted circulation. And while circulation rose with every costly promotion, sometimes dramatically, from a base of 184,000 in 1964 to a historic high of 247,500 in 1970, it had settled down to about 170,000 by the late 1970s. Over $70 million was spent between 1965 and 1975 on promotions to hold off what in retrospect was clearly the leading edge of a glacier. Costs crept up; revenues slowly fell; and the *Monitor*'s deficit began to grow at an accelerating rate.[24]

Writers' salaries, held down during the Canham–Hoagland era, were raised some, but did not keep pace with inflation. By the late 1960s, the rift between the editorial side and the business side at the *Monitor* was so great that one cub reporter fresh from England was instructed by his colleagues never to speak to anyone from management and to turn his back (as editorial staff did theirs) when anyone from the business side walked into the newsroom. Beginning in 1969, those who held the thankless job of manager of the Publishing Society were changed every two or three years for the next fifteen years, until 1983 when John H. Hoagland Sr.'s son, Jack, would reluctantly agree to take on the job.

The *Monitor* won its second Pulitzer in 1967 when John Hughes, the Welsh-born Canham protégé among those featured in the fiftieth anniversary film in 1958, was honored for his coverage of Suharto's coup in Indonesia. Two more Pulitzers came in 1968 and 1969 for the in-depth, even-handed investigative pieces, of the kind the *Monitor* was best known for, on the overload in the U.S. court system and the management of national parks, respectively. Many on the editorial side felt they were doing their job under increasingly pinched conditions, but that, somehow, management—and, ultimately, the Church Directors—were failing to figure out the math.

An intelligent early attempt to rethink the *Monitor*'s format for delivering news and public affairs to a wider public came in a 1970 memo from Dick Nenneman, for several years business editor at the paper, who left in 1974 to become a senior vice president at the Girard Bank in Philadelphia. Nenneman, a Harvard graduate and student of international relations, foresaw that electronic delivery of information to the home would soon make daily newspapers an anachronism. He proposed a weekly publication of news background, opinion, social analysis, and culture, with a format something like that of the London *Economist,* but broader in its attention to human affairs. Nenneman's suggestions were shelved without extensive discussion, but they resurfaced in the debate in the late 1980s that ended with the dramatic exit of the *Monitor*'s then Editor, Katherine Fanning.[25]

Between 1968 and 1974, the Mother Church carried out a massive building program around the existing buildings, creating a sweeping eleven-acre campus designed by an I.M. Pei associate. On the north side of a handsome, 670–by–100–foot reflecting pool, a long, five-story edifice was created to house various Church administrative activities. At its east end is a seventy-five-foot square fountain, in summertime full of squealing neighborhood children in bathing suits, surely requiring a hefty insurance policy. Under the pool that once cooled water for the massive central air-conditioning system, a 500–car garage was built. On the south side of the pool rose a new twenty-five-story Church administration building and, at the west end, an amphitheater and Sunday school space. Across Massachusetts Avenue, tenements were cleared—not without some hard feelings—and Church Park, a large, plain, mixed-income apartment complex with shops at ground level was built.[26]

The original estimate for the whole project was $15 million in the dollars of that day, but costs multiplied as the project proceeded. The final price tag was around $88 million, or about $197.5 million in 1992 dollars, and the undertaking, paid for in cash, put a severe strain on Church finances. Some 600 employees were laid off at the Publishing Society and in the Church administration. For short periods there was borrowing from dedicated funds to meet cash flow needs and, in particular, to cover payroll. Eventually, the cash-flow crisis passed, and Church income again exceeded expenditures—sometimes by a considerable amount—until the late 1980s and early 1990s, when the moves into radio and television, combined with the newspaper's spiraling deficits, again made cash in hand scarce.

In early 1977, John Hughes, acting briefly as both CSPS Manager and CSM Editor, responded to a request from the Trustees and Directors for a plan to confront the mounting deficits at the paper, which had only just switched format from broadsheet to tabloid. Hughes considered and rejected transforming the *Monitor* into a weekly. He also mentioned three other bold possibilities, none of which, he felt, was agreeable: piggy-back printing with the *Wall Street Journal,* putting out a significantly thinner paper, or printing weekly while using radio to maintain the daily franchise. To make the status quo work, Hughes urged fixed cost reductions, getting members to contribute to an endowment fund and push subscriptions, somehow increasing circulation, somehow holding the line on ads. In sum, an impasse: untenable present, unattractive alternatives, unrealistic hopes that further deterioration on the business side could be halted without sweeping changes.[27]

A proud face was turned to the world, and, characteristically, the *Monitor* stayed at the cutting edge of technology by continuing to install computerized information systems—some of which had the initial effect, there as elsewhere, of causing confusion. By 1976, electronic photo typesetting was in place. But the Church's growing annual "contribution" to cover the newspaper's deficit became an important non-topic among Publishing Soci-

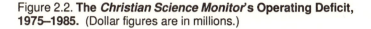

Figure 2.2. **The *Christian Science Monitor's* Operating Deficit, 1975–1985.** (Dollar figures are in millions.)

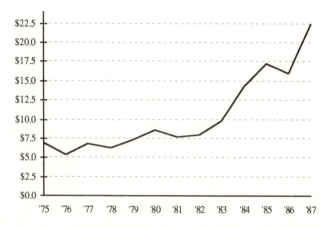

Source: The numbers on the newspaper's operating deficit are from Publishing society records and have been verified by the Church Treasurer's office.

ety employees, discussed in quiet tones or by indirection, and much on everyone's mind. Between 1977 and 1980, there was an unprecedented 100 percent turnover on the five-member self-perpetuating Church Board of Directors.[28]

1978–1982: The Search for a New Business Formula for the Monitor

So proud a face was turned toward the world beyond the Boston headquarters, that when Harvey Wood answered the call to become a Church Director in 1977, he had no idea that income had not been covering expenses at the *Monitor* for some time, and that for fifteen years, the gap had been widening at an accelerating rate. At fifty-two, he was one of the youngest ever to serve on that august five-member board. Like most Church members worldwide, Wood, his family, and his community looked to the *Monitor* as a beacon of excellence, a guide to which social and political issues needed Church members' prayerful attention, and, above all, the movement's healing outreach to a troubled world: the gift of balanced, caring, and healthful understanding.

In mid-turnover, the Directors asked for—and got—an unvarnished view of the *Monitor*'s financial condition. The incumbent Manager, a number-cruncher with a flair for the dramatic, produced an accordion-style report tracing the newspaper's profits and losses from 1908 to 1978: at one year per page, the report is said to have stretched fifty feet across one whole side of the light and informal boardroom on the twenty-fifth floor of the Church Administration building. It showed that the *Monitor* had made a clear profit returnable to the Church in only two of its seventy years—in other years, any modest excess of revenues over operating expenses had been put back into plant or personnel.[29]

Although the scenario foreseen in the *Manual* was that Publishing Society activities would return an annual profit to the Church, the fact that the situation had reversed itself had historically been deemed acceptable because the *Monitor* was seen as the Church's main service to mankind.

The slowly accelerating growth of the deficit since 1962 had, however, gradually destabilized even the revised assumption that the newspaper could after all lose some money in some years, and the Church would absorb the costs. The mammoth accordion report concluded by projecting the accelerated growth of the deficit into the future, and purported to show the year in which, if nothing were done, the *Monitor* would wholly bankrupt the Church. Yet the Manager's recommendation was for half-measures: to build more remote printing plants throughout those parts of the world where subscribership was the heaviest, to achieve still-faster delivery of the daily paper. An admirably hardheaded review concluded with operational recommendations based on wishful thinking—the unfounded hope that conventional operational adjustments could stop further fiscal deterioration. They could not.[30]

The 1978 accordion report was the final harsh note of an alarm that had already been heard by the Directors, loud and clear. The Directors finished replacing themselves within the next year, and the new Board—composed of men and women not tied personally to the policies of the past—began a search for bold solutions. Not for several more years, however, would their search turn toward radio and television.

Moving Beyond "Monitor Exceptionalism"

What might be called "Monitor exceptionalism" has confused and deflected much discussion of the Christian Science Publishing Society's attempt to reposition and diversify for the age of electronic information. Participants and onlookers, friends, skeptics, and foes have too often favored explanations of that high drama which overemphasize what is unique about the Monitor experience—that is, that the project was being bankrolled and managed by a church, and a somewhat unusual church at that, in terms of majority experience in mid-twentieth-century America.

In truth, more than anything else corporate culture at the *Christian Science Monitor* in the early 1980s resembled the corporate culture at other American newspapers. Though less so than most other media of the day, the Monitor organization was still overwhelmingly white and male at all levels. The paper had been shaped by editors who were strong and competent as well as by some who were not, and over the years, editors and writers with political preferences from moderately liberal to moderately conservative had been given jobs and a platform. In the *Monitor* shop as elsewhere, there had developed an almost ritual antagonism between the editorial and the business sides of the paper, and all concerned had had occasion to wrestle with how and when the owners should expect to influence editorial policy.

Like their counterparts at other journalistic enterprises, *Monitor* management and staff had been swept up by the great tide of enthusiasm for the Allied cause in World War II, and during the McCarthy era, they, too, found that the liberals among them were vulnerable. The rising costs of newsprint, labor, plant, and distribution, the flight of the public to television with advertisers in hot pursuit, and the aging of those readers who remained, left *Monitor* executives, exactly like management at most other American newspapers, knowing they had to take decisive action—yet facing what seemed a desperately limited set of options from which to choose.

By the early 1980s, the *Monitor*'s truth-telling mission was in serious jeopardy because the business arrangements that had sustained it for three generations were failing. A half-effective code of silence with respect to the growing deficit was maintained inside and out, but the signs of decline were becoming unmistakable. Yet the causes of these disturbing trends were not mysterious, and they were in no way unique to the *Monitor*.

It is not easy to grasp the effects of broad shifts in business and technology while they are still in motion. Some at the Publishing Society and beyond placed blame on managements past or present, or with the unhappy ad sales and marketing teams, or at the door of the circulation department. Others took refuge in denying that any fundamental problem existed, redefining the newspaper's historic mission so that it would seem to conform to present realities, otherwise too painful to bear. Still others, knowing that Church membership was declining and aware that members had accounted for much of the newspaper's full-rate subscriber base, thought the unthinkable and despaired: could it be that the *Christian Science Monitor*'s long and distinguished tradition as a beacon of excellence for journalists and opinion leaders worldwide was in fact drawing to a close?

Chapter 3

Renewed Vision

1982–1987: Monitor communications as a broad public service

The future came to the *Monitor* first.

—*Jack Hoagland, 1993*

A Renewed Vision of Monitor Communications Emerges

During the 1970s, not quite $100 million was spent to pump up the *Monitor*'s circulation and cover the growing deficit. By the early 1980s, full-rate circulation had settled at about 165,000 and, without continued aggressive marketing and promotion, it was believed, would fall to a "natural" base of 125,000. By then, the *Monitor*'s losses had risen to $8 million a year on combined circulation, ad sales, and syndication revenues of $30 million.[1]

As the crisis deepened, the newspaper's historic charge to disseminate balanced, in-depth news and public affairs widely to men and women of good will collided head-on with the realities of late-twentieth-century information markets. From that punishing collision emerged a controversial—and costly—new vision of Monitor communications.

Optimism and Technology in the Early Years

At the turn of the last century, Mary Baker Eddy and her followers, even more than other Americans, believed that technological change would play a key role in easing the suffering of mankind. For this reason, from the first prototype issue displaying a page-one picture of the Wright brothers' airplane at Kitty Hawk, technology had been followed closely and held in high regard at the *Monitor.*

To Erwin Canham, it seemed that the paper covered technology with almost indiscriminate enthusiasm in its formative years, because it had welcomed a number of inventions that, with time, did not prove viable. In this connection, he downplays the *Monitor's* February 2, 1910, mention of "a new process called television," which would allow both image and voice to be received from a distance, adding a visual dimension to telephone communications.[2]

Nevertheless, a profound optimism regarding technology marked the movement from its inception, and in the 1980s, once the status quo was deemed intolerable, diversification to new communications media was welcomed without difficulty among many at the highest levels of the otherwise hidebound Publishing Society and among top decision-makers at the church that owned it.

Early Forays into Electronic Journalism

The Publishing Society's hands-on experience with broadcast communications began without fanfare in the 1930s, when a small number of *Monitor* writers worked for several years with a non-profit radio station in Boston to produce educational programming for distribution abroad. Early in World War II, a determined senior member of the *Monitor's* editorial staff almost singlehandedly wrote, produced, and broadcast a nightly news program beamed to Europe via shortwave radio. By 1943, a number of *Monitor* writers and editors in Boston expanded the operation, anchoring a highly professional nightly news round-up carried on the Mutual Broadcasting Network, with live reports from *Monitor* correspondents in Europe, North Africa, and the Pacific.[3]

After the war, the *Monitor's* radio journalists quietly returned to full-time newspapering. Between 1950 and 1980, certain *Monitor* journalists, along with their counterparts from other newspapers, were regulars on TV news-in-review shows. From the fifties and into the sixties, Erwin Canham hosted a weekly show called *Starring the Editors* on Boston's NBC affiliate. During the 1970s, the *Monitor's* overseas editor appeared regularly on Boston's PBS station, and another of the *Monitor's* most distinguished journalists was a frequent guest on *Washington Week in Review.*[4]

Television as a vehicle for *Monitor* journalism was given serious if brief consideration in 1968. A twenty-page memo from the Church's public information department to the directors suggests drawing on the staff and the resources of the *Christian Science Monitor* to develop an ongoing TV documentary series dealing with current world problems. The memo noted that there was reason to believe that such a series would be welcomed by television stations across the country and thus given good promotion and air time as a public service. The advantage to the Church would be simply to affirm its long-standing spiritual and institutional concern for quality news and public information.[5]

A detailed internal study in 1969 suggested two ways the *Monitor* might move into TV journalism: first, some of the newspaper's investigative series could be developed as TV documentaries as well, at the rate of three or four a year (ABC had informally expressed a strong interest in broadcasting such programs). Second, the Church might accept a long-standing proposal from WGBH, Boston's highly successful PBS affiliate, to do a biweekly TV news show, with the *New York Times* hosting in alternate weeks. The *Times* had already accepted and had begun broadcast. In the end, though, for reasons that are not clear, neither suggestion was acted upon at the *Monitor*. There the possibility of disseminating *Monitor* journalism via the new electronic media rested for another decade.[6]

The Catalyst: A Commitment to Professional Management

Harvey Wood was a man of high energy, widely known at the time of his 1977 appointment to the Church Board as a charismatic teacher and a practitioner with a long list of documented healings to his credit. True to his Texas roots, he was a first-rate public speaker. During the 1970s, he consciously identified with younger members of the Church, even growing sideburns as many of them did, and wearing informal dress. By the early 1980s, Wood had become an articulate advocate of change on the Church's brand new Board of Directors.[7]

One of the new Board's first acts was to call in professional consultants to evaluate the management of the entire Church Center, then staffed at 1,300 (down from 1,900 in 1970) with a total annual budget of about $30 million. For this they turned to Hoagland, MacLachlan & Company, Incorporated, a successful Boston consulting firm with associates in Europe and Japan, whose principals, both active Church members, had advised clients, including IBM, Bendix, United Technologies, Air Transport Association, International Harvester, Saab-Scania, American Motors, Aerospace Industries Association of America, Renault, and McGraw-Hill, in business matters ranging from office automation to diversification of product to international marketing.[8]

Jack Hoagland acted as the contact for his firm. In several rounds of detailed recommendations over the next two years, he advised streamlining and reducing the Board's direct executive responsibilities, encouraging departments to solve problems on their own and in cooperation with each other, centralizing staff services and developing a strong data processing and word processing capability throughout, keeping support functions to 50 percent of personnel or under, strengthening the controller function, integrating planning with budgeting and upgrading personnel and training.[9]

Hoagland's early recommendations for the *Monitor* included setting up a five-person editorial policy advisory committee that was to meet weekly. Designed as a working committee, with agendas set and meetings chaired by the newspaper's editor, the other four members were the paper's chief editorial writer, a Church director, a trustee of the Publishing Society, and the Publishing Society's Manager. A budget advisory committee was proposed to oversee Publishing Society finances, with detailed monthly reviews and a mandate devise a three-to-five year plan for deficit reduction.[10]

Hoagland's final report in early 1982 began bluntly: "The Christian Science Publishing Society is not well managed at the present time, by normal organizational standards." His recommendations: greatly strengthen the hand of the Manager in a long list of specific ways; place a Managing Editor reporting directly to the Publishing Society Manager on the staff of the newspaper to track expenditures on a daily and weekly basis; concentrate on rationalizing and upgrading management of the paper's two key revenue centers—advertising and circulation—as well as the two key cost centers—editorial and production. Hoagland provided comparative data showing that *Monitor* editorial costs were by then not only far above their historic levels, but badly inflated when compared to other American newspapers. He also permitted himself to wonder how many other serious newspapers attempted to cover the world without using the Associated Press.[11]

The Church's Board of Directors so appreciated the services Hoagland rendered, that they sounded him out about assuming the expanded post of Manager of the Publishing Society himself. He declined, partly in deference to his elderly mother, a well-known Christian Science practitioner who feared that the contradictory demands of the office would crush him, as she felt they had her late husband. Soon after her death a few months later, however, a Church Director whom Hoagland particularly respected confronted him with reasons he could not set aside. Jack Hoagland, understanding full well that the opportunity was highly circumscribed by a tradition he loved, did accept his father's old post and began to report to work at the handsome, high-ceilinged eighth-floor offices of the Manager of the Christian Science Publishing Society. It was December 1982.[12]

Within months, the austerely modern campus in Boston's Back Bay was being crisscrossed by a brisk and urbane new breed of manager—all dedicated Church members, to be sure, but also recognized professionals who had made money and earned credentials in for-profit business and publishing. Like Hoagland, who had been president of the Glee Club at Yale, a Whiffenpoof, and member of a secret society as well as president of the Christian Science college organization, they were hard-driving people who found no contradiction between the demands of their faith and the pleasures of excelling in the secular world. Honored and excited, they answered the call to come to Boston and put their shoulders to the wheel, almost always, like Hoagland himself, accepting significant pay cuts in the bargain. Key among the new faces were Don Bowersock, Dick Nenneman, and Kay Fanning.[13]

Don Bowersock came in as the Publishing Society's Controller. A Navy man in World War II, he graduated from Brown in 1947 and went from engineering with Babcock and Wilcox to sixteen years at Arthur D. Little (ADL), a mammoth high-tech consulting firm with headquarters in Boston. At ADL, he moved from management of technology to general business management and eventually became head of R&D. He eventually moved to an ADL client, ITEK, to create conditions for turn-around, then worked for several years as an internal consultant at Gulf Oil. Bowersock was also a long-time active supporter of the Boston Symphony.[14]

Dick Nenneman was brought in as Managing Editor of the newspaper. As an undergraduate at Harvard, he had earned his degree in American intellectual history and converted to Christian Science, continuing for an M.A. in International Studies. As an army recruit, he lived with his wife and young children in Germany for several years, then moved back to Boston from 1965 to 1974 to serve as the paper's business manager. When Hoagland called him to join the team, he was a senior vice president with the Girard Bank in Philadelphia, where he had headed its investment policy committee for several years, and had authored several books on international relations, with emphasis on the geopolitics of the two Germanies.[15]

Kay Fanning was recruited to be Editor of the newspaper. In 1966, newly divorced, Fanning renewed her commitment to Christian Science under Harvey Wood's tutelage, then with her new husband bought and eventually ran Alaska's *Anchorage Daily News*. Though it operated at a loss, the *News* won wide recognition for its courageous liberal stands on local issues; Fanning was also beginning to rise through the ranks at the American Society of Newspaper Editors (ASNE) as a professional protégée and close friend of Tom Winship, influential editor of the *Boston Globe*. By 1983, she was head of the ASNE's Ethics Committee.[16]

David Anable and John Parrott were intelligent and articulate young Englishmen who had come to the *Monitor* in the 1960s, straight out of Cambridge. Anable became Fanning's well-regarded second-in-command at the paper, and Parrott, who had moved from editorial to the business side of the paper in the 1970s, found himself being tapped by Hoagland for a dizzying succession of high-priority assignments.[17]

As operational reform gathered momentum, four key players developed an informal system of contacts that allowed them to evaluate and integrate policy at the top on an ongoing basis. Harvey Wood, fellow Church Director and avid reformer Hal Friesen, Jack Hoagland, and Don Bowersock began to meet for working lunches at least once and often several times a week in a corner alcove of a quiet restaurant not far from their offices. Hal Friesen, a World War II army paratrooper who had left a solid business in California real estate to become a full-time healer and respected metaphysician, would act as a spark behind the scenes in the years to come. It was he who persuaded Hoagland to leave a prospering business to take on the *Monitor* job, and it was he who would fire those around him with enthusiasm for rapid, radical organizational change in the name of traditional values. Occasionally, those who were slow to take his points were treated to a show of temper.[18]

This self-described "gang of four" reformers continued to consult each other over lunch until the early 1990s. Throughout that time, Wood remained a Church Director and Hoagland remained Manager of the Publishing Society. Bowersock was Controller of the Publishing Society from 1983 to 1985, a Publishing Society Trustee from 1985 to 1987, Church Treasurer from 1985 to 1992, and Managing Treasurer until his retirement in 1994. Hal Friesen, as a Church Director always an enthusiastic supporter of Hoagland's sweeping recommendations, became, in 1988, one of the Publishing Society's three trustees.[19]

More and more pieces fell into place. To no one's surprise, the *Boston Globe* under Tom Winship had given favorable coverage to the appointment of his close friend Kay Fanning as the *Monitor*'s new Editor. It was not long before Fanning arranged a lunch for three at The Ritz to bring Harvey Wood and Tom Winship together, for the expressed purpose of instituting a measure of peace between her two great mentors and their institutions. Winship, in his early sixties, was at the height of his power: it was generally recognized that he had almost single-handedly built the *Globe* into the first-rate regional paper it became during his twenty-year tenure as Editor, and though local television was beginning to make inroads, the paper still accounted for the lion's share of ad dollars spent in New England that year. The lunch went very well indeed, and the *Globe* backed off from its long habit of needling, ill-will, and condescension in the coverage of Church affairs.[20]

Reform was long overdue, but not everyone was happy. While Jack

Hoagland's impressive new team prepared to usher in a new era, Netty Douglass, long Director of Circulation, then the Publishing Society's operations manager overseeing the early moves to automation, was preparing her resume and beginning to look for work elsewhere. Like many managers in place when the era of reform was ushered in, Douglass was tarred with the brush of the past, and Hoagland's reports had been uncharacteristically sarcastic when he described how the Publishing Society's circulation function had been handled.

Outright dismissal under Hoagland's stated "no casualties" policy was unlikely, but when Netty Douglass suffered a lateral move at the end of 1983, she interpreted this, correctly, as a vote of no confidence and resolved to spare herself further humiliation by moving on.[21]

Netty Douglass's fortune within the organization would soon take a 180-degree turn for the better. Indefatigable, a quick study in matters from technology to finance to public communications, she absorbed the Publishing Society's fast-multiplying agendas with ease. Douglass became Jack Hoagland's most trusted associate and right hand for operations in the heady decade to come.

Reaffirming Mission: "To Live for All Mankind"

Not only Harvey Wood, Jack Hoagland, and their close colleagues, but many others, too, came to believe that the dire straits into which the *Monitor* had drifted as a business, threatening to drag the rest of the Publishing Society and the Church with it, were inseparable from a larger crisis of mission within the movement. In this view, the well-to-do Church membership had become isolated from the general human condition. The newspaper now catered mainly to the aging faithful and a shrinking elite of others, and the market reflected this underlying weakness.

If the bones and sinew of revitalized institutions were to be sound professional management, the reformers and their allies believed, its heart and soul would be a renewed engagement with the suffering and confusion of the rest of humanity. To support their belief in pragmatic outreach as a moral imperative, the reformers could and did cite Mary Baker Eddy. A clear sense of the need for revitalized mission had begun to galvanize the inner circle long before any consensus emerged about how to act on it. It would be the better part of three years before a decisive shift in emphasis to electronic journalism at the *Monitor* made its way onto the agenda.[22]

In December 1983, a year after Jack Hoagland became manager of the Publishing Society, he gave a widely distributed speech at a large branch church in Chicago. In his speech, titled "The *Christian Science Monitor*—

Its Mission for the Rest of the Century," he asserted the need to keep the *Monitor* abreast of the times as a functioning business in the marketplace. He identified advertising and circulation as critical to the newspaper's ability to carry forward its historic mission and asked his listeners—representing membership beyond Boston referred to as "the Field"—for their active support for the changes under way, designed to breathe new life into the newspaper's pivotal business functions.[23]

Since World War II, as the well-to-do membership shrank and branch churches gradually closed, liquidated real estate holdings and bequests had become an increasingly significant income stream for the Boston headquarters and an opportunity for astute investment in stocks and bonds. The Church's portfolio, managed conservatively by Boston banks, had on the whole done well.[24]

As the 1980s began, the Church had considerable funds at its disposal, and opinions varied as to how, or even whether, these resources should be used. Harvey Wood, Jack Hoagland, and their close colleagues had a clear opinion in the matter: in their view, the Church's cash-rich position created an obligation in effect to share this treasure with the rest of humanity, by reviving the Church's historic outreach to mankind—somehow—through the *Monitor*'s even-handed, factually rich brand of journalism. Legally and in practice, all power at the Mother Church in Boston is vested in its five directors, who are expected to act in a highly autonomous manner. To succeed in the long run, though, spiritually and materially, the reformers knew that the Field must at some level understand and at least tacitly endorse any important change of direction.[25]

Although a modest weekly newscast from the *Monitor* began to be distributed via American Public Radio in 1983, the ailing newspaper remained the focus of the reformers' deepest concerns. An updated design for the paper, under way when Katherine Fanning was brought on as Editor in June 1983 and completed under her enthusiastic direction, was unveiled to polite applause from *Business Week, Time, Newsweek,* the *Wall Street Journal,* the *New York Times,* the *Boston Globe,* and others.

All these commentaries noted that the business situation at the *Monitor* had deteriorated in recent years, but significantly not a single one reported it as part of a broader industry trend. As late as 1983, then, some of the most sophisticated observers in the publishing world clearly did not yet grasp the connection between the generation-long shift from print to electronic communications and decline in the *Monitor*'s readership—a powerful confluence of events which was about to change how their own companies did business, too, radically and forever.[26]

Late in the summer or early in the fall of 1984, Harvey Wood had an inspiration. Why not hold a teleconference—*a worldwide teleconference*—to link the membership, let them hear directly that challenge and change were in the air, and invite them to join in! When Wood took his idea to Hoagland, Bowersock, Freisen, and the other directors, no one knew for sure how they would carry off such a feat of advanced communications derring-do, or where exactly such a precedent-shattering event would lead, but they found the prospect both appropriate and exciting.[27]

Preparations for what was to be perhaps the largest worldwide teleconference ever, by any organization, private, governmental, or commercial, began immediately. When the woman responsible for technical arrangements left for a three-week family vacation in Mexico, she asked Netty Douglass to act as contact with the outside consultant who had been brought in for the duration. Thus, opportunity knocked, and Douglass, her resume already out to potential new employers, was there: she flung the door wide open and happily strode through.[28]

By the time the nominal project head came back, Netty Douglass was very much in control of the technical side of the teleconference and working closely with Jack Hoagland and the Board to coordinate the event. In the course of the next few weeks, Douglass came to see the reformers as visionaries worthy of her loyalty. For their part, the increasingly entrepreneurial leadership quickly came to appreciate Douglass's natural aptitude for technology; her ability to organize, to improvise, and to lead under pressure; her iron constitution; and her enormous appetite for meaningful work.[29]

The December 1984 teleconference, "To Live for All Mankind," was a live two-hour broadcast to over 100 sites worldwide from São Paulo to Lagos to Dublin, Stockholm, and Honolulu, translated simultaneously into nine different languages. Only Australia and New Zealand had to wait for delayed transmission.

The theme sounded was revitalized service beyond the confines of Church membership, and rededication to the healing of all mankind. In Greenwich, England, much time was given to a distinguished panel of *Monitor* journalists, chaired by Dick Nenneman. In this, their first-ever appearance on television, men and women who had spent their professional lives at the newspaper spoke for the most part easily and eloquently, displaying the broad factual knowledge and deep ethical sensibility about world affairs, economics, political ideology, and non-Western cultures for which Monitor journalism had long been known.

The video record of the teleconference shows the younger selves of many who would line up as allies and adversaries in the coming years—Harvey Wood, large, articulate director of the Church—his straight dark hair showed the Cherokee blood in which he takes such pride; Kay Fanning, newly appointed editor of the newspaper and Wood's pupil in theology, intelligent, patrician, hair swept back, a radiant smile; Don Bowersock, former Arthur D. Little executive, active backer of the Boston Symphony Orchestra, eventually to assume a pivotal role as Church treasurer, looking in 1984 at least twenty years younger than he would in 1992.

And there was Jack Hoagland, rushing in for a brief, tightly choreographed appearance as manager of the Publishing Society, who spent most of the day down at the electronic "command central" in the basement of the tiny original church one floor below, having the time of his life. Netty Douglass, in her thirties, was not a speaker at the event, but she was in the thick of the action in the basement: with the help of the outside consultant, it was she who had pulled the whole technical side of the extravaganza together in eight weeks flat.

The tone of the teleconference was exuberant and ecumenical. Nowhere in the course of the proceedings was there any intimation that a major shift to radio and television was in the offing, but clearly, the Church's leaders were calling for individual and institutional energies to be redirected outward to a world in need. The event cost $3 million and, in the eyes of its organizers, was an unqualified success. The next morning, Wood told Nenneman he felt he was coming to work with a whole new sense of Church.[30]

The *Monitor*'s traditional mission to bless all mankind had been reaffirmed dramatically and publicly, and the worldwide Field was on notice to expect renewed dedication from a reenergized Boston headquarters. It remained to discover the means.

By 1984, communications technology was already ubiquitous and increasingly diverse: Most of the population was accompanied everywhere by seductive electronic companions, in their cars, at work, at their gyms, on wilderness hikes, in bed, in baths, in schools, on airplanes. Even in 1984 when the Monitor's new leadership team began to turn everything on its head, one simple fact dominated the rest: This was the general public's growing appetite for audio and video communications, rather than for print.

Soon a close-knit core of four men—Jack Hoagland, Harvey Wood, Don Bowersock, and Hal Friesen—joined shortly thereafter by Netty Douglass, defined a mission that appeared rational and straightforward: The goal was to make a significant contribution to public communications in the twenty-first century. To ensure that they could, they soon resolved to diversify the product of the Publishing Society beyond the respected but faltering newspaper. Eventually, the eleven-acre headquarters in Boston's Back Bay would house—besides the newspaper—public radio, international shortwave radio, a monthly magazine—and state-of-the-art facilities for television.

Up Against the Limits of Professionalism

The success of the December 1984 teleconference did not translate into a shift of resources away from the newspaper the following year, however, or even the next, or the next. Nor did anyone foresee that it would.

Between 1982 and 1984, Hoagland, backed by the Church Board and the Publishing Society Trustees, moved ahead with far-reaching professional reforms at the Publishing Society. At the paper, change was informed by the careful research that had been done into the *Monitor*'s strengths and weaknesses from the readers' perspective. Soon, under Dick Nenneman's watchful eye, the paper's business operations were better managed, the paper itself had been made more readable thanks to Kay Fanning's execution of the prescribed reformatting, and more sophisticated publicity, promotions, ad sales, and circulation campaigns proceeded apace.[31]

By 1985, Hoagland's management reforms at the *Monitor* were in place, financed at a generous level, as they would continue to be until early 1989. Advertising and circulation had been consolidated and organized on a regional basis, and recruitment and training had been upgraded. There had been a series of salary increases for top performers on the paper's editorial staff, and a number of new bureaus had been opened in the United States and overseas. Katherine Fanning was a well-liked ambassador for the new *Monitor* within the newspaper profession, and with the *Globe*'s Tom Winship as her mentor, she continued to move steadily up through the leadership posts at the American Society of Newspaper Editors. Top editors and writers from the *Globe* even came to two or three lunches with their *Monitor* counterparts in the Trustees' handsome boardroom at the Publishing Society.[32]

State-of-the-art market research was ongoing, and the resources dedicated to marketing the paper, never small in recent decades, had been increased. Kay Fanning and Jack Hoagland traveled together to New York to talk to Dow Jones about piggybacking the *Monitor* on the *Wall Street Journal*'s distribution system, an initiative that was explored with interest on both sides for several months, but which eventually fell through. However, a dish installed on the roof of the old Publishing Society delivered the images and the text of the daily paper to four remote printing plants around the country via satellite, improving delivery time dramatically in the Western states.[33]

All the causes seemed present, yet the desired effects did not take place: the educated public did not return to reading the *Monitor* as a second or a third daily paper in sufficient numbers to make a real difference on the business side. Each new subscription cost more to bring in than it returned in direct revenues and advertising. While this was disappointing, in 1984, all concerned—among them, Hoagland, Wood, Bowersock, and Fanning—

still assumed that the changes at the paper would eventually bring new readers, especially the all-important younger readers.

Meanwhile, Harvey Wood, Jack Hoagland, and their associates expanded tentative moves into electronic journalism that had begun in 1983. An approach from American Public Radio (APR) that had roused only mild interest in December 1982 was revisited with enthusiasm six months later when the first round of market research had been analyzed: among other things, it showed that public radio listeners were precisely the *Monitor*'s target demographic with one exception—*they averaged 35 years old, whereas the average age of the paper's current readers was 57!*[34]

John Parrott, until then Hoagland's director of research, was instructed to pull together a weekend news show for launch on APR the following January. He did so, notwithstanding twenty-year-old equipment, passive resistance from the small incumbent recording staff, and sarcastic murmurs from the paper's newsroom. MonitoRadio's news won quicker acceptance from the public network's member stations than anyone had dared hope for: by November 1984, ten months after launch, it was already being carried by 130 public radio stations around the country. The Monitor's APR contacts were delighted and impressed.[35]

Katherine Fanning, eighteen months into her job as Editor, officially supported reform at the paper and the move into radio, but the chorus of murmurs behind her in the paper's newsroom grew very loud indeed. In May 1984, the Church Directors pulled out notebook and pencil and listened with workmanlike attention to a three-hour presentation of respectful criticisms subscribers and occasional readers had offered about the newspaper, in an extensive and well-executed market survey of the paper's non-Church readership. The following day, the same presentation was given at the paper, but the reception was different indeed. Most writers and editors chose not to take the survey results as constructive criticism that they, too, might welcome and act on. Instead, the survey and its results were understood as unwelcome meddling in editorial matters from the business side. The messenger, Parrott, was skewered and roasted for his troubles by a vocal majority, and his head was sent back to Hoagland. Such professional intransigence left the Church Directors and the Publishing Society Trustees appalled.[36]

Developing an Entrepreneurial M.O.

As new media outlets for *Monitor* journalism were introduced and resistance stiffened at the newspaper and elsewhere, Hoagland began to tap non-traditional managers and assign them to building new working units from scratch, under timetables that stretched the modest human and mate-

rial resources he put at their disposal to the limits. Early forays into electronic journalism had been under the newspaper's editorial control, officially, but now the new efforts were set up as parallel structures with their
own editors. Soon, management's urgent interest in change demanded high
energy, focus, and flexibility right down to those who filled entry-level
jobs. At first, ad hoc teams were created outside established chains of
command; eventually, these were supplemented by new divisions instructed
to be responsive to market forces, at the very least—and, as possible, to
begin to turn a profit.[37]

The management style developed at the new radio and television operations would characterize radical innovation at the Monitor, particularly the
fast-growing new media projects, for the next seven years. Middle management assignments changed frequently; resources might be shifted around
with little notice; hours were long; lines of responsibility were not always
clear. Top management would disappear for weeks, closeted with the next
new project, and would suddenly reappear, astonishingly familiar with the
details of operations they had seemed to ignore, again taking a hand in
everything.[38]

Overseeing the succession of major technical build-outs that followed
one after another from 1985 into the 1990s fell to Netty Douglass, working
with the same outside contractor who had been behind the scenes of the
"For All Mankind" teleconference. Days after that teleconference, Hoagland asked her to explore the usefulness of shortwave radio as a medium for
international communication, then, in short order, instructed her to put a
global shortwave radio network in place. Between April and July 1985,
Douglass also oversaw the design and building of state-of-the-art radio
studios on the fifth floor of the long, low Colonnade Building, later to be
renamed the Broadcast Center. Specifications for shortwave transmitters
and antennas were developed, and in August and September, equipment
was purchased from a Swiss supplier and installed.[39]

In October 1985, a site in Maine was identified that was appropriate for
shortwave transmission to Eastern and Western Europe, most of the Soviet
Union, and most of Africa. Building the Maine facility was contracted out
in January 1986 and completed a year later. In that same year, the fourth
floor of the Broadcast Center was expanded to include complete television
production facilities. A second shortwave site was purchased, this one in
Erwin Canham's old ambassadorial outpost on the island of Saipan in Mi-
cronesia, for broadcast to most of Asia, Australia, and New Zealand. In
February 1987 an uplink to the Maine shortwave station was put on the roof
of the Publishing Society, and the next month "The World Service of the
Christian Science Monitor" began. In June of that year, a third shortwave

site, this one in South Carolina was chosen for a facility to broadcast to Canada, the Caribbean, and Latin America. Netty Douglass was hitting stride and loving it.[40]

For a while, John Parrott's titles seemed to change every few months: Director of Research, briefly Editor of Radio and Television, then Editor of Radio, then creator and on-air host of MonitoRadio's *Weekend Edition* and five other programs. He was unfazed. MonitoRadio first offered daily news inserts for commercial radio stations across New England in May 1985. Then in July, MonitoRadio's weekly show went daily. Parrott also learned to turn on a dime when Hoagland needed him as a troubleshooter, and from time to time he was sent on tours around the United States, Europe, and Africa to present the rationale for change at the Publishing Society to the Field.[41]

Nor were shortwave radio, public radio, and commercial radio inserts everything. The *Monitor*'s former Editor and former Manager of the Publishing Society, John Hughes, became the first anchor of *Monitor Reports,* a monthly half-hour television show launched over WPIX in New York in July 1985. A second public radio series, *Conversations with the Monitor,* began to be distributed that fall. Weekly television news began broadcast a year later, in July 1986—on schedule.[42]

Hoagland, with strong backing from the Church Board, began to question personnel policies that perpetuated inefficiency and editorial practices that had helped isolate the *Monitor* from its prospective public over the years. Which customs rested on important principle, and which were just longstanding habits? Increasingly, the pedigrees of a number of sacred cows came under scrutiny.[43]

In 1986 a radio series on AIDS was produced, which in time would win praise and important prizes within the public radio industry. This was a bold move. Not unlike other Christian churches of the day, nor, for that matter, the overwhelming majority of religious communities worldwide, the First Church of Christ, Scientist, flatly disapproved of homosexual activity. Of course, decade after decade a certain number of closeted gays worked quietly and professionally at the newspaper, in other parts of the Publishing Society, and in the Church administration. But in 1981, a year before Hoagland became Manager, the mossy silence on the subject in the newsroom had been interrupted by a particularly ugly incident: a woman writer's private voicemail messages had been purloined, and eventually, after an ill-considered series of confrontations, the employee was dismissed and the matter ended up in court.[44]

The AIDS series demanded a thoughtful update of the Monitor's longstanding reluctance to emphasize the physical dimension of any disease or report any subject in a way that might abet public hysteria or despair. The programs followed the mental and spiritual journeys of several brave individuals facing premature death, and it had the active approval of management as well as the tacit approval of the Church Board. Eventually, the series was awarded the industry's coveted Gold Medal of the National Radio Festival prize. For years, a kind of proud hush surrounded that award, and well into the 1990s, the plaque that MonitoRadio had received for the early series on AIDS, among many on a wall of awards, was quietly pointed out to professional newcomers and industry visitors on tour.[45]

The immediacy of electronic media forced MonitoRadio to reexamine some of its other old taboos. There was so little lead time! When an earthquake devastated Mexico City or the *Challenger* went down in full view of all America and MonitoRadio was on the air, human suffering and disaster had to be met head-on. Reporters, producers, and editors at MonitoRadio worked hard to bring a practical and, if possible, a positive approach to the most difficult stories. When Christa McAuliffe and her colleagues died on live TV with tens of thousands of the country's schoolchildren watching, then died again and again in hundreds of replays in the following hours and days, MonitoRadio interviewed psychologists, clergy, and other experts and by implication, through the collage of concern they created, offered their own real contribution to the healing. Praise for this response came from the general public around the country as well as from fellow professionals in public radio.[46]

Personnel at the Publishing Society's new operations soon became a hot topic. Hoagland at first intended to follow the newspaper's practice, staffing the Monitor's new media ventures with Church members plus occasional talented outsiders who met Monitor journalism's standards for objectivity, erudition, and an ability to frame stories in a way that helped leave readers confident and empowered to act. In the summer of 1986, accordingly, two dozen or so recent graduates of Principia, an independent college in Illinois run by Christian Scientists but not formally affiliated with the Church, were hired in junior positions to learn the ropes of electronic journalism on the job. Few recent Principia graduates made the cut. Some were found wanting in energy level, others, in willingness to take direction.[47]

By contrast, a number of older Principians were key players on the entrepreneurial team. Among them was David Cook, a highly intelligent, hard-working pragmatist, son of a Church and Publishing Society employee, born and raised in the shadow of the Publishing Society, who in 1994 would become Editor of what remained of the collapsed communications empire. When daily television was launched, the sensitive task of making judgement calls or checking with the Board if questions arose about editorial content, fell to Cook.[48]

Another Principian who survived and thrived under pressure, climbing easily up the learning curve and competing unapologetically for influence within the Publishing Society, was close Douglass friend and associate, Gail Pierson, who had been at the *Monitor* since 1976. Pierson had finished Principia in two and a half years, then gone on to graduate school at Columbia. It was she who oversaw the installation of modern information architecture throughout the Publishing Society on both the business and the editorial sides between 1986 and 1992.[49]

There were others, but many more of these second and third generation Christian Science youth were eased out. They had carried with them to Boston an enormous sense of entitlement, the entrepreneurial leadership found, yet they were neither trained professionals nor suited by temperament to the improvisation and long hours needed.

In May 1986, Hoagland tried out a modest but significant structural change, creating the Monitor Syndicate, a for-profit corporation managed by the Publishing Society, which would oversee the two existing shortwave facilities plus WQTV, a small commercial television station purchased that same month at a bargain-basement price of $7.5 million for facilities, signal, and an inventory of syndicated reruns. At the same time, the Syndicate took over responsibility for ad sales across all media, including the newspaper. Doing business on a for-profit basis was, to Hoagland and his allies, a logical extension of the push toward professionalism.[50]

WQTV/Channel 68, the seventh station in Boston's seven-station market, was a UHF with a weak signal and a minuscule viewership whose most popular programming in recent years had been reruns of public domain movies. Acquiring the station guaranteed Hoagland and his new cadre of managers a hands-on education in the world of working TV—the muscular unions, the fast-talking syndicators, the unforgiving ratings services, and the dynamic, hell-for-leather world of cable, on which by 1986 it was clear that all broadcast stations large and small depended to reach the most desirable viewers. In the years ahead, the station would function as a laboratory, a preview theater, and the showcase of first and last resort for the *Monitor*'s television programming.[51]

The Syndicate's main offices were set up in commercial space on Boylston Street, three blocks from the Publishing Society. WQTV-68 was a ten-minute drive away in a small, drab, workaday strip housing auto dealerships, liquor retailers, a giant office supply center, and fast-food restaurants near the Charles River at the Brighton-Watertown line. The physical distances reflected management's intention that the new generation of *Monitor* managers distance themselves from what Hoagland styled the "Chapter 11 mentality" that he felt the Publishing Society had fallen into over the years.

Neither the Syndicate nor, certainly, the Publishing Society could hope to turn a profit for the foreseeable future, but this was an intentional first step in that direction.[52]

August 1987: The Truth from the Marketplace

At the end of the fiscal year in April 1987, shock waves rippled through the Publishing Society: the newspaper's losses had climbed to a whopping $22.6 million.[53]

Five years of managerial reform and heavy investment in circulation, ad sales, marketing, and editorial had not had the expected effect. Some improvements were beginning to be visible, and Kay Fanning, David Anable, and others committed to print communications argued that more patience and more resources would eventually turn the paper around. The Publishing Society management and Trustees and the Church Directors, however, saw themselves face to face with a different prospect entirely: perhaps all the intelligence and discipline and prayer in the world could not turn the venerable newspaper around. Perhaps the public communications playing field had tilted for good against a small daily newspaper with a widely scattered readership, which could provide neither a clear regional nor a strong national ad base.[54]

In mid-August, Jack Hoagland made a carefully prepared, day-long presentation to a meeting of the Publishing Society's Trustees, consisting of presentations by Hoagland himself and his six or seven top business-side managers, complete with ninety-page briefing books. Data were presented on the newspaper's circulation, ad sales across media, the ongoing technical installations, responses to the first five months of shortwave broadcasts, evaluation of the paper's weekly international edition, the process of getting clearances for existing radio and TV programs, the emerging strategy for programming WQTV, financial planning, and planning for daily TV, and for a possible monthly magazine.[55]

The proceedings were videotaped and sent "across the pond" along with more briefing books, for the Church Directors' immediate attention. Fanning and her top associates at the newspaper were aware that a Trustees' meeting was taking place, but it would be weeks before they understood that, in effect, the outlines of a new vision of Monitor communications had been quietly, methodically, put out on the huge old black walnut table for the trustees' (and the Church Directors') consideration.[56]

The morning session was devoted entirely to the newspaper: circulation, advertising, expenses and operations were set in an industry context. In the previous twenty years, the population had increased, national newspaper circulation had remained steady, and the number of viable daily newspapers, particularly those owned independently, was dropping at an accelerating rate. Surviving dailies, except for the *Wall Street Journal* and *USA Today,* shared a similar business profile: they dominated a metropolitan market, met circulation costs with circulation revenues, then covered the rest of their operating costs and perhaps made a profit with ad revenues. Ad sales cost 5 to 7 percent of ad revenues, and almost 90 percent of ad revenues were sales to local and regional businesses in the single market they dominated.[57]

By contrast, in recent years the *Monitor*'s ad sales had cost 85 to 125 percent of the revenues they generated, and circulation revenues alone could not, under any of three aggressive promotional scenarios, be expected to cover the paper's editorial and production costs. The deficit was structural and with reduced expenses for marketing would settle in at about $20 million a year or, the Manager's team concluded, $85 to 92 million over the next five years.[58]

Some managers had been asked to look into the possibility of bringing the *Monitor*'s international edition into the U.S. market, either as a standalone or in combination with the daily paper, but they reported that, for a variety of reasons, this would not affect the deficit or the size of the readership. Electronic delivery of the daily newspaper through a "black box" placed in the subscriber's home had been explored and a prototype produced, but it was expensive and, to be feasible, required a change in reader habits that seemed unlikely. One alternative scenario put forward in the briefing books phased the daily paper out entirely in three years' time.[59]

Shortwave radio received an optimistic review. In four and a half months of operation with only one of three transmitters broadcasting, "The World Service of the *Christian Science Monitor* "had received 5,400 letters from Europe, the Middle East, Africa, and even the United States, where reception was spotty. The programming was still rudimentary, consisting of hard news and soft rock during the week and religious features on the weekends. Shortwave audiences worldwide could not be measured, still the possibility of corporate sponsorships to defray costs seemed real. Hoagland urged that the remaining transmitters be installed and made operational in South Carolina and in Saipan without delay, and that programming begin broadcast in Spanish and Portuguese as well as in English as soon as possible.[60]

MonitoRadio was successfully broadcasting in 200 markets across the United States by then and had developed a strong working relationship with its partners at the American Public Radio Network. However, there was little room for growth, and the Monitor's programs had no realistic prospect of paying for themselves. Unless substantial corporate sponsorships could be found, one scenario also had MonitoRadio being phased out over the following three years.

Television seemed to hold out more promise. According to the management team's calculations, through weekly television, Monitor journalism was already reaching a cumulative audience six times greater than the newspaper's readership, assuming an average of three readers for each daily copy of the paper. Television's reach was expected to double with the move to daily broadcasts. The Publishing Society's team was still struggling with distribution, trying to learn on what terms to deal with the hundreds of station managers and news directors nationwide who stood as gatekeepers between Monitor's new television efforts and the viewing public. A working description of a proposed daily television news program was put forward.[61]

Hoagland recommended that, in the future, the Publishing Society concentrate its resources on the two or three most effective media vehicles for Monitor journalism: shortwave internationally, television domestically, and, perhaps, a monthly magazine as yet only in the earliest stages of development. His arguments turned, finally, less on net revenues than on a related index: the relative cost of reaching a single person. Just such measures had favored television over print since the fifties, of course, in the calculations of the newspaper's former national advertisers.[62]

Don Bowersock, by then both Publishing Society Trustee and Church Treasurer, sat opposite Hoagland at the other end of the long table, with the other two trustees: one, a thoughtful English bulldog, and the other, a Dutch-born senior vice-president for international sales at Wang. Bowersock did make it clear that the deficit as such was not his primary concern, but that like Hoagland he treated information from the marketplace with great respect for other reasons. As Hoagland put it, the message of the deficit was that the newspaper had distanced itself from humanity. At the argument's core was a sort of democratic pragmatism: why not favor those media that could spread the blessings of a balanced, unsensational worldview most effectively to the widest possible public?[63]

Hoagland's conclusion was firmly embedded in the data: to be of service to the public, Monitor journalism would have to be made available through a radically changed media mix. He ended the day by proposing a well-financed blue-ribbon task force with the ability to bring in top-quality outside consultants to challenge his conclusions and report back in a year. Kay Fanning was suggested, with Don Bowersock and Hoagland himself, as the review committee that would oversee the process.[64]

At the same time, Hoagland urged the Trustees and Directors to "accept and not resist the possibilities that have become evident to us to reach more of humanity more rapidly and frequently," and to "recognize and build on the expanded reach, influence, and effectiveness of the new (to us) publishing media." He concluded:

If I were to go back to one of the guiding principles for me in everything that's happened here . . . it's something that was said by Peter Drucker a long time ago: that resources must flow to opportunity and not to problems. There's a temptation in a non-profit enterprise to say, "if only we threw more effort, more money, more dedication at these intractable problems, they'd crack."

It could be that those intractable problems are telling you, by reversal, some of the right ways to move. . . . Because there's an element of listening and an element of humility in doing that . . . to look at a thirty-year experience, we've been in deficit over thirty years, and we've had people . . . of great capability and great experience in these jobs, and we need to listen to what that has told us over this period of time, and see where we're being led. Because in the final analysis, the mission . . . is vastly greater than any one medium. . . . It really is time for us to accept our future.[65]

Eight weeks later, between October 6 and 19, 1987 the stock market took a 508–point dive, coming to rest with a thud at 68 percent of its August values. The Church's $228 million in funds in hand were, miraculously, out of danger. Something about the way key stocks had been behaving back in August prompted the ever-watchful Don Bowersock to liquidate virtually the entire portfolio of investments and take the Church out of the market. No direct losses were sustained, the organization continued soundly cash-rich by any measure, and the entrepreneurial leadership remained confident that they could move forward boldly in pursuit of their more and more sharply focused vision of what Monitor communications could be.[66]

Thanks to Bowersock's perspicacity, the financial resources for the major shift into electronic communications were available. But the economy would handicap the Monitor's entrepreneurs nevertheless: for over the next four years, the nationwide recession that followed in combination with other factors would wreak havoc with Hoagland's projection that the Publishing Society could cover a significant portion of what it would cost to reposition and diversify with revenues from advertising.

Chapter 4

Sharpened Focus

1987–1988: A quality news service for television

Metaphysics resolves things into thoughts, and exchanges the objects of sense for the ideas of Soul.

—*Mary Baker Eddy* Science and Health with Key to the Scripture, *1875.*
(Quoted by Jack Hoagland to describe the essence of the Monitor's transition to electronic journalism.)

High-End Vehicles and the First Wave of Outsiders

Despite limited human resources, despite internal opposition, despite the newspaper's continuing losses, and despite the significant additional expenses to be incurred, the Monitor's entrepreneurs moved directly into week-nightly television news broadcasts. They had become aware of a compelling business reason to do so.

Hoagland, Bowersock, and their team understood earlier than most the increasingly pivotal role of distribution. To capture a wider public, it might be necessary for Monitor journalism to be on television, but it was not sufficient. Hoagland's salespeople had been reporting back from the marginal world of small, independent television stations, that daily shows and *only* daily shows could get favorable viewing hours or local promotion. To secure acceptable time slots, rather than languish in the after-midnight-to-pre-dawn hours, it was imperative to go daily. Without good placement and promotion from client stations, no viewers, and without viewers, no ad sales. Without moving to daily television, not only would break-even be forever out of reach, no worthwhile organizational mission would be served.[1]

When word got around the Publishing Society that a daily television news show was in the works, some thoughtful voices among those committed in principle to the move into electronic media raised issues of pace and scale in the transition. One economical format considered, then set aside, was a daily morning news program in which *Monitor* correspondents would give their perspectives on events of the previous day, events that could be shown with syndicated tapes and perhaps with live feeds from Asia. As planning moved forward, some loyal staffers did their own projections and warned that management's production budgets were low, and the revenues projected were high—which would indeed prove to be the case. Burnouts were already beginning to occur, and others pointed out that the pool of personnel available could not be stretched yet thinner while still maintaining high journalistic standards.[2]

Hoagland's efforts continued to be reviled by the majority at the newspaper, who expressed outrage at any change other than pumping more money into the paper itself. Anonymous letters in the telltale editorial style of the religious publications circulated periodically in-house and to the Field. By mid-1987, the Monitor's entrepreneurial leadership took less and less interest in distinguishing thoughtful criticism from the cacophony of angry print fundamentalists, conservatives whose religious views (or institutional interests) led them to oppose any vigorous outreach, and congenital nay-sayers. Hoagland, Douglass, and their action team of the moment always worked flat out, and now they began to respond to internal opposition in an increasingly summary manner.[3]

Eventually, Hoagland and his associates came close to taking a "you're-either-with-us-or-you're-against-us" stand—hardly surprising, given the magnitude of the changes under way, the constraints of a twenty-four-hour day, and their clear mandate from the Church Directors. The Monitor's entrepreneurial leadership deviated from normal business practices mainly in their reluctance—or inability—to fire outright those at the paper, at the religious periodicals, or at Church archives who more and more openly worked to undermine the policies they were struggling to execute.

By September 1987 planning was under way for both daily television news and a new monthly news analysis magazine. During that fall, *World Monitor News,* the television show, and *World Monitor Magazine* came to be conceived of as handsome, high-end vehicles, with quality content boldly reflected in exceptionally attractive production values. To make sure these stylish new products would be top-of-the-line from the start, Hoagland brought a new kind of manager to the Publishing Society: the high-powered, highly paid outsider. The fact that these outsiders were compensated according to communications industry standards rather than on the *Monitor*'s modest pay scale raised hackles, especially among Publishing Society "lifers." Less important, yet something that was noticed and discussed, was the fact that many of the influential newcomers who absorbed management's days, nights, and weekends, and had a strong hand in shaping the *Monitor*'s important new products, were Jews.[4]

Herb Victor, a San Francisco–based broadcast consultant, and Danny Wilson, his long-time friend and a man with an enviable reputation for high-quality documentaries and specials—not, however, for conventional newscasts—came on board. Victor and Wilson were, with Hoagland and Douglass, the designers of *World Monitor News*. Both men were pleased to support Monitor values as translated into the new medium: there would be no character assassination and no graphic depictions of violence and disaster, and there would be more in-depth pieces than conventional TV made room for, emphasizing the long-term causes of events and demystifying crises.[5]

Initially, the plan was to use a system of bonuses that would allow the newspaper's correspondents and stringers worldwide to appear on camera with television versions of their print stories. Television would also have its own reporters and develop its own stories, and radio, as it gradually downsized, would be able to broadcast edited and/or enhanced versions of the soundtracks of television pieces. The policy, designed to contain costs and to give visibility to the newspaper's journalists, was called "synergy."[6]

Victor and Wilson brought the sensibility of lifelong broadcast television professionals to *World Monitor News:* this meant a national-class animated logo, musical signature, and transitions, a format alternating longer pieces with shorter ones, and a visually important set and highly professional camerawork and editing were all essential. While Monitor regulars from the newspaper, the radio, or the earlier television series would report from around the world, with some new staff as needed, Victor and Wilson wanted the show to have an anchor who would give it instant visibility nationwide, an icon of intelligence and integrity, a promotable star. But who? Nobody in-house met these specifications.[7]

Danny Wilson assured Hoagland that, "with the networks abdicating their responsibilities and winding down their newscasts, there [were] good people available," and the search was on. Eventually, NBC and CBS veteran John Hart, serious son of a Methodist minister, known for integrity and an independent cut on events, was suggested. Wilson met with Hart in New York, set up a Boston visit, and over dinner with Hoagland and Douglass at the hotel across from the Back Bay campus that first day, as Wilson put it, "Everyone fell in love." In April 1988 the new show—by then actively shopping for a cable venue—was announced. Hart was introduced as anchor at a press conference at the Hotel Pierre in New York and the story got good national play in the print press.[8]

For executive producer, Hart pushed Sandy Socolow, a respected, popular senior producer who had left CBS amid the cost-cutting frenzy mandated by the network's new owner in the previous year. "The best of what news journalism is," Wilson said of thirty-two-year old network veteran Socolow, calling him "an ace." Hoagland, himself, had called Socolow, as well, on the strength of what was said about him in Peter J. Boyer's book, *Who Killed CBS?* Despite reservations about Hart's temperament, Socolow came to Boston and took charge of shaping the news staff for the new program.[9]

Douglass set up the Monitor's new television operations in Washington and abroad. In January, she signed an agreement with NHK (Japanese National Broadcasting) for use of studio facilities in Tokyo. By February, arrangements were in place in London for television studio facilities as well as news footage service. A Washington, D.C., studio was lined up in March.[10]

By February, Victor and Wilson had initiated discussions on the Publishing Society's behalf with several cable networks, and by late spring they shook hands on terms with Arts and Entertainment. At the last minute, the Discovery Channel made an offer that might mean more money for the Monitor, and A&E was dropped—a move Hoagland would come to regret. Herb Victor began long, sometimes acrimonious negotiations to iron out the details. As talks dragged on, Hoagland fretted: if Discovery slipped through their fingers, the Monitor would be left with a big star, a big new show, an expensive worldwide electronic news-gathering operation in place—but no distribution. He stepped in and closed a considerably less favorable deal than the one Victor had hoped to land—unnecessarily, at least from the consultants' perspective. Under the circumstances, though, for Jack Hoagland, having the Discovery deal in hand was a whole lot better than no deal at all.[11]

In fact, the agreement signed cost the young founders at the Discovery Channel considerably more than they had been accustomed to paying in the three years since their own launch. Discovery agreed not to place ads for alcohol or for pharmaceuticals during *World Monitor News* and to make "reasonable efforts" to get its cable affiliates to follow suit. Advertising and promotional costs were to be borne equally.[12]

World Monitor Magazine was scheduled to begin publication simultaneously with the launch of *World Monitor News* in the fall of 1988. Malcolm Netburn and his partner Frank McGill, pleasant and intelligent publishers' consultants from New York, had been working with Publishing Society managers since 1985 on the logistics and costs of distributing the paper, and with Dick Nenneman on overall strategies for reducing the paper's deficit. Now they were asked to help design the handsome new monthly magazine, and they eventually stayed on to try to jump-start its advertising and circulation.[13]

The new magazine's editor was Earl Foell, editor of the newspaper from 1979 to 1983 and one of the finest of the *Monitor*'s old school. Initial operations were set up in rough-and-tumble offices several blocks off campus.[14]

The new magazine's concept would emphasize the newspaper's tradition of giving a platform to those in public life who took a constructive, factually grounded approach to the burning issues of the day. *WMM* was conceived of as written, not by Monitor staffers, but by opinion-leaders for opinion-leaders, with special emphasis on issues of global import. Foell, intelligent and debonair, long-time president of the U.N. press corps, drew on his own wide network of personal contacts and parlayed the *Monitor*'s reputation to line up impressive contributors beginning with former presidents Gerald Ford and Jimmy Carter, who wrote pieces for the first issue giving their advice on foreign policy to whoever would be elected the new president a few weeks hence.[15]

The New Vision Comes into Sharper Focus

By 1987, three years after the global teleconference, it had become self-evident to the fifteen or so men and women in the eye of the Monitor's entrepreneurial hurricane that, to honor the paper's historic mission "to serve all mankind" with balanced, ethically informed, factually rich news and public information, it was imperative to diversify into whatever media the public used. The Monitor, they came to realize, was not in the newspaper business—but the communications business!

A long list of vexed questions remained to be worked out in practice. How flexible could—or should—the Publishing Society's eighty-year-old corporate culture be? If intellectual capital of a very special sort was the institution's real treasure, how could that be protected in the transition? Should the newspaper be phased out, or integrated closely and actively with other media, or just left alone? Who would guarantee the quality of the content broadcast? And who was keeping track of how all that money was spent?

As the outlines of the new vision of Monitor communications emerged, Jack Hoagland, Harvey Wood, Don Bowersock, Netty Douglass, and their close associates moved without delay to implement the decisions that followed from it. As individuals and as a team, they thrived on the challenges.

For some less free-wheeling souls who reported to them, it was a different story. Professional turf was invaded on a regular basis, and employees at all levels had to change and upgrade their skills or be left behind. It was common knowledge that those who moved to television and the new hires from the outside were better paid than those who stayed on the newspaper or with the religious periodicals. The old order, imperfect as it had been, seemed almost unforgivably violated by the appearance of large numbers of well-paid strangers, people who were not Church members, people who probably lived quite differently from themselves, and who more and more assumed positions of authority.[16]

Such feelings were amplified by a pro-print, anti-TV bias still very much abroad among educated Bostonians of the day. Boston-area intellectuals and professionals of all faiths and philosophies, including some of the highly literate employees at the Christian Science Center, were proud to care little about television, except to deplore its effects on the rest of the population.

Synergy—specifically, encouraging journalists in print to double as on-air radio and TV commentators—was central to management's new vision of Monitor communications. It proved difficult to implement in practice. Typical print journalists still worked alone, year-in, year-out, and in their world, individual responsibility for the thoughtfulness and information content of the final communication put before the public seemed crystal clear. By contrast, TV journalism is accomplished by ad hoc teams whose members may move in and out of a project on a given day or in a given week, as needed; each team member is responsible for a different aspect of the end communication, and the sort of authorship writers take for granted evaporates. Print or electronic, they might be seasoned journalists all, but in the 1980s and perhaps especially at the Publishing Society, they worked in wholly different professional cultures.[17]

Other factors amplified the clash of cultures, including, on occasion, mischief made by Hoagland himself. For example, at first Kay Fanning's Managing Editor, David Anable, not only supported reform, but in principle the policy of synergy as well. But Fanning and Anable lost their enthusiasm for synergy quickly, when it seemed too often to be used as an excuse to raid the newspaper's staff, enticing those who performed well in electronic media to move over to radio and or to television with salaries that the newspaper could not match.[18]

Likewise, the electronic information systems introduced by Douglass's associate Gail Pierson at the Monitor, linking print and electronic journalists, editors, producers, and archives, were difficult for some writers to adjust to. When it became clear that the networks being put in place would link personnel first throughout the Publishing Society's Boston headquarters, then the Washington bureau and bureaus overseas, and eventually, for some purposes, sites and sources beyond the Monitor organization itself, many at the paper became convinced that their professional autonomy would—somehow, surely, eventually—be compromised.[19]

Moreover, the very look of network television that *World Monitor News* introduced offered much to offend old-guard Monitor sensibilities. The network star system personified by John Hart emphasized physical attractiveness and glamorous pose rather than inward mental qualities. Similarly, the high-end, "uptown" look of the program's handsome blue and mauve set was just too rich, too material, for comfort.

Historically, the bedrock upon which the *Monitor* had built its worldwide reputation for excellence in the decades since its founding in 1908, was its editorial standards. Never had there been a standards-and-practices manual at the paper, however, and newsroom lore had it that it took a newcomer, even one raised in the Church, a full ten years to understand what made a *Monitor* story different from journalism by other people of conscience. Some *Monitor* writers amiably admit that the heavy mystique surrounding the newspaper's editorial standards was often one part nonsense to one part deep principle, but even such friendly debunkers understood very well that there was much precious that could be lost in the shuffle of new faces, new technologies, and new work habits.[20]

At the newspaper, the five-person editorial board Hoagland established in the early 1980s did demystify editorial control somewhat and, by consent of all concerned, diminished the presence of the "owner" in daily and weekly decisions about content. Only editorial-page essays and cartoons were submitted in advance to a designated Church director. When editorial responsibility for radio and TV was made separate from the newspaper, the Church's influence was exerted far less formally and most often only *after* a piece had been aired, if at all.[21]

In the early years of radio and television, Hoagland, as Manager of the Publishing Society, often involved himself in thrashing out matters of editorial oversight, sometimes acting as a conduit for questions and answers between the editors and producers in radio and television and the Church Board. The prevailing opinion on the Board and among Hoagland's closest associates at the Publishing Society was that the newspaper's editorial policy labored under too many taboos, too many encrusted habits of self-censorship, particularly in reporting sickness, medical treatments, death, and natural or manmade disasters. As part of their program to make their communications more accessible to the general public, the reformers intended little by little to free Monitor journalism of quaint linguistic conventions and embarrassments not certifiably based on principle.[22]

Although the Church Directors exercised authority with a very light touch where the embryonic radio and television operations were concerned, it was clear to them, to Hoagland, and to the editors, producers, and reporters that they were dealing almost daily with sensitive new issues. Much of the success of the whole effort would revolve around finding a principled, humanitarian Monitor style for reporting human tragedy: the death, destruction, sickness, natural disaster, and human brutality that are normal fare in the rest of the electronic media. The goal was to develop techniques and approaches that would inform the public without provoking a sense of terror, aversion, or despair. The radio's AIDS series and *Children of Darkness,* an important joint print and radio documentary series about children worldwide raised among the worst horrors known to mankind, were bold and creative steps in the process.[23]

When plans for daily television were set in motion, Dick Nenneman proposed that the executive producer of a show would be responsible for production only, while a Monitor-trained editor, usually a member of the Church, would assume responsibility for editorial content. Acknowledging that the line separating production values and editorial message was often impossible to draw, Nenneman advocated discussing the unusual arrangement in advance with outside hires, giving neither person the final say, and urging both parties to make developing good chemistry between them part of their professional drill.[24]

And who was keeping track of the money? For all the broad scope and dizzying speed of the decisions being made, fiscal matters were conducted in a wholly conventional manner. Don Bowersock ran a tight ship from his new post at the Treasurer's office. The Publishing Society Manager and division heads generated detailed operating budgets in the weeks before the start of each fiscal year. These, with quarterly and monthly year-to-date expenditures covering the newspaper, radio, television, information services, the religious periodicals, technical installations, and so forth were distributed to the five Directors, the three Trustees, and some division heads and others.[25]

Douglass and Pierson often found themselves locked in combat with Bowersock behind the scenes over the extent of the Publishing Society's authority to get information about its own operations directly from within the organization, rather than having it routed through the Treasurer's office, but they, too, were completely at home in the world of budgets, spreadsheets, reports, and detailed projections. And so, of course, was ex-banker Dick Nenneman.

Jack Hoagland's ability to make business decisions was constrained by the fact that he reported on an ongoing basis to not one but two well-informed working boards, the Publishing Society Trustees and the Church Directors. He could not make major moves without bringing them along, nor did he try. But he was a brilliant analyst of public communications, and by the late 1980s he was several years ahead of most communications industry observers in his understanding of what the future would hold. And he could be persuasive.

The Opposition Smolders

The recommendations put forward at the August 1987 meeting, including the muffled threat to the very existence of the newspaper, became known to Kay Fanning and her allies several weeks after the fact. Fanning was understandably furious. She demanded and received copies of the Trustees' ninety-page briefing book and the videotaped record of the proceedings that had been made for the Church Directors. The alternative scenario suggesting that the internationally distributed daily newspaper might one day be superfluous leapt from the page. She demanded and received the chairmanship of the revived task force, with funding at a level that would allow her to use the best outside advice money could buy. She was determined to devise a vision of the future that the *Monitor*'s newspaper professionals could live with.[26]

On December 1, a *Globe* writer recently arrived in Boston published a substantial story that accurately reflected the ferment inside the Publishing Society across town. "We can't continue writing just for a small elite— that's not what it's all about," Hoagland was quoted as saying. "That's why we have to open up our thinking." In the article, Bowersock said money as such was not the issue, but effective use of resources was. Fanning said that although there was talk at the top of closing the paper, that option, to her, was "unthinkable." But, the *Globe* writer opined, noting the proliferation of new media and the fact that many of the newspaper's writers were already regulars on radio, whatever emerged from the task force, the *Monitor* would lose its historic position as "primary standard-bearer" for the Publishing Society's mission.[27]

The next day, Hoagland appeared in the *Monitor*'s newsroom to face the furor, and for two hours took hostile questioning from its denizens, some of it ugly and quite personal, while the Editor and Managing Editor stood silently by. An audiotape of the confrontation was sent over to the Directors who, outraged at the rank incivility of the staff's remarks, reprimanded Kay Fanning in writing for her failure to control the tone of the meeting. To create support for their sense of outrage activists in the newsroom circulated transcripts of the meeting, with their rudest remarks given tamer expression, among colleagues in the *Monitor*'s bureaus and elsewhere.[28]

~~~

The rumor mill ran overtime. Among other things, it cranked out the notion that Hoagland's employment with the CIA during his twenties could somehow be at play in the repositioning of the Publishing Society; after all, no one ever really left the Agency, did they? Didn't Yale's historic ties to the Agency point in the same direction? What about all the electronic paraphernalia being set in place under the Monitor's aegis in the United States and abroad? Was the Agency a secret partner and did that help explain some of the new faces around the place?

Mary Baker Eddy was quoted right and left. How the past should inform the present is always and everywhere a legitimate discussion, but it became an obsession at the Boston center. The organization's history was cited, interpreted, and re-interpreted. Eddy had founded a newspaper: moreover, a daily paper, a paper with advertising, one that set its sights on global reach. So should not this legacy be honored, no matter what? Or did the counsel to "keep abreast of the times" militate in the opposite direction?

~~~

In early spring 1988, San Francisco's left-leaning public radio station KQED threatened to take MonitoRadio off its air unless the Publishing Society pledged publicly to respect the federal government's Equal Employment Opportunity Commission (EEOC) guidelines and make hires without regard to race, gender, age, religion—and sexual orientation. When Hoagland and Douglass were informed of this, they petitioned the board to permit the Publishing Society to operate under the EEOC guidelines beginning immediately, even though, being Church-owned, no requirement to do so existed under the law. The board's answer—*yes!*—came back in a matter of hours.[29]

It remained for Parrott, Hoagland's liaison, to fly to San Francisco and inform the assembled KQED higher-ups that MonitoRadio would be pleased to comply voluntarily with EEOC guidelines. What KQED management had no way of knowing was that, beginning in the 1970s and carried forward under Hoagland and Douglass, voluntary compliance had more or less been an accomplished fact. Some at the San Francisco station were embarrassed to find that sexual orientation was not, as they had thought, protected under the EEOC. But their point had been made, and taken without a beat missed, by the entrepreneurial leadership in Boston at both Church and Publishing Society. The move did not go unnoticed among those opposing reform.[30]

～～

In April and May 1988, a part-time writer for the newspaper submitted a piece about racial unfairness in the schools of Estill, South Carolina. Estill just happened to be the community where the Monitor's shortwave transmitter was to be located, where the Publishing Society continued to negotiate key issues, and where good will in the community, which Hoagland's working team had labored many months to cultivate, would have an impact on the smoothness of the operation and possibly its costs for years to come.

The writer and her editors at the paper were, in their version of events, unaware of any connection to the Monitor's planned shortwave facility when the story was first proposed and the proposal accepted. In any case, by April 18 at the latest, two days after interviews had begun, everyone concerned—the writer, her editors, local officials in Estill, and Publishing Society management—was completely informed. Only Fanning, who was traveling, was out of the loop. Her consummately competent second in command, David Anable, decided not to kill the story, but assured Hoagland that it would be handled with appropriate care.

By the time the Estill story appeared on May 16, it had been on the desks of various editors in the Boston newsrooms for a week. The portrait of the community was highly unflattering and, Anable later admitted in a memo to Fanning, unfair in the sense that it failed to note the ongoing efforts of town fathers of both races to overcome the heavy legacy of class and racial divisions. Hoagland's request that it be softened or shortened was rejected. Anable had also quietly contacted a senior reporter at the *Boston Globe* to alert him that there was a controversial story in queue that might be killed by the manager's office; that reporter had called Hoagland directly, identified the *Monitor*'s own Managing Editor as his source, and asked for more information. The *Monitor*'s newsroom gave the story a first-page promotional box and a two-page spread with three photos on the inside.[31]

Kay Fanning was blindsided—she first learned that trouble was brewing the day before the story ran. Was the Estill incident really, as she later wrote to Hoagland, just "an unfortunate chain of coincidental events?" Or was the story conceived and pursued to embarrass management and, perhaps, put a little sand in the gears of the effort to diversify beyond print, as Hoagland and Douglass believed? Or was it, as David Anable asserted, a story that got under way with no harmful intent, but then, once the conflict of interest became clear, turned into a necessary exercise in editorial independence? Or were Fanning and Anable both set up by troublemakers in their news-room? Whatever the composite truth, it hardly mattered: the Estill episode left more poison in the well from which everyone at the Publishing Society would need to drink, in order to survive.[32]

In June, one of the Publishing Society's religious periodicals printed a sly lampoon of a foolish Church member whose professional particulars resembled Hoagland's. The hapless fellow nearly lost his life attempting to talk to those outside the faith. The moral: Trying to communicate with the rest of the world is a fool's errand, and dangerous.[33]

Over the summer, as *World Monitor News* and *World Monitor Magazine* headed for September launch, Robert Peel, the Harvard-educated dean of Christian Science intellectuals, weighed in publicly against the Publishing Society's policies. He fulminated in print against "the very latest expertise in management, strategic planning, advertising, public relations, psychology, marketing, electronic communication, computer science, global tele-thons, together with a more relaxed standard of traditional moral and intellectual values." Peel's argument was heavy with quotations from Mrs. Eddy's immense oeuvre, a number of which could as easily have been cited to support an opposite opinion. His tone was unself-consciously elitist—a call (like the parable published a few weeks earlier) to stay safe inside the fortress of one's faith.[34]

Harvey Wood took the unprecedented step as Chair of the Church Board of Directors of distributing advance copies of Peel's diatribe to all employ-ees, regretting the "cloistered nostalgia" of the views expressed in it and reaffirming the directors' own conviction that the Publishing Society's ex-citing new ventures would and should move forward "on behalf of a hu-manity in great need."[35]

A July retreat of top Publishing Society managers at Loon Mountain, New Hampshire, threw more fuel onto the flames of dissent. Hoagland's consultants argued openly for making the paper a weekly; Hoagland countered emphatically that there must always be "a daily print product." Two years earlier, he had developed a primitive prototype of an electronically delivered newsletter in the belief that text and images could soon be delivered inexpensively via the home TV. Two members of Fanning's task force present at the retreat drew their own alarmed conclusions that the reference to "a daily print product" in this context could only be yet another scarcely veiled threat to the paper.[36]

The September launches of daily TV with John Hart and the monthly news analysis magazine drew near. On a number of occasions during those weeks, David Anable pointedly asked Jack Hoagland and others, "When will we know that television has failed?" The implication seemed to be that then, when the entrepreneurial management looked good and foolish, the Publishing Society could return to concentrating on the newspaper.[37]

World Monitor News Launches: Reaching for First-Rate Television Journalism

On September 12, 1988, John Hart turned to the camera from the sweeping set and began, "Tonight on *World Monitor News:* Saying 'no' to dictator·ship in Chile, saying 'yes' to democracy in Burma, and the children of wartime love, rejected in peace, looking for a welcome home."

First came a visually gripping, seven-minute piece from old *Monitor* hand James Nelson Goodsell in Santiago, chronicling events that would end a few weeks later with the exit of dictator Augusto Pinochet and the installation of democracy. Goodsell's voice-over copy was spare, punchy, and full of key facts. The show continued with Burma footage and expert commentary via satellite from another old *Monitor* hand, Takashi Oka, speaking from the Monitor's Tokyo bureau for a total of another seven minutes, then, briefly, headlines from Damascus, West Germany, Northern Ireland, and the Pope in Africa. The third and final story of the broadcast was a look at mixed-race children left behind in Vietnam by American soldiers, five minutes long, by African-American *Monitor* correspondent Meredith Lewis. The show ended with an unimaginative minute-and-a-half homily on Rosh Hashana from a New York rabbi. Although awkward in spots, the show was held together by the tough, transparent web of Hart's prose and the natural authority he communicated.

Solid from the first broadcast, the program's longer, feature-style pieces, its international, multiracial, multireligious flavor, with visuals—and ideas—emphasizing the beauty of people and of places far from America signaled clearly that its producers were aiming for a different kind of television. The reviews in the national press were uniformly favorable.[38]

Kay Fanning's Vision Evolves: Closing the Gap or Disguising the Differences?

By October 31, 1988, when Fanning's task force on the future of the newspaper reported to the Publishing Society Trustees, there was no question in anyone's mind that the simultaneous launch of *World Monitor News* on the Discovery Channel and publication of the new *World Monitor Magazine* had been a smashing success.

Fanning, visibly tired but looking authoritative in a deep-blue business suit, convened the meeting. The videotaped record, six tapes in all, shows a severely utilitarian room on the seventeenth floor of the Administration building. Cafeteria-style tables and unupholstered chairs were arranged along three sides of a rectangle facing a movable podium, an overhead projector, and a screen.

Fanning introduced herself to the camera, then her four-man core team: David Anable, her Managing Editor and executive alter-ego; the Publishing Director, responsible for circulation; the President of Monitor Syndicate, responsible for ads across media; and the Assistant Managing Editor. She introduced the task force's principal consultant, Chris Urban of Urban and Associates, respected advisers to the American Society of Newspaper Editors as well as to some eighty individual newspapers nationally. The Diebold Group, consultants on applied communications technology, would arrive after lunch. She introduced the Publishing Society's three new trustees, also Don Bowersock, Church Treasurer, and Harvey Wood, sitting in as the Board contact.

Fanning forgot to introduce three other people who were present: Jack Hoagland, Manager of the Publishing Society, Netty Douglass, by then Assistant Manager of the Publishing Society, and Dick Nenneman, then General Manager of Print Publishing.[39]

Everyone had a good laugh over the unintentional lapse, but it was an uncanny reflection of the central weakness of Fanning's message. After months of study, the very management principles and procedures that had been so reviled and resisted at the newspaper for so long were now accepted and incorporated into her proposed vision of the future. Yet, not once throughout the day was it acknowledged that among those present were the very reformers who had insisted on these reality-based principles and procedures in the first place. No remark was made conceding that Hoagland and his team had been right, or even partly right, and that the new converts on the task force had persisted for several years in views they now saw were wrong, or partly wrong. In fact, after Hoagland introduced himself and his colleagues, neither his name nor theirs were mentioned again in the five hours of presentations that followed.

In her opening remarks, Fanning invoked tradition to limit in advance the possible policy outcomes she would consider. First, she recalled some of what Mary Baker Eddy and her close associates had said in founding the *Christian Science Monitor* eighty years earlier. Then she went on to assert that the founders would have wanted these parameters to remain essentially unchanged in the present circumstances. Tradition could not be honored, she asserted, unless the *Monitor* remained a newspaper that was published daily, distributed internationally, carrying advertising, and so forth.

Urban and Associate's research confirmed in detail much of what previous studies had already found: that most of the public could not be persuaded to read another daily paper, nor would current subscribers tolerate a price increase. The key contribution Urban made to the day's discussion was her finding that Hoagland's August 1987 report to the Trustees understated the *Monitor*'s reach by 50 percent. According to her numbers, each *Monitor* subscription was read on the average by three adults every day, and by six adults, cumulatively, in the course of any given week.[40]

A funereal gentleman from the Diebold Group pronounced the current use of technology at the newspaper to be lean, mean, and appropriate. No technological innovation beyond those already in place could help reduce the deficit for the next several years, he declared, by implication endorsing Hoagland's policies to date, but ruling out electronic delivery to the home as a cost-cutting measure anytime in the next fifteen years. John Diebold, the Diebold Group's founder and a close adviser to the American Society of Newspaper Editors, arrived for the presentation and sat next to Fanning.

The task force foresaw a major redesign to make the paper more friendly for general readers. Market research would be a key tool in the process. A chalk-white David Anable outlined major, carefully reasoned cuts in editorial staff. Advertising would hold the line and pay for itself. Circulation strategy was something new: the report recommended deliberately building in "churn"—that is, temporary subscribers attracted by cut-rate offers who were unlikely to renew. By averaging discounted subscriptions and full-rate subscriptions, they thought circulation could make some money. Finally, all department heads would be taught to manage marginal costs, on a decision-by-decision basis.

The newspaper, as the task force saw it, would be "the anchor" in the larger configuration of the Monitor's multimedia communications, with a key role as the guardian and arbiter of traditional editorial standards.

Under the task force's draconian plan, the paper's deficit would be reduced from $20 million to $10 million a year. If the consultants were lackluster, the core team's presentations were riveting. The tensile strength of the collective intelligence of the managers who gave presentations that day, every bit of it bent to the job of saving the newspaper they loved, can be felt across the years through the videotaped record.

Fanning's team remembers feeling proud and happy, knowing they had labored long, hard, and well, sure that they had presented a plan that could and would be accepted.[41]

At the end of that long day, Harvey Wood spoke, and his brief remarks punctured any bubble of hope that the presenters might have had that their efforts were well received. He did not congratulate the task force for what they had accomplished. He said flatly that the paper's deficit must be cut still further, still faster, and he declared that their report had confirmed, not disproved, the assumptions in Hoagland's August 1987 report to the Trustees.

Fanning answered Wood's provocation in even tones, promising a follow-up the next day. She asked for other questions or comments, and there were none. She asked again, cajoling, but was met with silence. She closed the meeting. As she slowly gathered her papers up, her face giving away nothing of her thoughts, the other participants could be seen filing out behind her. Then the camera switched off.

A six-page addendum to the task force report distributed the following day did indeed challenge some facts and some assumptions put forward at the August 1987 Trustees' meeting and shed light on the curious willingness in the previous day's report to subsidize short-term subscriptions by whatever means necessary, including cuts in the editorial staff. The alternative assumptions put forward and the budget trade-offs made did not merely affect the absolute size of the paper's expected deficit, but also, specifically, improved cost-per-person-reached ratios. Even though the newspaper might reach a narrower segment of the public, it was still more cost-efficient per person reached in this calculation than television was likely to be in the foreseeable future.[42]

While some parts of the argument put forward by Fanning and her team were weaker than the whole, their analytical efforts and professional courage in attempting to square the circle can be described, without hyperbole, as heroic. A business model susceptible to discussion and analysis had been produced, and the policies proposed addressed the difficult issues facing the *Monitor* within the parameters of the model.

The task force plan or something close to it might well have been acceptable had the fabric of human relations not already been so badly frayed. The addendum was marred by a quarrelsome, almost contemptuous, tone. Fanning's quality team had, as they said, learned a lot in the course of the previous year's work. What they did not say was that they had learned the methodologies and accepted most of the general goals of the very people to whom they were presenting their report. Because the task force had given itself such a good education, the objective differences between them and management had narrowed significantly.

Sadly, Kay Fanning and her allies lacked what they most needed at that juncture—the human skills to deal diplomatically with colleagues and employers they heartily disliked, at least in part because those colleagues and employers had grasped the new economics of newspapering three or four years earlier than they did themselves. Fanning and Anable, especially, were too proud and too angry, and at that point perhaps too exhausted, to make the task force report the occasion to proffer an olive branch and sue for peace.

The Newsroom Explodes: The Directors Dig In

The task force's impolitic addendum was distributed on Tuesday, November 1, 1988. Two days later, the Church Board canceled its regularly scheduled meeting with Kay Fanning, and early the following week, Harvey Wood simply failed to appear for his regular biweekly lunch with her.[43]

When Fanning finally met with Hoagland and Wood on Thursday, November 10, they presented her with a new organizational chart for the Publishing Society. Based on their outside consultant's recommendations and designed to give the Manager authority commensurate with increased accountability for the bottom line, under this plan, Fanning would report to Hoagland. Hoagland, as Manager, would have a clear mandate to function as publisher, with the Church, as owner. Hoagland and Fanning then met with Nenneman, who showed her the redesigned newspaper he and another consulting group had developed, with no ads, still deeper editorial cuts, and its circulation allowed to drop to about 120,000 or so core subscribers—long described by the reformers as the *Monitor*'s "natural" circulation level. Fanning objected strenuously to the proposed new reporting lines, but agreed to consider matters over the long Veterans' Day weekend.[44]

The next morning, Friday, a *Globe* columnist reported the task force story at length from Fanning's point of view, saying that the Church had suffered substantial losses in the stock market crash a year earlier (it had not), that for this reason and because of general media expenditures, money was tight (by most measures at that point money was abundant), and that if the Church Board endorsed the Nenneman plan, Fanning might be forced to quit. In closing, hope was held out that a compromise might be reached over the coming three-day weekend, which "could keep Fanning at the paper and get the *Monitor* out of the red."[45]

On Sunday evening, Wood telephoned Fanning at home, and she again rejected the idea of reporting to Hoagland, but said she was ready to compromise on matters of the paper's format, staffing, and circulation policy.[46]

On Monday morning, Fanning was told that many of the differences between the task force model and the Nenneman model were indeed still on the table, but that the proposed new lines for reporting were not. The Directors could exercise their editorial preferences through the manager, insofar as they chose to. Fanning still expected to argue her alternatives in front of the full Board before a decision was made. Just before noon that day, however, Fanning was informed that the full Board had adopted the Hoagland–Wood–Nenneman plan, and that she would not be asked to appear. She resigned, along with David Anable and the Assistant Managing Editor, David Winder.[47]

Kay Fanning wrote her resignation in a way that made many believe she expected to be called back: "If there comes a time that I can again serve—in a more normal atmosphere of openness and mutual trust—I stand ready." David Anable's long and thoughtful letter of resignation also left the door ajar: "I have no doubt that the current fermentation will eventually bring to the surface what needs healing, and the Church will move on purified and stronger. I remain dedicated to the Church and to its mission." [48]

The *Monitor* newsroom exploded. Personal loyalty to Fanning and her respected deputies ignited a highly combustible mix—anger over the newspaper's decline and confusion about what, if anything, could be done to halt or reverse it; distrust of the process of reform itself as much as dislike of particular reforms; historic industry-wide antagonism between newsrooms and managements at daily newspapers; and fury over the Publishing Society's exponentially increasing commitments to new media. A back room was taken over by frantic staffers who copied, faxed, and mailed out to their counterparts at dozens of newspapers and magazines around the country any and all arguments and internal documents they felt supported their case against management's policies. Many on the newspaper's editorial staff seem not only to have expected writers and editors at other papers to come to their defense vigorously and publicly—but also that this, amplified by the anticipated chorus of demands from the *Monitor*'s readers, would somehow lead to Fanning's reinstatement on her own terms.[49]

Editorial control was one of Fanning's loudest rallying cries, but the matter was not as clear-cut as her protestations—sincere though they probably were—made it seem. For decades, the *Monitor* newsroom had worked with little direct influence from the Church Board on the reporting of most of the news, most of the time. For one thing, many writers and editors at the *Monitor* were Church members, after all, and competent collectively to draw their own conclusions about how the news should be reported. Most of all, the professional culture in the *Monitor* newsroom resembled that in newsrooms at the best papers nationwide, where writers and editors traditionally make systematic efforts to rely on their own news judgments whenever possible.[50]

Ironically, years of principled self-censorship had left the *Monitor*'s journalists in general more conservative, particularly in reporting the world's suffering or in covering medicine, than the current Church Board or the Publishing Society's Trustees or the Manager and his allies or for that matter their readers, wanted them to be. In the end, the swing issue—whether Fanning would agree to report to Hoagland—was personal.[51]

Late Monday morning, when Fanning, Anable, and Winder read their resignations to the assembled writers, editors, and staff of the *Monitor* newsroom, the *Globe* columnist who had written the previous Friday's article was present, accepting documents and interviewing everyone in sight. After Fanning, Anable, and Winder shook hands all around and "had been hugged blue" by their colleagues, many of whom were in tears, they went to lunch at a Cambridge restaurant high above the Charles River looking back toward Boston, where the *Globe* man joined them for a long interview.[52]

In the *Globe*'s 1,000–word story the following day, Fanning and Anable pinpoint the beginning of the crisis as the drafting of a five-year plan in 1985, which included some options downgrading the newspaper, but they also confirm that the issue that precipitated their exit was indeed Fanning's unwillingness to accept Hoagland as her immediate superior. That same day, Tuesday, another *Globe* writer published a 900–word appreciation of Fanning as a person and as a professional; the story's principal source was her old friend, retired *Globe* editor Tom Winship, who still wielded considerable power behind the scenes in his old shop.[53]

On that day and the next, Hoagland met with the paper's newsroom, accepted some criticisms of the new media that had been launched six weeks earlier, and sought to reassure on business matters bearing directly on the newspaper. On the second day, he naively supplied specific numbers and charts and graphs: the materials—which revealed much about the Publishing Society's current budgets and projections, staffing levels, and intentions—were, as so many other documents had been the preceding day, promptly faxed around the country to any and all parties who the angry journalists believed might take up their cause.[54]

All three articles on the crisis at the *Monitor* in Wednesday's *Boston Globe* bear the marks of work done against deadline in the thick of breaking events. That Sunday, however, a *Globe* business writer published an article setting out the issues clearly: whether Monitor journalism should have a broad reach or a narrow one and whether, if the daily newspaper could not find a viable niche in the marketplace, it should be subsidized in its present form at whatever level necessary, indefinitely. Hoagland was quoted as saying the newsroom staff "were living in a dream world with regard to all the financial issues that were being faced hour by hour by another group of workers here, and that if the other group of workers were to raise the issues they would be accused of being negative about the paper."[55]

The national press reported the upheaval at the *Monitor* evenhandedly, running most stories with pictures of Fanning. In contrast to the uniformly naive coverage of the *Monitor*'s financial difficulties in 1983, by 1988, the *New York Times, Newsweek, Business Week, Time,* and others all framed the *Monitor* story to some extent in terms of the broad generic changes in public communications that were, for good or for ill, at play. *Time* magazine paired the *Monitor* story with the dismissal of *Atlanta Journal and Constitution* editor Bill Kovach, over who should control the newsroom budget, noting: "Hoagland reflects a view that seems to be sweeping the newspaper industry. Confronted by a long-term slump in circulation and intensifying competition with other media for advertising revenue, many newspaper executives are beginning to demand that editors join the management team, rather than pit themselves against it."[56]

Her critics claim that like many on her staff, Kay Fanning thought her resignation would set off a chain of events that would quickly bring the Directors to their knees. In this scenario, Fanning would return to her editorship, triumphant in the matters of principle she cared about so deeply. In the Directors' view, though, Fanning had been demanding to function as her own publisher, as she and her second husband had at the *Anchorage Daily News,* and as her first husband had at the *Chicago Sun-Times*—but this time with the Church footing the bills. Her refusal to accept changes the Directors felt essential in order to broaden Monitor journalism's outreach "to all mankind" was, to their way of thinking, short-sighted and left her unqualified to hold the job she loved.[57]

In the following months, fifteen or so resignations, two dozen early retirements, and a few more emigrants who moved over to electronic media reduced the paper's editorial staff, all told, by approximately one-quarter. In January, a slimmer edition of the *Monitor* with color photographs appeared.

While it represented less of a change than Nenneman's group had recommended, it was, as expected, hugely unpopular with the core readership of aging Church members. The aggressive promotion and marketing of the previous six years ceased, and circulation to those outside the Church fell.

When he resigned in November, David Anable had felt he had expenses on track to reduce the deficit to $15 million. At the April end of the fiscal year, due mainly to one-time costs of severance and conversion, the deficit, though reduced, stood at $18.7 million.[58]

Chapter 5

Setting the Course

1989–June 1990: The logic of 24-hour access through cable

> Genius ... means little more than the faculty of perceiving in an unhabitual way.
>
> —*William James,* The Principles of Philosophy, *Ch. 19*

Setting the Course: January 1989–January 1990

Fanning was replaced by eminently qualified, long-term staffer, Richard Cattani, who, it was hoped, could help rebuild bridges across the yawning chasm between the newspaper on one side, and the Church Board and the Manager's office on the other.

Jack Hoagland was increasingly preoccupied with creating the conditions for success in the fast-growing television operations. He had been pondering unwelcome advice from the Boston consultants who had stood him in such good stead during the evaluation and reform of the newspaper: now, they were saying that the Publishing Society would do well to unload WQTV, the small UHF station acquired in the summer of 1986. Progress had been made with ad sales, but there was no coherent programming package, the Boston TV market remained extremely competitive, and prospects for growth were limited. The station might reduce its current $10 to $11–million annual loss, but it was not likely to break even.[1]

Returning from World Monitor TV's Tokyo bureau on a Sunday in the second week of January 1989, Hoagland joined Netty Douglass at a Gannett printing plant in Scottsdale, Arizona, to finalize contractual arrangements

83

for the reformatted, full-color edition of the newspaper then already in its second week of production. That done, mentor and protégée headed back to Boston on an overnight coach and began to discuss what Hoagland had come to see as the necessary vehicle: a 24-hour cable TV channel. Douglass had worked out a list of 25 to 30 operations slots to be filled if, as anticipated, radio was cut back and television programming expanded. She had already penciled in names for most positions. In the five or six hours between takeoff and touchdown, Hoagland and Douglass outlined the concept for what would eventually be named The Monitor Channel and worked out a rough-and-ready long-range plan and a list of immediate action items that included specific program ideas, approximate timetables, and personnel.[2]

The ambitious new cable programming venture would not be announced until some sixteen months later. By the time of its May 1991 launch, The Monitor Channel would have been in intense development at all levels for over two years.

The broad new vision of Monitor communications that had emerged during the previous five turbulent years remained unchanged: the Publishing Society would present the *Christian Science Monitor*'s traditional brand of balanced, in-depth journalism to a wider public than the paper could reach, repositioning and diversifying through new vehicles, including electronic communications. The Publishing Society would concentrate on distribution over its own shortwave radio network abroad, and would use television to bring Monitor journalism to the public across North America.

What Hoagland and Douglass proposed later that week to a meeting of the Directors and Trustees, with the Boston consultants as well as Herb Victor and Danny Wilson, the architects of *World Monitor News*, sitting in, was that the Publishing Society take a giant step beyond the half-hour nightly newscast to develop a platform from which the whole range of information found in the newspaper could be televised on a twenty-four-hour basis. This meant not just hard news and breaking stories, but also the features, editorials, family pages, longer series, and guest opinions that had always given the paper its distinctive thoughtful, cosmopolitan yet homey flavor.[3]

Hoagland had come to believe that network-style "television by appointment" would continue to cede to a newer format known in the trade as "lifestyle programming," in which audiences were tuning in, not for a specific show, but for a programming genre. By 1989, that trend already dominated radio: the most successful major market stations provided a single type of communication—all sports, all news, all soft rock, nonstop. Cable narrowcasting, including huge successes like CNN, MTV, and The Weather Channel, were the television equivalent, the kind of specialized information providers likely to survive and be effective in the electronic communications environment of the future.[4]

Beyond this, Hoagland's idea diverged sharply from even the most far-sighted industry analysts. The *Monitor*'s new channel, Hoagland maintained, would not provide "lifestyle programming" for a conventional demographic defined by age, gender, education, and income, but for a psychographic: precisely those world citizens, high and low, whom the newspaper's first editor had identified as the readers he sought—those "good men and women everywhere, interested in the betterment of all human conditions." The concern uppermost in Hoagland's mind was how to reconnect with the audience mandated by tradition, and expand it.

And so, less than three months after the successful launch of a nightly newscast hailed by industry pros as a class act, Hoagland had concluded that the only way the Monitor's news and public affairs programming could really work was to offer it continuously, seven days a week, around the clock. Ted Turner had stumbled onto the same fact of life in the cable business ten years earlier. In Turner's case, the twenty-four-hour format meant being able to defray the enormous costs of producing the news, while Hoagland's overriding interest was to make Monitor communications accessible and compelling to new generations, people of conscience and good will, but with radically new information-gathering habits. Both roads, the focus on the bottom line and the focus on audience-building, led to the same tactical insight: in the contemporary marketplace, only a full twenty-four-hour clock of programming could work.

WQTV, reaching under two million homes in the great Boston area, would be the test bed, the incubator, the preview theater. An early February news release said simply that the tiny station would soon shift its emphasis to a news and public service format. For the next fifteen months, The Monitor Channel would be developed without publicity under the rubric, "TV: Special Programming," as if intended for broadcast in the Boston market alone.[5]

The First Wave of Launches

In her five years near the top of the Monitor organization, Netty Douglass, the cheerfully competitive tomboy, had become Netty Douglass, the super-sharp, tireless, effortlessly multitasking executive with a sense of humor. The game plan Hoagland had outlined on the flight from Phoenix was to develop low-cost programming, staffing up initially by shifting employees already on the Publishing Society payroll from other jobs, particularly radio, then to move as quickly as possible, repeating programs two or three times a day, to fill the entire twenty-four-hour clock. One key hire would be an outside pro, a combination teacher and drill sergeant, someone who could do for "TV: Special Programming" what the avuncular Sandy Socolow was doing so very well for *World Monitor News,* but with far more modest human and material resources.

That key hire was Lyn Chamberlin, Boston-based producer/director, sometime teacher of television production, and mother of two young children. She was the daughter of Ward Chamberlin, an important player in the early development of public television under President Johnson. At nearly six feet tall, Lyn Chamberlin cut a formidable and fashionable figure. Endowed with a ready temper as well, she made it clear she would brook no opposition from those who reported to her, from potential rivals, or from anyone else. Like Douglass, she was indefatigable, decisive, and had an exceptional ability to work simultaneously and at top speed on multiple tasks. Hired first as a consultant, within months Chamberlin was named Director of Programming for the new undertaking, and she was, arguably, exactly the kind of person needed to get the job done at the fractious Publishing Society.

Hoagland and Douglass recruited some of the best minds and voices at MonitoRadio, as well as a few writers not considered particularly heavy hitters from the newspaper, to become on-camera hosts. John Parrott, once Douglass's rival for the seat at Hoagland's immediate right hand, was removed from top management but given, in his words, "the opportunity of a lifetime" to put together a weekly "big ideas" show. Production facilities were expanded at the Publishing Society itself, rather than at heavily unionized WQTV. Once a week, a Washington-based talent coach gave crash courses to those crossing over from print and radio to on-camera roles on the basics of grooming, gesture, voice modulation, and how to divide attention effectively between the guest seated beside them and the camera's powerful but idiosyncratic eye. Chamberlin and Douglass cranked out the formats, assembled the teams, and cobbled together six new television shows for launch in less than four months.[6]

The new shows were a mixed bag. *Today's Monitor* had two competent young men discussing the stories in that day's newspaper from a set built smack in the middle of the newspaper's newsroom, with writers and editors stopping by to share their thoughts on key stories. *One Norway Street* was a well-paced talk show, and the host, an intellectual omnivore, clearly enjoyed drawing out guests from the book circuit, from Boston's vast academic and artistic community, and itinerant politicians of all stripes and nationalities. *El Monitor de Hoy,* also a discussion of the day's paper with an emphasis on Central and South America, was hosted—in Spanish—by

Jim Goodsell, the white-haired, long-time correspondent in Latin America for the paper, soon joined by the thirty-something daughter of a Venezuelan diplomat; earnest, a bit awkward, it was Boston's first-ever Spanish-language television show.[7]

Inner-City Beat was hosted by a courtly black man who had been with the paper more than a decade, but who spoke too slowly to meet the expectations of conventional television viewers; before many weeks elapsed, a camera-ready young man, also black, began to appear regularly to help pick up the pace, as formats changed, and changed again, in the search for a workable formula. *Affairs of State* tied with *Inner-City Beat* for the most painful of the new offerings to watch, yet it too had merit: a rumpled, legally blind host, words issuing forth in staccato bursts, questioned politicians, civil servants, activists, lobbyists, and educators with disarming candor. The host was an old *Monitor* type with an extensive network of personal contacts that went back many years in political circles. Big names trekked in because they knew that on a television show under the *Monitor*'s auspices, hosted by this familiar figure whose encyclopedic knowledge of their business they respected, they would be accorded an intelligent and fair forum.[8]

By May, WQTV's Monitor-produced programming, with some repeats, accounted for sixteen hours of the clock. This included thirty-five minutes of religious programming at the beginning and at the end of the broadcast day, five minutes to read the newspaper's traditional daily religious article, and a half-hour Bible lesson. Selections from old inventory that had come with the station, such as *Pink Panther, The Littlest Hobo,* and *World of Disney,* played from 2:00 P.M to 6:00 P.M. during the afterschool hours. *World Monitor News,* which a clause in the Discovery contract allowed WQTV to broadcast, played to Boston audiences at 8:00 P.M., and again at 6:30 A.M. the next morning.

The May 1989 launches were worse than uneven in quality by national television programming standards, but Hoagland, Douglass, the Trustees and the Directors were pleased. To them, cosmetic considerations were a distant second to their sense of journalistic mission, and this was an important beginning. They did not, at first, fully appreciate the power of television conventions whereby credibility is signaled with a prescribed look, just as surely as stock villains were once identified by their mustaches. For her part, Chamberlin had no idea yet that the shows she was helping create were intended for national distribution. Well into the second year of development of the "TV: Special Programming" lineup, she felt that Hoagland and Douglass themselves were handicapped by a too-literal fidelity to the newspaper, partly due to their own personal standards and loyalties, and in part because they hoped against hope that they could somehow prove the worthiness of their enterprise to the opposition.[9]

Parrott's weekly *Monitor Forum* launched in the early fall, and, if it was hardly exciting by conventional commercial standards, it did approach the more relaxed standards of public television. An hour-long interview each week, initially with no accompanying video clips and no field production, it broke all the rules. The first guest was Sissela Bok, ethicist wife of Harvard's president, and for anyone curious about the world of ideas, it was a treat. Subsequent shows gave some of the world's best and brightest—from Judge Robert Bork to Professor John Kenneth Galbraith—an unhurried chance to explain their views. Guests appeared regularly on *Monitor Forum* who dealt with medical issues and matters of faith at length and in depth from perspectives that differed in one degree or another from that of the Church. Pediatrician T. Barry Brazelton and new-age physician Deepak Chopra were among the early arrivals. *Monitor Forum,* later renamed *Frontiers,* was closely watched by Church members, conservatives, and progressives alike.

In December of that year, *Fifty Years Ago Today* was launched, with a long-time Hoagland friend, MIT political historian Lincoln Bloomfield, as host. The set design was arresting and the concept was strong: a day-by-day look back at world affairs and lighter matters as they had unfolded half a century earlier in the *Monitor.* More costly editing was allowed than had been afforded the earlier shows, and eventually old newsreels and other archival film footage were used to bring the gathering storms of 1939 and 1940 alive. A young volunteer in the U.S. Navy during World War II and later a close adviser to President Carter, the craggy-faced Bloomfield exuded authority.

A busy man and active Unitarian, Bloomfield worked out a disciplined weekly routine: he set aside time each Sunday after church to review the broadsheets from old issues of the *Monitor* that would be used in the taping scheduled for Wednesday, making notes for his producer on what to use and what to research. On Tuesday evenings, having prepared his observations and done some background research of his own, he drove into Boston and stayed at a hotel. Wednesdays, *the Fifty Years Ago* team would tape five half-hour shows, to be edited with archival materials for broadcast two weeks hence.

By the time two more new shows were in development and moving toward their January 1990 launch, the general on-camera look of the Publishing Society's mysterious "TV: Special Programming" lineup had improved noticeably. Chamberlin managed her people and her projects with protective intensity—reassuring, shunning, playing favorites, dispensing invaluable professional advice, helping with hires, and making summary changes as necessary in consultation with Douglass. A pattern emerged: on-camera presences in the first two years were predominantly Church members, while behind the camera, under the sharp-eyed tutelage of Chamberlin and Douglass, hiring was done without regard to affiliation, and a significant admixture of newcomers was soon on staff.

One Norway Street, the most professionally produced of the first wave, was going strong, its young staff setting high standards behind the scenes. The host did not have the all-American big-hair, big-teeth look of conventional television talk-show talent, but he did have training in the theater as well as in the law, took direction well, and was willing to work whatever hours necessary to prepare well for each and every visitor on the eclectic list of guests who came to the set daily.[10]

A national-class graphics team responsible for the stunning look of *World Monitor News* now worked flat out to create equally handsome animated logos complete with distinctive musical signatures and transitions for each of the new shows, and the results were exciting. An integrated look began to pull the new programming together.

Pitching to Prospective Cable Partners: The First Throw Lands Short

In October 1989 remarks to a forum of business executives, Hoagland reaffirmed the Publishing Society's determination to maintain a global reach and in doing so to use whatever media the Monitor's public found "accessible and compelling." Of *World Monitor News,* he said, "The main purpose of our . . . nightly program is to extend the international awareness of the American audience by providing a deeper and more penetrating view of the world." His central theme, the Publishing Society's resolve to serve traditional goals through boldly adapted means, was vintage Hoagland, but not a word was spoken about the all-Monitor cable channel, by then almost one year into development.

The missing strategic piece was a strong cable partner. Since the late 1970s, the cable television industry had moved toward vertical integration, with groups of the larger cable operators joining to support the development of programming content that would differentiate them from broadcast television and enable them to sell subscriptions. By the late 1980s the major cable programmers were virtually without exception owned by consortiums of their distributors. Such a partnership would involve some cash investment and would help The Monitor Channel meet costs until break-even. Even more urgently—since money could be found in many places—a partnership was needed to ensure that cable operators nationwide would carry the new channel. Given the structure of the market, the big cable operators were the gatekeepers: without cable distribution, there would be no national all-Monitor news and public affairs channel.[11]

Under the terms of their agreement with the Publishing Society, the Discovery Channel had the right to coproduce any new programming. From Hoagland's perspective this was more than acceptable, for Discovery's owners—TCI, Cox, and Newhouse—were among cable's heaviest hitters, and directly and indirectly they controlled access to a third of the country's cable households. Although CEO John Hendricks obligingly put the Monitor presentation on the agenda for Discovery's December 1989 board meeting in Bethesda, and Hoagland and Douglass set forth the concept of a high-quality news and public affairs channel emphasizing in-depth reporting and background pieces, the event went curiously flat.[12]

Some Discovery board members were also part-owners of CNN. Because two key players, the board members from Cox and TCI, were absent on the day that Hoagland and Douglass made their presentation, the proposal was left on the table with an invitation to respond within sixty days. Hoagland remembers that as the meeting broke up, Discovery President Ruth Otte, a strong supporter of *World Monitor News,* stood near him amid the general pleasantries and found a moment to deliver a firm warning: "Don't ever, ever become our competitors!" Competitors of the Discovery Channel? Competitors of CNN? Both? Hoagland and Douglass left wondering.[13]

In the end, the Discovery Channel board never made a formal response to the Monitor's proposal. Hoagland thought perhaps the bad publicity still echoing from Kay Fanning's exit a year earlier made a closer alliance less attractive, or perhaps Hendricks himself wanted to be the idea man, or perhaps, he feared, the original Discovery deal made the Monitor team look as though they had no instinct for the bottom line.[14]

By late January, Hoagland took action and the Publishing Society began to move the Monitor Channel forward on its own. In point of fact, whatever other considerations may or may not have been at play, the Monitor's solitary start-up conformed to the industry norm. In 1990, most successful cable programming services—including CNN and Discovery—had moved through development and launch without financial participation from the operators. The industry preferred to move in only when a service had proved attractive to viewers, the founders' money was short, and the price was right.

The Second Wave of Launches

Two new launches in January 1990 were high-quality shows, with important visual advantages over the talking heads that had dominated the first wave of programming. *Good Green Earth* covered gardening and ecology. With host Peter Tonge, a devout native South African with bright blue eyes, white hair, and a ruddy complexion, Tonge was pleasantly surprised to find that he was a natural television talent. Together, Tonge and his hip, hard-driving producer, a woman who had survived years of ups and downs on the production side at the Monitor's radio and television operations, turned Tonge's sprawling garden and a makeshift greenhouse into places where good-natured, pragmatic, visually beautiful communications were turned out week after week, gradually supplemented by field trips to sites that ranged from innovative sewage treatment plants to managed forests.

After two months in production at a rented studio, an entire new set for *The Children's Room* was built at the Publishing Society and filled with big, brightly colored toys and a slide. The show was jointly hosted by a popular male storyteller hired away from public television and by Hoagland's diminutive, mildly eccentric secretary, both of them dressed in primary colors and sitting on the floor to read stories to the children in the television audience. Feelings occasionally ran high behind the scenes, in part because the secretary insisted on being first among equals on camera and off, and in part because choosing books for children was a matter of great sensitivity. There was no interest in making religious points as such, but proposed works were screened to omit stories of illness, or serious magic, or ghosts, or death, any of which might be offensive to conservative Church members. Yet the show was a delight to behold, and would last in syndicated reruns, it turned out, far longer than the star-crossed Monitor Channel itself.[15]

About the time these two handsome additions to the lineup began broadcast, John Parrott devoted an entire weekly show to interviewing Dr. Herbert Benson, renowned author of *The Relaxation Response* and director of the Mind-Body Institute at Boston's Deaconess Hospital. Benson's life work had been devoted to expanding the conventional medical model to include therapies in which the mind helps heal the body. Protests came in as if on cue from conservative Church members angered that Dr. Benson, while convinced of the efficacy of mental healing, approached it as a secular phenomenon. But Parrott and his producer, who had acted on their own in scheduling Benson, never heard any complaints about this or any other show from their bosses. Apparently the Publishing Society's entrepreneurial management and those who stood behind them were content to provide a respectful venue for the whole range of "big ideas" in the marketplace.[16]

Launch Money: How Much Was Needed?

Moving toward the April 30 close of fiscal year 1990, Church Treasurer Don Bowersock watched the growing investment in television journalism carefully but without alarm. The Church's balance sheet was strong, and for the time being it could afford the $30 to $35 million annual shortfall it was incurring.

As anticipated, the Church's cash in hand was being spent down. At an all-time high of $228 million at the end of fiscal 1988, one year later, in April 1989, working funds available to the Church had stood at $204 million, and, in April 1990, cash in hand was at $168 million.

Income from all sources—gifts, trusts, and investment earnings—replenished available funds at the rate of $60 to $70 million each year. Church administration accounted for about $30 million a year in expenses, and in fiscal 1989, the Publishing Society was subsidized at about $66 million. In the fiscal year ending in April 1990 the size of the subsidy—or investment—had not increased, although the pattern of expenses was shifting, predictably, toward television.[17]

The jobs to be tackled seemed manageable: move full speed ahead with the development of television; hold or reduce losses in other media; and continue the search for suitable cable partners. To clarify the nature of the fiscal challenge—and to prepare to approach sophisticated investors—the next step was to identify reliable industry-wise experts to help develop a full-dress business plan and project profit and loss through start-up to break-even.

The Entrepreneurial M.O.

Hoagland and Douglass ran the new television operations at the Publishing Society under their own can-do version of zero-based budgeting. For the first two years or so, neither Chamberlin herself nor the shows her team was creating had annual budgets, but were given whatever resources Douglass saw they needed—within the bounds of what she knew was possible—to reach the goals Hoagland and the Trustees had set and the Directors okayed. The Hoagland–Douglass style, which evolved to some degree in response to the disruptive opposition with which they had to contend, was like a tennis set played entirely with disguised shots: it kept opponents and employees alike perpetually off balance, wondering where on the court the next ball would be drilled.

Neither Hoagland nor Douglass seemed to mind that their modus operandi created the appearance of extravagance and caprice among those who had never been part of an entrepreneurial start-up, or those whose ideas about costs were derived from print or from radio, or those who wondered if they were operating totally free of any real plan. As it happened, the truth lay in exactly the opposite direction. A coherent master plan, one with room to maneuver in its execution, was very much in place but unannounced. In

1989 and 1990, expenditures over budget in fast-growing *World Monitor News* and "TV: Special Programming" were held to about 10 percent of the annual budgets totaling $29 million (which Douglass had worked out before the year began), with the difference covered to some degree through ad hoc economies in print and in radio.

Ironically, neither Hoagland, nor Douglass, nor their backers, nor their enemies ever appreciated just how parsimonious the Monitor's television operations were by industry norms. Real costs for television news and public affairs programming were treated as top secret at the networks and were not fully reported even in annual reports at CNN. But as the embryonic Monitor Channel grew and took shape, expenses were—and would remain—at a fraction of the costs incurred in comparable television news operations industry-wide, broadcast or cable.[18]

Revenues, by contrast, were off projected levels from the beginning. For one thing, management did not devote much attention to developing television ad sales until 1991—there was nothing to sell, really—and even in maturity the Monitor's vehicles would be the kind of sell that often took considerable lead time to close. In addition, the country lay in the trough of a severe recession that had caused the worst ad sales slump in decades, wreaking havoc at well-established magazines, newspapers, and radio and TV operations nationwide. Yet another reason for the failure of the Monitor's ad sales team to meet revenue projections between 1989 and 1991 for television (or at the handsome new magazine) was that the projections themselves were chronically high.[19]

Competing Professional Cultures within the Publishing Society

In the spring of 1990, a year and a half after launch, the *World Monitor News* team had met or exceeded the standards of network newscasts by every measure but audience size, on a budget of $22 million. That figure was something like one-fifteenth or one-twentieth of a typical network evening news budget, depending on who does the counting. The show was a solid success, with a growing list of industry prizes to prove it. A record six Gold Awards for broadcast design had been conferred by the Eleventh Annual International Broadcast Design Competition, and John Hart had been named Best Anchor on Cable Television, with one judge declaring him the best anchor on television—cable or broadcast.[20]

World Monitor News ran a lean, highly professional operation worldwide, with bureaus in Washington, London, Tokyo, Moscow, Santiago, Berlin, and eventually Manila. There were thirty to thirty-five full-time editorial staff working abroad, with another twenty-five in the United States outside Boston, and at least 85 percent of what appeared on *World Monitor News* was shot by the Monitor's own people. In contrast, the three networks were still quietly bringing people home, shutting down bureaus, and using news service materials taken off the satellite. Their global presence was coming perilously close to a showbiz illusion.[21]

Because the deployment of the Monitor's television correspondents from the bureaus was planned carefully in advance when possible, because the journalists involved typically had a thorough knowledge of the areas they covered, because once deployed to a location from the bureau they did not one, but four or five, substantial pieces, the *World Monitor News* operation was exceptionally cost-effective. The cameramen were among the best in the business, and a finished five-minute segment could be done and delivered back to Boston for an unheard-of $5,000 to $6,000 in variable costs above the costs of ongoing salaries, rents, and equipment.[22]

World Monitor News professionals labored to expand the credibility of their newscast in the national market under what the network veterans among them knew were strapped circumstances by the standards of ABC, CBS, and NBC. Many were not amused by the new "TV: Special Programming" launches. The new shows competed for scarce resources, and some producers stretched their own minuscule production budgets—with management's encouragement—by recycling footage shot on location around the United States and abroad by *World Monitor News* teams. Even though broadcast of these productions was (they thought) to be confined to the Boston market, to them, the production values at "TV: Special Programming" were a professional embarrassment mixed with a touch of insanity, serving (so far as they could tell) no conceivable business or editorial purpose.[23]

Most on the *World Monitor News* staff stuck to their beautifully designed cool blue and gray quarters on the second floor of the Colonnade building, by then renamed the Broadcast Center, and held themselves aloof from those scrambling to pull together the new WQTV lineup in the crowded, orange-carpeted warrens on the floor above. A few remember that they were curious. Some suffered mortification-by-association in silence. Many just shrugged off the new programs and worked harder, still grateful for the sense of adventure, the editorial excellence, and the great breadth of vision they felt a part of by dint of working within the Monitor tradition.

But John Hart, never easy, now more and more deprived of access to Jack Hoagland, got edgier, his dark moods darker. For a year and a half, the soft-spoken Sandy Socolow functioned as Hart's "handler." In December 1989, though, Socolow, Walter Cronkite's producer at the old CBS, got an offer he could not refuse: the opportunity to work with Cronkite again, putting together a long look back at the twentieth century. Hart was given the replacement he wanted in NBC's Bill Chesleigh, but as Chesleigh and Managing Editor Dave Cook formed a tight working relationship, Hart withdrew from them both. About this time, some Church members opposed to the move into television began to target Hart, telephoning him and sending him materials purporting to expose misdeeds in Don Bowersock's personal life and other information, some slanted, some imagined, all designed to alienate the anchor from his employers and undermine the Monitor's effort to diversify.[24]

When displeased, Hart could be "downcast," as Cook put it, on camera. In April 1990 an exclusive interview with President George Bush was set up. Hoagland originally wanted the event to be two on one, with the newspaper's Editor and Hart both asking questions. Hart politely but firmly refused to go forward with this display of synergy among Monitor media and was given the interview with the president one on one. When the big day came, Hart slouched in his chair, unsmiling, at his most self-indulgent. Question after question illuminated Hart's own worldview rather than eliciting a significant statement from the president about how he saw things. Finally Bush said, "John, I don't share your sense of despair." Tastes differ in the news business, but by the standards of Monitor journalism, Hart had misused an opportunity that had been no mean feat to arrange. Monitor journalism favored a constructive, respectful intellectual posture and self-effacing journalism, not stars, let alone stars who brood, Hamlet-like, in public view.[25]

Not surprisingly, morale at the downsized newspaper was low. Immediately after Fanning's exit, Douglass had set about streamlining operations throughout the Publishing Society. By August 1989 a total of 205 positions had been cut: a third of these employees accepted management's offer of enhanced pension benefits and left voluntarily; a third were terminated, most also receiving enhanced pension benefits; and about a third were transferred to other jobs. The Monitor's editorial staff was reduced from 177 to 103. Seventeen of those who left had moved to other jobs in-house. Three or four of the best writers who accepted the Publishing Society's layoff package eventually went to work for the Boston Globe.[26]

By the spring of 1990, a number of the senior writers and editors who had stayed on at the paper regularly gave gracious and creditable performances as guests on the new television programs, and some, including a thoughtful woman foreign editor, the New York–based movie critic, and the jazz and rock critic (a woman with her own band) were first-rate. It was difficult, though, to feel that the paper itself was a vibrant, vital enterprise, or that its writers and editors were respected as a working unit by those who had decreed that their hallowed newsroom would, for an hour or two each day, double as a television set with themselves visible working in the background, willy-nilly, appearing as extras. And to most in the newsroom, the new color format in no way conformed to their idea of what a "real" newspaper should look like.

After several years of reform at the *Christian Science Monitor,* grief and confusion were the legacy. In the absence of the multimillion-dollar promotions of the mid-1980s, circulation was falling. After a particularly harrowing day in the newsroom, the impassive Dick Nenneman, to whom the task of consolidating reform at the paper had fallen, came to Hoagland in the Manager's office, sat on the edge of his desk and, voice choked with emotion, said simply, "You can't begin to imagine what it's like down there!"[27]

Some writers tried to use the pages of the paper as their personal platform for attacking management policies, with mixed results. A piece on management by fad ran; an article was killed supporting Fanning's contention that editorial independence was threatened because the Editor now reported to the Publishing Society Manager. There were other examples.[28]

~~~

Hoagland's vision of synergy among professionals in different media was proving elusive. Several hundred highly ethical working people, all sharing a commitment to balanced, factually rich public communications, passed in the halls and used the same elevators, restrooms, cafeteria, and garage, but barely interacted on a daily basis. They were separated by life experiences in radically different professional cultures and by salary differentials that paralleled those in the marketplace.

World Monitor News represented the best of the pre-1985 network news culture, and the burgeoning Monitor Channel resembled nothing so much as a classic cable start-up—half-trained, hungry, and facing forward. Tiny MonitoRadio proudly marched to the same quiet drum as the public radio networks.

At the newspaper, fifteen years or more of enervating collective denial had almost completely ended, but no alternative, no new sense of professional purpose—no effective new vehicle—had emerged. Stories of layoffs, shutdowns, and mergers elsewhere in the newspaper business gradually provided perspective on the events that had shattered their world.

World Monitor Magazine by then occupied a pleasant, high-ceilinged space a few hundred feet down the hall. The magazine in effect contracted out its editorial work, as many other contemporary magazines do, fielding high-profile contributors no other general circulation magazine could match for the sheer power, prestige, and variety they represented in the world of affairs.[29]

Standards and Practices: The Print Media Cover Repositioning at the Monitor

When they left the *Monitor* in November 1988, Kay Fanning, David Anable, and a number of other former employees cast their dispute in heroic terms, as a battle against unprincipled adversaries to preserve "editorial independence." Explanations in terms of a plain-vanilla power struggle over budgets and reporting lines would not do, nor even the story of highly skilled and dedicated workers caught unawares by technological revolution and economic change in their industry.

For months, former *Monitor* employees solicited print journalists at other publications around the country through a campaign of faxes and phone calls, urging them to take up their cause. The *Washington Post*'s Howard Kurtz and the *Los Angeles Times*'s Tim Rosentiel told Monitor Television's press contact that they had never before been subjected to such an outpouring of unsolicited materials and persistent lobbying by fellow members of the press as they received from former *Monitor* writers, editors, and others critical of the *Monitor*'s repositioning. Some answered the call of their guild and some did not. But the upshot was a certain amount of coverage that emphasized personalities and "he said, she said" accounts sympathetic to Fanning and dismissive of the Publishing Society management's efforts to give Monitor journalism a voice that could be heard and a chance to become once again a significant provider of news and public information to the world.[30]

For example, when a story depicting Fanning as the victim was killed by the *Monitor*'s new Editor, it was immediately forwarded to the *Washington Journalism Review,* which printed a sympathetic note on the event. In February, a staff writer at the *Los Angeles Times* did a long piece under the headline, "High-Tech Heresy at the Monitor?" based on "confidential church documents, videotapes, financial data, and interviews," suggesting that the shift in emphasis from print to television at the Monitor might be both ill-advised financially and a departure from a long and honorable tradition in journalistic terms. The March–April issue of the *Columbia Journalism Review* carried an article by a sometime *Boston Globe* contributor titled, provocatively, "Can the Stripped-Down *Monitor* Stay Afloat? A Close Look at Why Katherine Fanning and Others Jumped Ship." This article reflected the views of the departed editors and questioned the wisdom and the efficacy of the Publishing Society's emphasis on new media.[31]

For a while, one former Monitor editor, a former Church administration employee, and a former Church legal counsel set up a command central in an office not far from the Publishing Society to coordinate the opposition. The three worked with others to collect the articles critical of the Publishing Society's policies that they and their colleagues had helped generate, duplicated them, and mailed the copies out to Church membership throughout the United States, England, and Germany. They urged the faithful to express their indignation to Church directors and even to withhold contributions and bequests to the Church. Much of this opposition activity was funded by well-to-do activists at a branch church in New York City, at least one of whom had been in opposition to Church policies since well before Hoagland came on as Manager.[32]

During most of 1989, the *Boston Globe* published very little about events across town at the Publishing society, mainly chronicling, briefly and straighforwardly, the departures of three or four more long-time employees, including former Editor/Manager of the newspaper John Hughes. Then in December, a year after Kay Fanning's resignation, the *Globe* published another long, flattering profile complete with photo. The article emphasized her track record in turning the failing Anchorage paper into an editorial, if not financial, success. The *Globe* writer, hired two years later for on-camera work at The Monitor Channel, alleges that Fanning's friend and professional mentor, retired *Globe* Editor Tom Winship, personally directed her to do the story and that Fanning repeatedly insisted that the profile highlight her devotion to Christian Science. Not a single sentence refers to the stormy events at the *Monitor* a year earlier—a highly conspicuous omission under the circumstances, to say the least. To some, this curious article read as if it were an open letter from Fanning and her allies to Church Directors and to the Field, saying, loud and clear: she's tan, she's rested, she's ready.[33]

Fanning was not invited back. By the same token, though, neither did the opposition campaign let up: key former employees, their well-wishers, and their wealthy backers continued to work to discredit the Monitor's entrepreneurial management and the Church Board behind them. Over the next two and a half years, it would take a heavy toll.

Standards and Practices: World Monitor News *Covers the Twitchell Trial*

Only a few months after the *Globe*'s second profile of Fanning, Monitor journalism faced a public test of its own editorial integrity. David and

Jennifer Twitchell, a young Boston couple whose two-year-old son died because the parents had relied on Christian Science practitioners and prayer instead of seeking medical help to treat a blocked intestine, were being tried for manslaughter. How should the Monitor's several news vehicles cover the case?

World Monitor News ran its first Twitchell piece two weeks before the trial began, outlining the issues in a detailed, dry factual way. Trial coverage continued dry and factual to the end, consisting mostly of footage from the proceedings themselves and interviews with the attorneys and witnesses. During the trial, a seasoned journalist who was not a Church member covered the courthouse daily, and as the trial dragged on into its second month, *World Monitor News* also functioned as pool reporters, providing footage to other local television outlets. When the Twitchells were found guilty of involuntary manslaughter, an unusually long piece was run, at John Hart's urging. The final editing was done with Hart, Chesleigh, Cook, and the programs' NBC-trained senior producer all supervising.[34]

For Monitor journalism, the Twitchell trial was the moral equivalent of the challenge NBC News must confront as a professional organization when it covers (or fails to cover) controversies involving its parent company, General Electric. NBC's ability to meet this ethical challenge is the subject of perennial criticism. NBC's performance in this matter is characterized by a minimalist sense of obligation to keep the public fully informed about controversies that involve GE.[35]

By contrast, *World Monitor News* probably gave the Twitchell tragedy more national play than all other national news organizations, print and electronic, combined, and that coverage was full and fair. From the viewers' side of the television, the only bias evident was strictly professional: the clear determination of the Publishing Society and of the *World Monitor News* team to protect the credibility of the fledgling television news operation at all costs.

The Twitchell trial provided the occasion for creating a Monitor standards and practices code. Just as the Twitchell coverage began, Hart had submitted his resignation, then withdrew it, saying what he really needed was a written standards and practices code he could agree to. The guidelines for the comportment of the Monitor's television journalists were developed for, among other things, coverage of the Church and of medical news. In providing the catalyst for the standards and practices code, produced quickly in successive drafts circulated among Hoagland, Douglass, Cook, Chesleigh, and Hart over a two-week period, Hart rendered Monitor journalism a great service. These guidelines would be an invaluable tool for all concerned, as the Monitor's television operations grew and matured.

Two and a half years later, John Hart, a stormy petrel throughout his long career, claimed in the *Columbia Journalism Review* that the Twitchell coverage—and in particular, Cook's conduct as Managing Editor—left something to be desired in a number of essentially minor, largely procedural details. Hart raised the important questions—the connections between ownership, authorship, and truth in the media—but then came up with answers snarled in minutiae and denigrated his former colleagues, both Church members and outside professionals alike, in the bargain. A close review of the tapes of the Twitchell coverage, as well as of other coverage Hart eventually criticized, shows that *World Monitor News* was not merely doing well but exceptionally well in these matters, by any standards. For whatever reasons, Hart lost sight of the forest, lost sight of the trees, and made much of the patterns he discerned in the twigs.[36]

If NBC has cultivated what might be called a "minimalist sensitivity" to the issues of ownership, authorship, and truth, *World Monitor News* coverage of the Twitchell trial chose maximum exposure of the embarrassments of the ultimate owner. More than enough (some might say a surfeit of) scrupulously balanced information was furnished to permit viewers to form independent judgments in the Twitchell case. In the spring and summer of 1990, thanks in part to Hart, the *World Monitor News* team moved through a brutal rite of passage with rare grace and integrity.

"Coming Soon: The Monitor Channel"

A brief, carefully-crafted announcement on page four of the May 1990 issue of the Publishing Society's handsome monthly newsletter finally broke the big story:

> In the tradition of the *Christian Science Monitor* international newspaper, *The Monitor Channel: A Television Service of The Christian Science Monitor* will soon be available on cable television 24 hours daily.
> The *Monitor Channel*'s target audience includes high-quality viewers of the 1990s—people characterized as busy, thoughtful, demanding, committed, and caring about quality of life in the community and the world—globally minded people who are looking for an unbiased, trustworthy source of news and information in the age of media giants.
> The *Monitor Channel*'s goal is to provide, instantly and continually, everything the viewer needs in order to maintain an enlightened, constructive view of the surrounding world:
>
> - a continuous daily view of the world, its events, and the trends, cross-currents, and ideas at work in an increasingly interconnected globe;
> - news reports from resident correspondents in Monitor bureaus throughout the world;

- analysis and commentary by distinguished columnists, editors, and expert contributors;
- enriching, knowledgeable coverage of the arts—reviews of books, films, theater, new musical recordings, and fine arts;
- regular, in-depth reporting on science and technology, international sports, lifestyles, and personal finance—all with a global perspective;
- and distinguished, worldwide entertainment programming.

The Monitor Channel is also designed to serve a particular set of needs of the cable operator of the 1990s. Cable operators are becoming recognized as significant local citizens with a commitment to serving the community. In addition to providing quality programming, The Monitor Channel will work in close partnership with cable operators to serve community needs.

For example, the operator will be able to offer a daily commercial-free current events program to local schools, complete with printed materials supplied daily for classroom use. And there will be cultural and current affairs programs for local libraries and community centers.

The Monitor Channel will be an advertiser-supported basic cable offering which will launch in mid-1991.[37]

A succinct description of the product and its intended audience, and a clear statement of intent with respect to the cable industry, this issue was distributed to several hundred cable systems owners, programmers, and top executives around the country. The cable world was on notice.

Also on Notice: The Opposition

Three weeks after plans to launch The Monitor Channel were announced, a long article reporting the Twitchells' conviction appeared in a London newspaper. The Independent included a bizarre and vitriolic personal attack on Jack Hoagland. The author, an Englishman, was a senior member of the faculty at Boston University's School for Public Communications. A passage dropped into the middle of a discussion of the legal context of the Twitchell trial switched to allegations about Hoagland (who had no connection with the trial), which, if untrue, might easily be construed as willful defamation of character. Monitor Television's Washington law firm demanded and quickly obtained a printed retraction from the Independent, which was apparently unwilling or unable to defend what had been written.[38]

Hoagland, Wood, and others believed that this part of the article was destined to be excerpted, identified as information published in a respected London paper, reproduced and mailed around to Church members by opponents of the Publishing society's new policies. Rightly or wrongly, they saw a connection between this attack and the fact that David Anable and Kay

Fanning had been hired not long before as director and adjunct professor, respectively, at that same Boston University School of Public
Communications.

A Third Wave of Launches

The Monitor's electronic journalists used the newspaper's reputation to
attract distinguished guests for the kind of unhurried conversation the
Monitor's open television format permitted. There were exclusives with
King Hussein in Amman, with Nelson Mandela at home in his Capetown
garden, and Jean-Pierre Rampal, Vacslav Havel, Mario Vargas Llosa, Carol
Channing, Chita Rivera, Hal Holbrook, Ed Asner, Alice Walker, Tracy
Kidder, and Paul Theroux.[39]

Money and You, launched in May 1990, was a weekly half-hour on
personal finance and business hosted by Bill Bruce Dredge, good-looking
ex-football player in his forties, successful stockbroker and family man,
who had done eight years of nightly television for Dow Jones. The show
was competently presented, although in some weeks it lacked crisp defini-
tion and good working transitions between segments—perhaps the consequence of a revolving staff of producers and editors, a host who spent time
managing several investment portfolios, and constant skirmishes between
Dredge and Chamberlin about resources and reporting lines.[40]

Danny Wilson was by then well into production of an ongoing series of
one-hour specials, which, collectively, were the high point of feature programming on The Monitor Channel. *The Nineties: Our World in Transition*
was a series of visually beautiful presentations of the changes and
challenges facing mankind. The editorial technique was much quieter than
that of the networks, and the scripts were less factually dense than those of
most public television documentaries. In each show, a single carefully focused big question or cluster of questions was introduced, and in the course
of the hour at his disposal, Wilson gave visual evidence for the complexity
and the multitudinous ramifications of each issue and the importance of
struggling for answers, usually without pushing for any one answer.

Underlying all other messages and warnings, implicit in the on-screen
witnesses to struggle, suffering, and destruction, ran a strong visual message that somehow framed all the others: that this is a breathtakingly beautiful world in which we—the universal brotherhood of man—are privileged
to live. Wilson, a secular Jew with a strong social conscience like many
outsiders at the Monitor's new television operations, found that at the Monitor he had license to create the kind of thoughtful professional communications he personally found most meaningful.

Using some original footage, some purchased footage, and some footage from *World Monitor News,* Danny Wilson put his specials together for an average budget of about $50,000. The early titles read like a world citizen's handbook of what to think about, or, as some of his colleagues would have put it, what to pray about: "Japan: The Orient Express," "Super-Europe: 1992 and Beyond," "Africa: Odd Man Out," "South America: Dictators or Democracies?" "U.S.: The New Immigrants," "The Amazon: Paradise Lost," "Climate Control: Can We Do It?" and "Childhood: A Journey," a poetic but sobering three-hour look at the lives of children around the world today.[41]

A Message from Mandela

Early one Sunday morning in June, an emblematic event unfolded that for many in all the Monitor's journalistic endeavors summed up why they gladly came to work so early and toiled on so late. Nelson Mandela, accompanied only by four or five bodyguards, showed up unannounced, walked into the empty Church, and stood there, overcome with emotion to find himself at last at the far-off source of that must trusted newspaper, the home base of the journalists who had never forgotten him, the publication that had fed his hunger for balanced information with a global focus during a quarter-century of incarceration. The Editor of the newspaper, Dick Cattani, alerted, ran to find him inside the church. Many members of the newsroom came out into the courtyard to greet him. As word got around that day and the next, a renewed sense of privilege to be part of Monitor journalism spread, giving a special energy to the daily routines of employees, whether religious or not, across all media, business and editorial, print and electronic, old and new.[42]

Chapter 6

Launch!

June 1990–June 1991: Major course correction and flawless lift-off

> Future shock . . . .the shattering stress and disorientation that we induce in individuals by subjecting them to too much change in too short a time.
>
> —*Alvin Toffler,* Future Shock

Even as the pace of development at the Publishing Society's television operations quickened, the institutional framework around them shifted. The rebuff at the Discovery board meeting had meant that The Monitor Channel might not have strategic partners from the cable world until sometime after launch, scheduled for mid-1991. By early 1990, Hoagland and his team had quietly begun to respond to the newly perceived reality with a major mid-course correction.

In February, Hoagland had directed WQTV's General Manager and the station's ad man, working together in strictest confidence, to sketch out a preliminary business plan. Before long, too, a line of programming dear to the cable industry's sense of enlightened self-interest moved into development: educational fare delivered free of charge to public high schools under the Washington-based Cable in the Classroom umbrella organization. Cable in the Classroom, like C-SPAN, was an industry initiative designed to show that cable operators and programmers did not need to be regulated into being good citizens.[1]

In June, Netty Douglass succeeded Hoagland as Manager of the Christian Science Publishing Society and assumed day-to-day responsibility for its six or seven distinct media operations, its 900–odd employees, its $80 million budget, and its complex institutional goals. In terms of managerial skills and sheer energy, Douglass was among the best qualified ever to hold that position.[2]

Hoagland removed himself six miles away to WQTV and eagerly set to work under a new for-profit incorporation—Monitor Television. It was a bold stroke. For the time being wholly owned and subsidized by the Church, Monitor Television was now in a clear legal position to accept investing partners from the cable world or elsewhere. Hoagland himself was Chairman and CEO of the new incorporation; Douglass was its President. Don Bowersock, as Church Treasurer representing the company's lead investor, would sit on the board. Hoagland was already in conversation with top professionals and businessmen who could help him navigate the tricky waters that had to be crossed, inviting them to join the board.

The revised tactic was to launch the channel first, and sell the service hard, system by system if need be, in a grass-roots campaign to local cable operators. Now, the programming generated at the Publishing Society would have to prove itself sooner to wider audiences, but Hoagland, Douglass, Wood, and their allies were confident it could—they were proud of the beginnings they had made, and they had an abiding faith in the public's appetite for quality, if only quality could be put before this potentially willing public. It would be essential, too, for the Monitor to prove it could be a good team player within the cable industry for a year or more, through the school program, and in whatever other ways presented themselves. Then would come the time to work out the partnerships. If, despite all the industry-wide applause, a single, half-hour daily news show was not enough, it was well and good: Monitor Television would show itself willing to pony up the dues and become a full-fledged member of the cable club.

⁓⌒⌒⌒

One night early in 1990, Netty Douglass left her office in the Publishing Society well after midnight, as was her habit, to find that her car, parked in her reserved spot in the deserted garage, had been badly defaced. "Hi, Netty" had been gouged in big letters deep into the paint on the driver's side door.

New Players, Higher Dues

The Monitor's entrepreneurial leadership was moving forward at full throttle. The major course correction would require some new players and a somewhat higher initial investment. The price of the start-up would be greater and break-even pushed out farther into the future, but these were not, after all, completely uncharted waters: CNN, Discovery, and others had taken essentially the same route. From the perspective of June 1990 the new plan seemed a workable one—a stretch, but certainly workable.

If reaching a broad segment of the public was the goal that could not be sacrificed, there was no viable alternative for the Monitor to a twenty-four-hour news and public information cable TV channel. The reality of the emerging marketplace was that profusion had begotten enormous confusion among viewers: there were already as many as 100 cable channels available in some metropolitan areas, and *TV Guide* and other listings had become hopelessly complex. By 1990, the public was using single-subject channels like HBO, CNN, MTV, Discovery, and the Weather Channel as the easiest indexing device available to locate the kind of entertainment or information they wanted: that was how the connection between information providers and their audiences was being made.

Obtaining cable "shelf space" became the key to success as The Monitor Channel headed toward launch, and the new key hire would be an experienced hand in cable marketing. Hoagland had identified the person he wanted: a smart, aggressive seller with a rangy mind, a graduate degree in political science from McGill and two years of undergraduate work at Oxford, who as vice president of marketing had helped put Showtime's sales and marketing on the map. Barbara Bellafiore Sanden, member of a prosperous Christian Science congregation in Greenwich, Connecticut, played hard to get with Monitor Television through June and July of 1990, but when the package was right, she accepted the offer. The mother of two preschool children, Sanden proposed setting up the Monitor's cable marketing arm within easy drive of her home. Hoagland and Douglass tried for weeks to get her to move her family to Boston, then accepted her terms.[3]

What kind of money would it require? On the expense side, the major variable was the cost of the programming. On the revenue side, the major variable was the number of households reached, which in turn determined how much money would come in from cable fees and, potentially, from ad sales. By the early 1990s, between $30 and $80 million was considered a good ball-park figure for the investment needed to start a cable television channel.[4]

Television news is more expensive to produce than any other kind of programming, however—not just a little more expensive, but a lot more. It is in the nature of the beast. Much news programming is shot on location on schedules that are difficult to control, and most of it is a highly perishable product compared to a sitcom or a nature film, which can be recycled virtually forever. When Hoagland and his associates made their decision to move forward without partners for a year or two if need be, the full cost of CNN's notoriously frugal start-up in the early 1980s was not public knowledge. The Monitor's entrepreneurs had tracked their own expenses carefully, though, and they could project them forward, adjusting up for new programming and upgrades and down for purchased programming and reruns. In addition to an admixture of straight news, Monitor Television's programming included a combination of original shows produced at the Publishing Society—some of which were "evergreen," meaning they could be rerun— and additional properties acquired at a saving from other sources. For these reasons, the Monitor's programming might—if handled well—be appreciably less expensive than the CNN schedule emphasizing breaking news.

What did this mean in millions of dollars, though, over time? By the summer of 1990, Hoagland had two groups of professionals, Tendrel Associates on Long Island and Fleet Investment Bankers in Providence, working together to project expenses and revenues for the new channel.

The business environment into which Monitor Television was about to move was not exactly welcoming, but there was some room to maneuver. In building out and upgrading their delivery systems during the 1980s, the large cable owners, the Monitor's investors of choice, had gone heavily into debt. On the other hand, since the Cable Act of 1984, the industry was virtually unregulated, and it was continuing to take market share away from the broadcast industry at the rate of about 2.5 percent of the television audience each year. By and large, the dons of the cable industry were cautiously optimistic about the future. Their investments in new programming had slowed, but by no means ended.[5]

Exact cable fees paid to programmers were a closely-guarded secret, but could vary from three or four cents a month per subscriber to a rumored top price of around twenty cents, with strong programmers like ESPN and CNN commanding more, and the operators reaching the largest numbers of households demanding less. A programmer looking for carriage first negotiated a per household, per month price with corporate headquarters and got a "hunting license"—permission to talk to the local and regional men. Within the larger companies, big-city systems or subregional clusters of adjacent systems operated as stand-alone profit centers with some autonomy in programming. Although channel space was tight nationwide, an astute manager kept one or two extra channels in his hip pocket if he could, in case a programming service that might make sense in the margins, given the particular population he was competing for, came along.[6]

Cable's steady flow of monthly subscriber fees made the industry less vulnerable to economic ups and downs than most advertising vehicles. Ad sales, ignored by operators in the early days of cable—although not by Ted

Turner—were becoming an increasingly important revenue stream, both for programmers and for local and regional operators. In 1990, though, that cushion from ad sales was uncomfortably thin. While the nationwide recession might not affect the Monitor's prospects for cable carriage directly, it did mean that the big operators had less ready cash left over after debt service for investments in new programming.

In short, getting cable systems to carry new channels in the early 1990s—at any price—required a complicated ritual dance punctuated by bursts of improvisation, and the programmer's performance would be watched carefully and judged critically by a tight-knit community of industry insiders who had seen a lot of other dances in their time. Sanden, a self-made woman and a street-wise professional steeped in the rock-'em, sock-'em culture of the cable world, had her world cut out for her.

The Monitor Channel Team Bulks Up

Securing cable distribution would be the entrepreneurial leadership's most important strategic focus up until and well past launch, but to meet the competition in the early 1990s, the team had to be good at a long list of other agendas, too.

Program production under Lyn Chamberlin was well under way. Cable marketing—closely connected to affiliate sales in a cable start-up—would end up reporting to Sanden. Ad sales would be combined with *World Monitor Magazine*'s efforts out of offices on Fifth Avenue at Forty-Second Street in New York. Hoagland and Douglass, with ad hoc assistance from two dozen or more others inside and outside the organization, handled a long list of agendas: most program acquisition, Washington politics, equity partnerships, relations with the stakeholders in the Field, and, in concert with Sanden, contacts with those at the very top of the cable world. The Washington bureau chief of *World Monitor News* was already testing the waters for overseas distribution, and a small team coached by Coopers and Lybrand's Advanced Technology Group was beginning to explore aftermarket sales, from videotapes to CD-ROMs to a digitized archive of video footage. Monitor television's employees suddenly found themselves entered in the business version of a decathlon.[7]

Chamberlin's "TV: Special Programming" teams—excited that their programs were to form the core of a new cable network called The Monitor Channel—continued to fight their way up the learning curve, just as other production teams at other cable start-ups had before them. *World Monitor News*, the crown jewel, was pledged to run half an hour, five nights a week, on the Discovery Channel for four more years, and how that would

Jack Hoagland, Manager of the Christian Science Publishing Society (1982–1990) and Chairman and CEO of Monitor Television, Inc. (1990–April 1992), envisaged a multimedia future for the *Monitor*'s venerable journalistic tradition. Photograph by Sam Ogden.

Netty Douglass, Hoagland's high-energy executive right hand succeeded him in 1990 as Manager of the Publishing Society presiding over combined operations involving a total of 1,200 employees and annual budgets of $60 million; Douglass served simultaneously as President of Monitor Television, Inc. from 1990 to April 1992. Photograph by Bachrach.

Harvey Wood, strong-willed and genial Chairman of the Church Board of Directors, renowned teacher and healer, backed reform with Church funds and welcomed the hiring of scores of new employees with no affiliation to the Church. Photograph by Sam Ogden.

Dick Nenneman, Harvard-educated ex-banker and author of books on international affairs as well as on Christian Science, called for rethinking the daily newspaper in 1972, ten years after revenues had begun to slide. Photograph courtesy First Church of Christ, Scientist.

Don Bowersock, a Navy man and Dartmouth graduate, left a high-powered consulting career at Arthur D. Little to join Hoagland's entrepreneurial team, first as Publishing Society Trustee, then as Church Treasurer and Treasurer of Monitor Television, Inc. Photograph courtesy First Church of Christ, Scientist.

Danny Wilson, network documentary veteran and among the first high-profile outsiders to join Hoagland's team, helped recruit John Hart and Sandy Socolow for *World Monitor News,* then turned his hand to producing a spectacular series of one-hour specials, *The Nineties—Our World in Transition.* Photograph courtesy Daniel Wilson Productions.

David Cook, raised in the shadow of the Publishing Society and a Principia graduate, became Editor of *World Monitor News*; with the collapse of Monitor TV, he first became Editor of Monitor Broadcasting, then, in 1994, Editor of *The Christian Science Monitor.* Photograh courtesy First Church of Christ, Scientist.

John Hart, veteran of NBC and CBS nightly news, brought national visibility and immediate credibility to *World Monitor News*, which aired a half-hour nightly five nights a week on The Discovery Channel from the fall of 1988 to November 1991, eventually became disaffected and resigned. Photograph courtesy First Church of Christ, Scientist.

Gail Harris, Boston-based television newscaster with a degree from Harvard's Kennedy School, provided the fledgling Monitor Channel with a hard-headed, consummately professional yet upbeat anchor. The Monitor Channel news team hit stride in 1991. Photograph courtesy Gail Harris.

Mort Sahl, comedian and social critic, had been a favorite of Jack Hoagland's for many years. Sahl came on board in the summer of 1991 to do monthly two-hour specials for The Monitor Channel. Photograph courtesy Sandi Padnos, Padnos, Ink.

David Anable joined the *Christian Science Monitor* just out of Cambridge University in the mid-seventies, became Kay Fanning's loyal Managing Editor in the eighties, and resigned when she did, in November 1988. Photograph courtesy First Church of Christ, Scientist.

Kay Fanning, young wife of Marshall Field, heir to the Chicago department store fortune and owner of *The Chicago Sun-Times*. When she became Editor of *The Christian Science Monitor* in 1983, she was already Harvey Wood's long-time pupil in theology and protegee of *The Boston Globe's* Tom Winship within the American Society of Newspaper Editors' hierarchy. Photograph courtesy First Church of Christ, Scientist.

play out, nobody, least of all management, knew. But John Hart, temperamental network anchor of the old school, seemed mollified by the important new standards and practices code and pleased with the hire of the Canadian Broadcasting System's Peter Kent—a welcome sign that money could still be found for the nightly news.[8]

Between May and September 1990 a corporate superstructure of sophisticated advisers, directors, and strategic alliances was put in place. The inside Directors on Monitor Television's board were Hoagland, Douglass, and, representing both the interests of the Church and acting as Monitor Television's Chief Financial Officer, Don Bowersock. But unlike any other entity created previously by the Church or the Publishing Society, Monitor Television's Board also had outside Directors: John Koehler, Vice President of Hughes Aircraft, who would be instrumental in making it possible for The Monitor Channel to buy a transponder on the Hughes Galaxy V satellite in the fall; Eugene Sekulow, executive vice president international at NYNEX; and Stanley Cohn of Cohn and Marks, Monitor Television's Washington law firm. Also on the Board was Danny Wilson, overseeing the channel's important *Nineties* series of features. In December, Sid Topol, Chairman Emeritus of Scientific Atlanta and much respected in cable circles, would not only join the Board, but would serve in a full-time position with salary, as The Monitor Channel's Vice Chairman.[9]

The Monitor Channel's Editorial Advisory Board, in addition to Hoagland and Douglass, included two other highly respected insiders: Richard Cattani, who had replaced Kay Fanning as Editor of the *Christian Science Monitor,* and Earl Foell, who had preceded Fanning as Editor at the newspaper and who was currently Editor in Chief of *World Monitor Magazine.* Outside members of the Editorial Advisory Board included Hoagland's early mentors Sandy Socolow, now working in New York with Walter Cronkite, and Herb Victor, now back full time at Curran-Victor in California. Others were Hodding Carter, Assistant Secretary of State under President Jimmy Carter and noted television journalist; Stephen Salyer, President of American Public Radio and a long-time Publishing Society ally; Professor Charles Willie, a senior African-American faculty member at Harvard's Graduate School of Education; Peggy Charren, founder and President of Action for Children's Television; Diana Lady Dougan of the Center for Strategic and International Studies and former ambassador. Later, Horton Foote, author, playwright, television scriptwriter, and the only Church member among the outside directors and advisers on either board, would be added.[10]

The revolution picked up speed. If there were any doubts about whether the pace of innovation at the Monitor would be sustained over time, they were dispelled by the understated announcements appearing month after month in the Publishing Society's handsome newsletter.

Some individuals at the Publishing Society had always been at home among the talented and the powerful in all walks of life, but no one since the beginning of the century had demanded that the Publishing Society itself hold its own in the marketplace, or that it adopt the discipline of a business organization, let alone that it systematically seek constructive criticism of its journalism from knowledgeable outsiders. No one had ever rewarded sellers for performance, as Hoagland did in ad sales and, even more aggressively, within Sanden's cable affiliate sales group. Sweeping as the implications were, to the entrepreneurial leadership—Hoagland, Douglass, Bowersock, Wood, and their associates—everything seemed to follow step by step, as a logical continuation of the process that had begun with a renewed emphasis on professionalism in 1983.

The Cape Cod Meeting

A three-day retreat for senior television managers on Cape Cod made the change in plans official. Barbara Sanden described the Monitor team's new universe: the United States had 92 million television households, 85 million of which could get cable, with about 60 million actually hooked up. ESPN had 56 million subscribing households; CNN had 55 million; TBS had 54 million; USA had 53; Discovery had 51; and A&E had 46. For dozens of other services, the numbers dropped off precipitously.[11]

Sanden walked them through what her yet-to-be-formed affiliate sales and cable marketing groups would need to do: the initial negotiations with the central offices, the dozens and dozens of sales calls at the regional and subregional level, the big cable shows—New Orleans or Dallas, Atlantic City, Anaheim—and the smaller ones, the advertising, the public relations image-building, the mailings, the billstuffers, TV spots, radio spots, newspaper slicks, community relations including a free news service for high schools, then consumer marketing in the form of awareness advertising and direct marketing.

The current cable environment was nothing if not tough, as Sanden laid it out, hour after hour: monopolistic, known for indifferent service and dated equipment, facing consumer ire, uncertain regulation and uncertain competition, further encumbered by a preoccupation with the bottom line. Everything added up to one formidable fact of life for cable programmers, old and new: a serious shortage of channel capacity. She walked them through the rough chronology her new operations would follow.

Immediately following the Cape Cod retreat, Sanden began to recruit an affiliate sales staff and to develop rates. She made some first approaches to key cable players. She advised Douglass on setting up a two-part marketing operation to focus on the cable world only: one team, equipped with handsome small, medium, and large exhibits to cover the dozen or so trade shows a year where much of cable's business gets done; a second team, led by sharp, stylish cable public relations strategist Sandi Padnos and her associates, to focus on the trade press. The goal was to make The Monitor Channel "top of mind" within the industry even before launch.[12]

By November 1990, Sanden's team was banging at the cable clubhouse door, throwing The Monitor Channel into the fray, following the industry's rites of initiation to the letter: bring good value, wear a big smile, and keep elbows at the ready!

The Monitor Channel's Niche? "Television for the Global Citizen"

Fleet's February 1991 Private Placement Memorandum described the The Monitor Channel's target audience as politically independent, open-minded, socially conscious, and three or four times more likely than the general population to be involved at the local and national level in civic affairs.[13]

To the entrepreneurial leadership, holding in their minds and hearts a sense of mission first articulated eighty years earlier, this description of The Monitor Channel's niche seemed perfectly clear. Many of their top managers, trained to believe in the efficacy of appealing to a conventional demographic, however, were not convinced. To these experienced television professionals, the *World Monitor News* half-hour nightly concept was clear, the execution good to excellent, and they understood why its second anniversary was greeted with positive reviews in the *New York Times,* the *Los Angeles Times,* the *Washington Post, TV Guide,* and elsewhere.

But hoary tradition aside, the experienced newcomers asked, just what was The Monitor Channel concept, anyway? Was it PBS lite? A thinking person's CNN? Was it a cable-style narrowcasting concept that an identifiable viewership could find and adopt? Or just an omnibus for anything and everything that reminded Jack Hoagland and Netty Douglass and their allies of the peculiar upbeat, family-oriented, cosmopolitan, high-culture political mix of communications in the old newspaper? Monitor Television's professionals watched and worried among themselves. They feared that honoring tradition might prove an expensive luxury: successful targeting is a matter of life and death in the teeming public communications jungle, and what if the eclectic mix of programming produced and purchased under the aegis of The Monitor Channel did not, in the end, attract this hypothetical psychographic of "good men and women interested in the betterment of the human condition?"

The fall 1990 launches did nothing to lay to rest disconcerting questions about The Monitor Channel's market niche. A series that would eventually be billed *The Filmmaker's Art* began to run Saturdays and Sundays. Films chosen initially from WQTV's inventory—Alec Guinness classics or works by directors from Orson Welles to Woody Allen—were shown, minus an occasional obscenity, with opening and closing comments by the host, Bruce McCabe, a respected senior film and television critic at the *Boston Globe*. Within months, to his delight, the host's mandate was broadened: he could pick any classic, foreign, or art films he wanted to bring to the public—any at all—and, barring legal barriers, they would be made available. Only the occult, the producing team recalls, seemed out of bounds.[14]

Rod MacLeish's Week, a weekend magazine program broadcast from Washington and hosted by the veteran newsman, screenwriter, critic, author, and social conscience, would explore, with guests, the background of the week's news. The tone would be good-natured, whimsical, ethically focused, and politely persistent. Although MacLeish was not a member of the Church, the fit could not have been better: Monitor-style journalism was exactly what he had been doing throughout a long and distinguished career.[15]

The first of an important line of foreign acquisitions was *The Silk Road,* a forty-two-part series shot over ten years by Chinese and Japanese crews, which led viewers, one leg of the journey at a time, across the ancient trade route from China through the Middle East to Europe. The series, revoiced by the Monitor's own intelligent and amusing Takashi Oka, received mixed reactions from staffers when it began to air at the rate of one show weekly: the video materials were uneven by the standards of American TV, and, despite the fact that it had been the highest-rated documentary in Japanese television history, to the Western viewer, some episodes were as boring as others were engaging.[16]

With the introduction of *Monitor World Classroom,* two of Monitor Television's most urgent corporate agendas were served: the development of a line of quality communications for children and young people and the formation of strategic alliances within the cable industry. By way of a kick-off event, the *Monitor World Classroom* team hosted a fall workshop that presented the entire cable industry's in-classroom programming to 200 assembled public school teachers and administrators from across Massachusetts and Rhode Island. On a clear September day in the capacious Sunday School auditorium, looking east over the long reflecting pool, Discovery, CNN, Warner Cable, Continental Cablevision, A&E, and C-SPAN's Cable in the Classroom reps, as guests of the fledgling Monitor Channel, presented their respective offerings. The effervescent head of the industry's Cable in the Classroom program was in attendance, and an enthusiastic keynote speech in favor of educational television was given by Massachusetts' respected Commissioner of Education.[17]

Monitor World Classroom began broadcast, with its somewhat stilted news and public affairs programming for high school students, on WQTV; thirty-five Boston-area public high schools participated. For the first year, the program was little more than a repeat of the nightly broadcast of *Today's Monitor* with questions and study suggestions edited in, and written materials—including free copies of the *Christian Science Monitor*—available to the participating schools. Hugely successful from its inception as a cable marketing tool, by the beginning of its second year, *Monitor World Classroom,* with a brand-new format developed in consultation with the Harvard School of Education, was on its way to becoming a solid pedagogical resource as well.[18]

By the fall of 1990, The Monitor Channel's developing schedule—now combining breaking news and background features with diplomatic and military history of World War II, gardening-cum-ecology, art films, and quality programming for children and young people—guaranteed that the programming focus would remain far softer than conventional wisdom in the world of television marketing held was safe. Pleased and proud as they were with individual show concepts and the steady progress toward higher production values, the seasoned television pros at the Publishing Society still shook their heads over whether this would all add up to a coherent and popular identity in the marketplace.

Hoagland was unapproachable on the subject. He brushed aside their concerns, insisting that the Monitor's public was not an age-sex-economic status demographic, but a psychographic, and he had a gut feel for the range of communications that the target audience of men, women, and their children would want. Once again not unlike Ted Turner before him, and with the additional impetus of the Monitor's long tradition, Hoagland declined to make The Monitor Channel's programming lineup conform in advance to marketing lore: the public could hardly be expected to clamor for something they had yet to try.

The phrase The Monitor Channel would go to market with—"television for the global citizen"—kept the focus soft. How many Americans really made the Monitor's idea of "global citizen" an important part of their workaday identities by the early 1990s? That would be tested on air. A lot rode on whether those "good men and women everywhere, interested in the betterment of all human conditions" were really anywhere to be found in the American television audience.

A Fifth Wave of New Programming: Peace, War, and Russian Culture

Still in intense development and still available only to WQTV's 1.5 million Boston-area viewers and at odd hours to a scattered 13 million households via a microwave relay network controlled by WWOR in New York, The Monitor Channel ended 1990 and moved into 1991 with a renewed emphasis on news and public affairs.[19]

The year-end wrap-up, "An Agenda for the Nineties," featured an assistant secretary general of the United Nations, the United Nations' International Children's Emergency Fund Director of Information, the president of Conservation International, and representatives of the U.S. Drug Enforcement Administration and the Carnegie Endowment for Peace. The emphasis was on positive, pragmatic thinking about humanity's suffering.[20]

When the United States and its allies finally moved against Saddam Hussein on January 16, 1991, the seasoned *World Monitor News* team stretched the organization's resources and lived by their wits, determined to match the big networks' coverage in their own way, in the Monitor way. Close behind them were The Monitor Channel rookies, riding in their slipstream, learning their moves.

Hoagland, fluent in Russian, accompanied by the Washington-based executive working on international distribution for Monitor Television, had traveled to Moscow and Leningrad for a hugely successful series of meetings with Gostelradio officials and others in February 1991. One immediate result was a series called *Rodina* ("Homeland" in Russian), chronicling life in Soviet lands during the slow-motion collapse of the old regime.

Rodina was perhaps Monitor Television's most original single initiative in broadcast journalism—the harbinger, potentially, of a radically new way of gathering and reporting international realities for viewers in the United States. Beginning in March, young, enterprising television crews on Gostelradio's payroll fanned out to get footage of whatever struck them as significant in the whole rich, contradictory tableau of continuity and change. Material arrived on everything from the survival of colorful pre-Christian folk celebrations in rural areas, to the first attempts to convert weapons factories to peaceful uses, to a group of entrepreneurs making very good money by contracting to repair potholes in Moscow streets. Uneven, sometimes technically flawed, the material for *Rodina* was shaped into weekly one-hour programs by a gifted writer and producer in Boston.

During these same February 1991 talks in Moscow and St. Petersburg, plans for other projects were laid. Among them was a long, high-end documentary on the Hermitage Museum, including hundreds of art treasures hidden from view since the 1920s. Danny Wilson, like Hoagland sensing even bigger changes in the offing, began a long feature on the Gorbachev era for the *Nineties* series.[21]

Standards and Practices: "Re: Monitor Broadcast News Standards"

In early March, noting that with the April 15 preview launch or "soft launch" of The Monitor Channel the volume of news programming coming from the Publishing Society would increase dramatically, Netty Douglass, as Manager, circulated a fifteen-page, single-spaced memo to all radio and television staff outlining the Monitor's broadcast news standards. Drawing heavily in places on traditional pronouncements by the newspaper's founding editor, Archibald McLellan, and Erwin Canham, the editor who had steered the *Monitor* through its golden age, the guidelines set forth had been jointly authored by Douglass; Cook; The Monitor Channel's new News Director Harry King; Jack Hoagland; and others, and had been cleared in advance with Harvey Wood and the rest of the Board.[22]

The document sought to translate the unwritten canon of Monitor journalism into principles for all broadcast employees, and it addressed boldly and directly the issues of ownership, authorship, and the quality of truth that were a matter of pride as well as a source of intense uneasiness for the many non-Church journalists and production personnel on staff. The guidelines declared that the Monitor's broadcast journalism should be characterized by:

- A global viewpoint;
- Background, depth and perspective;
- No sensationalism;
- Focused resources (by which was meant, putting the news in a sound perspective, giving greatest emphasis to what is important and reducing the merely sensational to its place in an accurate system of values);
- No personal attacks (concentrating on issues rather than personalities or personal foibles, but also, specifically, maintaining a high standard of accuracy in reporting what public figures actually say).

The fact that the Monitor's broadcast activities were owned by the Church was not to influence the content of the product in any direct way:

• Concerning medical news coverage: "Our programs cover every issue of real public significance and concern and cover them in a depth and context which will bring enlightenment." It is significant, the guidelines note, that MonitoRadio won one of the industry's highest awards for its coverage of AIDS as an issue of public concern. The point, continues the memo, is not to induce fear or alarm, but to assist in intelligent public response to public challenges.

• Concerning obituaries: Here, the exigencies of broadcast journalism require a departure from the newspaper's custom of waiting a few days after the death of a major public figure, then publishing an appreciation of the person's life; a more immediate but still somehow measured response would be needed.

• Coverage of topics concerning the Christian Science Church: In serving a global public with journalism of the highest quality, setting standards of fairness, objectivity, impartiality, and decency, it is important to make the identity of the publisher clear, so the public can judge whether these high standards are being met; the Monitor itself and radio and television news broadcasts have one purpose, public service—there is no second purpose or hidden agenda, and there can be none if the public trust built up over the past eight decades is to be sustained.

• Finally, there is no subject Monitor journalism cannot cover, nor is there prior review of the contents of broadcasts by anyone other than designated editors and producers.

The rest of the memo presents matters treated in standards and practices manuals of most reputable broadcast establishments in an especially thoughtful manner: from camera angles and use of music, editorializing, conflicts of interest, gifts and favors, artists' drawings, recreations, eavesdropping, use of handouts, hidden cameras, interception of radio communications, interviews, use of polls, reporting pools, and so forth.

Was This Authentic?

To this observer, the protestations of disinterested service in the March 1991 standards and practices memo ring true exactly as stated. Having said that, themes that identify the philosophical roots of the owners and many of their top employees are present—and inevitably do have a bearing on the strengths and weaknesses of Monitor journalism.

Three such threads in Christian Science are particularly powerful influences. First, the Church teaches that each human life carries within it the spark of the divine, and so all human beings have the same absolute, irrefutable claim to respect. Second, thought itself is a powerful cause, indeed the most powerful cause, operating in human affairs. And third, a sense of proportion is key to understanding: it is essential to make daily and hourly a careful distinction between what is important and what is trivial, what is long-term and what is passing, what is an underlying cause and what is epiphenomenon.[23]

More New Players Join the Team

As the May 1 launch drew near, new members joined the Monitor Television team and old members moved into more prominent positions. Sid Topol, now working full-time as Vice Chairman of the Monitor Television Board, reported daily to his office down the hall from Hoagland's at WQTV. He worked closely with Hoagland and Sanden, planning approaches to the movers and shakers of the cable industry, most of whom were long-time friends or acquaintances of his: his old company, Scientific Atlanta, had grown and prospered selling the cable industry a goodly portion of the hardware it had needed for its spectacular national build-out during the previous decade.

A senior cable ad salesman—a reserved, intelligent professional—came on board to begin selling ad space on the still-to-be launched cable channel. A Boston television newscaster of East Indian descent, known for her snappy presentation, moved into a prominent role on the Channel.[24]

By February 1991 The Monitor Channel's first female news anchor, Gail Harris, a fresh and tailored on-camera presence, was on board. Since her decision several years earlier to step out of the fast track at ABC, Harris had both anchored and produced at Boston's public television station and had acquired a degree in public administration at the Kennedy School of Government. Harris had been watching developments at Monitor TV with great interest and sent word of her possible availability through Boston's professional television grapevine. Poised and pleasant, with a quick analytical mind, the minute the cameras rolled it was clear to everyone that she would be a perfect fit at Monitor Television. She juggled family and work happily and, like Hart, did all her own writing: "I get paid to anchor," she would laugh. "I do the writing for fun!"[25]

It was at about that same time that Harry King, the hardworking, street-smart mid-level *Globe* editor who had joined Monitor TV in October, was named The Monitor Channel's news director. King was given day-to-day responsibility for the half-dozen or so news programs that Lyn Chamberlin had carried through their initial development and launch. His assignment was to pull The Monitor Channel's news line-up together, refine it, and make it a more sharply professional whole from a newsman's perspective.[26]

King was not alone in his opinion that, while John Hart was good, Gail Harris was better. Before many weeks went by, John Hart, working within the separate and increasingly anomalous cloister that *World Monitor News* was becoming, and increasingly aloof among his colleagues there, complained to Hoagland and Douglass that he found Gail Harris a difficult presence.[27]

A Flawless Lift-Off Through Light Cloud Cover: April–July 1991

Soft Launch: Then Launch!!

The Monitor Channel launched without a hitch on May 15, 1991, probably the first programming service in the history of the cable industry to go up on satellite exactly on schedule on the first announced launch date without so much as a day's postponement. Helped by its ability to use WQTV as a rehearsal theater, the Channel had in fact quietly gone up in a preview or "soft launch" mode two weeks earlier, to let cable operators preview the programming before the official date.

The Monitor's entrepreneurs may also have been the only network in the history of cable television ever to celebrate such a triumphal event with a 5:00 P.M. ice cream party. All Publishing Society employees were invited to partake, and the crowd wound its way through the stately flag-decked entrance hall where at the time a handsome Library of Congress exhibit on the history of newspaper publishing was mounted.

The next day, a surprised Monitor Channel employee who had been at the party the previous afternoon, making a quick stop at Principia College's Illinois campus, heard the ugly rumors from a faculty member: word had it, on good authority, that The Monitor Channel's launch celebration had been a cocktail party held on Church premises and scheduled to conflict with Wednesday evening services! Shocking, but not true.

No matter: The Monitor Channel's flawless launch received modest but positive mentions in the national press and tentative applause in the cable industry's trade magazines.[28]

Financing the Development of The Monitor Channel

The business plans that Tendrel and Fleet had put together, based on assumptions about income and expenses drawn from what was known or could be inferred about the experiences of other cable industry start-ups, seemed to give a coherent picture.

An internal calculation done by Monitor Channel staff after the Cape Cod conference had shown a net investment to break-even of about $89 million. In late December, Tendrel Associates projected five different scenarios based on varying assumptions about expenses and revenues, which showed a net investment to break-even of between $101 million and $137 million. In February, working with Tendrel's numbers and refining assumptions in consultation with Monitor management and Don Bowersock, Fleet had come in with a figure of $91 million, spread over seven years. Investment was front-loaded—that is, heaviest in the early years and smaller each succeeding year—as revenues grew. Fleet incorporated its model into a business plan and began quietly to show it around to potential investors.

Programming costs were one variable to keep an eagle eye on. In the models developed in the fall of 1990 and the winter of 1991, programming was pegged at about $26 million annually—a conservative assumption, it would seem, given that in the fiscal year ending in the previous April, The Monitor Channel's programming costs were only $6.2 million and that in the coming April, when national launch and the close of fiscal year 1991 coincided, actual programming costs had come in at a little under $12 million. But there was an important catch: The Monitor Channel used free of charge footage that had been shot around the world for *World Monitor News*. *World Monitor News*, in effect held hostage by the contract with Discovery, had cost $22.6 million to produce in the year ending April 1990, and $25.9 million in fiscal 1991. Combined television production costs at the Publishing Society thus came to $28.8 million for fiscal 1990, and $37.9 million for fiscal 1991, and just how much of this should have been assigned to The Monitor Channel was unclear.[29]

On the face of it, this ambiguity might serve the new entity, Monitor Television, and its outside investors well, but what would it mean for the Publishing Society and for the Church? Internally, there was no mystery: complete information was compiled and distributed on a timely basis. Since the fall of 1989, Don Bowersock had been addressing these anomalies head on at the fiscal level with a monthly summary of expenses that covered all television, including WQTV, *World Monitor News*, and The Monitor Channel (formerly TV: SP), and these terse memos were distributed like clockwork to Church Directors, Publishing Society Trustees, and Hoagland and Douglass. It was understood that the Publishing Society produced and sold the Monitor's television communications and that, for the time being, the Church made up the difference.[30]

Sooner or later, these anomalies would have to be addressed at the business level. This would mean, for starters, covering costs for *World Monitor News*—either by negotiating a new deal with the Discovery Channel, or by ending the partnership.

Either way, clearly it would be unwise to get into a dust-up with Discovery, just as cable partners were being sought for The Monitor Channel. Then again, while the combined costs of all programming were high, if the

Figure 6.1 **Total Funds on Hand, 1980–1991.** (Dollar figures are in millions.)

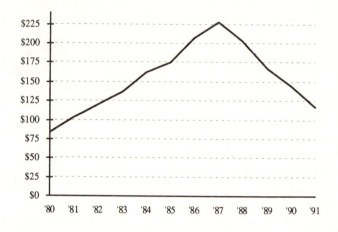

Source: Financial information reported at annual meetings. Summary courtesy of Don Bowersock.

two operations were fully integrated and such duplication as there was, ended, what would the true cost of the new channel's programming be? Twenty-six million dollars a year was a good-faith estimate by a team of sophisticated inside and outside players, but it was low.

Distribution was key. When Discovery and its owners did not immediately step forward and broker the Publishing Society's introductions to the rest of the cable industry, Barbara Sanden's affiliate sales and cable marketing operation became, of necessity, the engine that drove The Monitor Channel operation forward. Sanden's performance was high and her style, controversial—although among the Monitor's entrepreneurs, whose was not! Sanden's team and her expenses were growing, and by the end of April 1991, her operation was spending about $750,000 a month. Some of this went to one-time start-up costs such as the handsome small, medium, and large traveling exhibits for cable shows and the stunningly beautiful kick-off campaign with a New York agency where one paid for what one got.

Sanden's affiliate sales and cable marketing operation, Don Bowersock admitted, made him nervous. What was really happening as a result of the hurricane-force activities originating in Greenwich was hard to document in the beginning. Nor was there a network of informal back channels of the sort he had at the Publishing Society, so there was no independent information beyond what he heard from Hoagland and Douglass, coming from Sanden or any of her staff.[31]

A close comparison of The Monitor Channel's projected revenues and expenses with the historical experience of other programming services, even if it had been possible, would have had limited meaning. Because none of their programming in their early years was original, by scrambling hard the Discovery Channel had been able to reach break-even with a net investment of only $30 million. By contrast, CNN's true net investment to break-even can be estimated—conservatively—to have been at least $150 million in current dollars (over $200 million in 1992 dollars), and possibly much more. CNN's true cash-flow break-even probably came in the seventh year, with total expenses in the first six years, again conservatively, adding up to something in the neighborhood of $500 million.[32]

A $100–Million Answer to Prayer?

On a Wednesday evening in March 1991, as Jack Hoagland and his wife left services at the suburban church where they had been members since 1953, a familiar figure approached and gave Hoagland a penetrating look: it was a certain Mrs. Holbrook, trustee of a valuable Boston-area property housing Eddy memorabilia and a force to be reckoned with. "It will be a tragedy if all this money is lost to the Church," she said. At that point, Hoagland did not know what she was talking about, and he telephoned her at home later that evening to find out.

What Marian "Heidi" Holbrook, Vassar '32, was referring to was the Bliss Knapp estate: a little-known bequest that had been gathering dust—and compound interest—since the 1940s, and was by then worth almost $100 million. Bliss Knapp had written a controversial book about Mary Baker Eddy, which the Church Directors, in the forty years since his death, had declined to publish. Mrs. Holbrook, Knapp's devoted student and for many years his personal secretary, was a trustee of the wills of two family members, which provided that, if the Church published his book by early 1993, it would be the beneficiary—and if it failed to do so, the bequests would go to Stanford University and the Los Angeles County Museum. Time was running out. The following morning, Hoagland hurried to the Directors to get the background story.[33]

The molten core of the issue was exactly which primary and secondary sources about the life and teachings of Mary Baker Eddy should the Publishing Society make available to the faithful in the Christian Science Field? Even the Church Directors had found it too hot to handle except very, very gingerly.

In his eight years as Manager of the Publishing Society, Hoagland had already provoked aggressive opposition from Church archivists and others grouped around historian Robert Peel by moving steadily toward an "open-shelf" policy. It had been his long-standing contention that all Mrs. Eddy's writings and any memoirs by her contemporaries should be published, whether or not they might deviate in some degree from teachings that the Church considered correct. Those who opposed Hoagland, Wood, Friesen, and the remaining Directors in this matter asserted that to publish works was in effect to endorse them, that only "authorized literature" should be made available—and that in fact their own group was best qualified to serve as arbiters of taste in these matters.[34]

Before many days had passed, Hoagland sat down and worked through a long, concentrated night to draft a business plan for a "Twentieth Century Biography Series" that would include the Bliss Knapp book. He presented the plan to the Board. Hoagland, Wood, and Friesen argued that not only was including the Knapp book in line with the open-shelf policy they had been implementing gradually since the mid-1980s, it was also clearly their fiduciary responsibility to see that the bequest became available to help fund the attempt to reposition and diversify Monitor communications. The Board members and Trustees reached the same conclusion. The biography series was put in motion, and the Knapp estate was notified of the Church's change of heart.[35]

The End of Fiscal 1991

In the fiscal year that ended on April 30, 1991, the Monitor's television costs came in significantly over budget for the first time. At a net cost of $50.7 million for the total combined expenses of *World Monitor News,* The Monitor Channel, and WQTV, television was 30 percent higher than what had been anticipated a year earlier when the budget was worked out and first circulated.[36]

The reasons were three. Like other TV news operations, the Monitor found that despite the excitement and challenge of reporting war, in the end, war hurt: Gulf War coverage explained the lion's share of the $6.6 million of overspending at *World Monitor News.* Second, at The Monitor Channel, Sanden's operations, now central to the success of the whole enterprise, had been expanded after budgets had been set the previous year and were running at an annual rate of almost $10 million. This accounted for another $4.7 million of the variance. Overoptimistic forecasts of revenues from ad sales and syndication accounted for most of the rest.

Nevertheless, the Church began the new fiscal year in May 1991 entirely free of debt and with $145 million cash in hand. Although $100 million of that sum had restrictions on its use, the Knapp estate would soon yield another $100 million in unrestricted reserves. Church custom—an implied proscription against carrying any debt—would make it extremely difficult to raise more money with a mortgage or a sale/lease-back arrangement on capital equipment and real estate, but the Treasurer's office had done a study six months earlier showing that another $100 million or so might be raised that way, in addition to the $60 to 70 million a year that would come in from earnings on investments, donations, and other bequests. An outside investor could be expected to put in $20 to $30 million over a three-year period beginning at some point in the next year. As the recession finally eased, ad dollars would begin bringing revenues up and, eventually, cable subscription fees would kick in.[37]

Easy money was getting tight, but multiple solutions to the problem seemed available. Indeed, in June 1991 the Church was in a financial position that many businesses—including virtually all cable start-ups—would find enviable.

The Calm Before the Storm

As the summer of 1991 began, The Monitor Channel was well launched, available on the Hughes satellite to cable operators nationwide, already in 1.5 million homes in the greater Boston area and—under Sanden's hell-for-leather direction—had another 2.5 million under agreement and was poised to expand fast.[38]

Cable operators reported that initial viewer response to The Monitor Channel in competitive test-marketing around the country was good. The operators also seemed to accept the logic of the Hoagland–Douglass–Sanden positioning, which predicted that The Monitor Channel would appeal to the most active and civic-minded members of the local community, the very folks most likely to take a strong position one way or the other when it came to renewing local cable franchises. At the big New Orleans cable show in May, The Monitor Channel staged an invitation-only breakfast for about seventy-five operators in an indoor-outdoor space at the top of the Hilton—a stellar promotional event—in which the Monitor's jazz and rock critic, backed up by six local musicians, offered her brilliant original musical history of jazz from its African and Christian evangelical roots in the eighteenth and nineteenth centuries through wave after wave of innovation in the twentieth century.[39]

The industry continued to signal its recognition that the Monitor's programming was already of superior quality. *One Norway Street* was awarded an Emmy from the New England chapter of the National Association of Television Arts and Sciences for an outstanding program the previous November, before national launch, that had diverse segments including housing and other legal issues faced by gays; how AIDS had galvanized the gay community; issues of worker privacy in the age of electronic mailboxes; whether proposed changes in SAT testing will affect its current cultural/intellectual slant; an interview with the *Globe*'s children's book editor; and a look at music in Brazil. *The Children's Room* came away with the top award in "The Best Children's Series" in the commercial television category from Action for Children's Television. *Today's Monitor* and *Money and You* were recognized for reporting on issues that impact the rights and well-being of minority and disadvantaged persons with "Unity in Media" awards given out by Lincoln University in Missouri.[40]

As early programs matured, new programming continued to come on line. The first thirteen weeks of *The Filmmaker's Art* included Ingmar Bergman's *Wild Strawberries*, Jean Cocteau's original *Beauty and the Beast*, and Vittorio DeSica's *The Bicycle Thief*. Nearing launch was *The Mark of the Musketeers*, a Japanese-made animated film for children, which the Monitor edited into fifty-two half-hour series and re-voiced using American actors. *Opinion Page* would soon be filling the function of the newspaper's traditional daily op-ed space, with a fifteen-minute round-up of editorials from newspapers around the world, then segments with commentary and debate from studios in Boston, Washington, D.C., and London. *Monitor NewsDesk*, a snappy operation, had been giving news briefs at the top and the bottom of the hour for the past six months: now it would replace the usual newsbreaks with "News for Kids" segments during afterschool hours weekdays and mornings on weekends. *World Monitor News* was working on a six-part series, "Islam in America," because, following the Gulf War, as the producer put it, "We felt it was time to tell the story of mainstream Muslims who are not foreign to American society. They are our next-door neighbors."[41]

Rod MacLeish, Danny Wilson, and their production crew were back in Leningrad taping the treasures of the Hermitage, when Gorbachev was unseated and the Soviet era suddenly ended. MacLeish immediately flew to Moscow and began filing commentaries for *Monitor News* with Gail Harris. The young Russian crews under contract to the Monitor for *Rodina* materials shipped back an extraordinary view of the cataclysm from the grass roots, while *World Monitor Magazine*'s man in Moscow filed stories nightly for two weeks running covering the whole gamut of Monitor media: newspaper, radio, and television.

There would be no stopping for breath until cable partners were found and the inevitable crises of the start-up years had been weathered, but the ultimate success of The Monitor Channel seemed assured. By late June, Hoagland had a New York law firm he had used for talent contracts dotting the i's and crossing the t's on a final agreement with the Knapp trustees.

A well-lawyered business plan for Monitor Television was in hand, along with a for-profit incorporation, and a board of directors and an advisory board with solid outside credentials was in place. Sid Topol continued to approach cable investors. On June 12 a meeting had gone very well indeed with a particularly interesting potential partner, the privately held, uniquely cash-rich Providence Journal Company, which ran Rhode Island's best newspaper and owned a number of Boston-area cable systems. It might take a year or more of tire-kicking to close equity deals, with "Pro Jo" or others, singly or—preferably—in combination. In the meantime, Sanden's team was already fighting its way against the odds to respectable numbers in the fierce competition for scarce channel space nationwide.[42]

After years of suffering barbs at the hands of the *Boston Globe,* it was a relief to enjoy routinely respectful coverage of the Monitor's efforts in publications as diverse as *Multichannel News,* the *Hollywood Reporter, Cable World, Cablevision, Satellite Orbit, Variety, USA Today,* the *New York Times,* and the *Wall Street Journal.*[43]

During the next year, program development would involve less storming and more fine-tuning, and no doubt more programming would be purchased, much of it abroad. The physical infrastructure of a state-of-the-art electronic communications production shop was close to completion—six radio studios, three television studios, four editing suites, the Scitex editing system that could turn a TV image into pictures for print and the fiberoptic spine connecting all editorial departments across media. A few more technical installations at WQTV itself were being considered.

The Monitor Channel was breaking ground internally and, in some ways, for the industry. The standards and practices code was in place for the editorial side, and criteria for ad content were being worked out in practice on the business side. With Douglass, Pierson, Chamberlin, Sanden, and others, including the head of technical operations and the head of the new multimedia aftermarket sales group, there was probably a higher percentage of women in key executive positions at The Monitor Channel—strong, competent, competitive women—than at any other national television operation, cable or broadcast.

At the end of the day, though, the only question that mattered (or so it seemed) would be answered in the marketplace. In that late-twentieth-century marketplace, moreover, the success or failure of the Monitor's diversification and repositioning would turn on a matter of objective fact that was ultimately beyond the power of anyone at the Monitor to influence in significant degree: was a contemporary counterpart to the Monitor's traditional public—those "good men and women everywhere"—really out there? Did that global citizen, that psychographic whose existence was virtually an article of faith for the Monitor's entrepreneurial leadership, really make up any significant part of the contemporary television audience? Could The Monitor Channel's peculiar programming mix build audiences in sufficient numbers over a four- or five-year period to make it a viable business proposition—or even, for that matter, a break-even proposition? By July 1991 straws in the wind were yielding some positive—if very preliminary—evidence in this pivotal matter.

A Denver-based analyst, well known and trusted in the cable industry, did some polling in the Boston market to evaluate reaction to the embryonic Monitor Channel fare that WQTV had been broadcasting for the previous two years. On the negative side, he found too much scatter: those who valued the international news most were, statistically speaking, less likely to want the "back of the book" features on gardening and ecology, minority affairs, programming for children and young people, and so forth. Still, in his opinion, there was definitely a niche, a viable niche, for what the Monitor wanted to sell.[44]

A second source of early information was so-called beauty contests, a purely cable-style institution that had evolved in the 1980s as the local operators' way of letting subscribers help choose among the new services competing for increasingly scarce channel space. These competitions were organized as elections of sorts, with two or three to as many as a half-dozen new services, or existing services looking for wider carriage, broadcast back to back on designated channels. The public was invited to watch and give candid feedback to the local system. Sanden—like her bosses, sure beyond the shadow of a doubt that the audience The Monitor Channel needed to connect with was indeed out there—was fearless in throwing The Monitor Channel into direct competition in these arenas as early and as often as she could. Never mind, she argued, that half the Monitor's shows were still in development: cable audiences have always seemed intuitively to know where a programmer is heading and are known to be forgiving of less-than-polished early products.

In the year following launch, The Monitor Channel would be entered in about ten such local beauty contests around the country. The early trials were in cable systems under a variety of ownerships in Missouri, Kentucky, Minnesota, and upstate New York, and in each case, The Monitor Channel—heavily promoted by Sanden's team—had been the viewers' first choice. An analysis of the results suggested that three groups in particular favored The Monitor Channel: church-goers, teachers at all levels, and politicians and other influentials.

In mid-June, Jack Hoagland's four grown children and their spouses saw to it that he and his wife Sally celebrated their fortieth anniversary in style, with a blow-out party for 200 at the Wellesley College Club. Guests included lifelong friends dating back to Hoagland's days as a famously teetotaling Yale Whiffenpoof. The children flew in Mort Sahl—a great favorite of their father's who was by then under contract but not yet in production at The Monitor Channel—for a stand-up routine that had the crowd in stitches.[45]

It was the calm before the storm.

Chapter 7

Clouds

July 1991–February 1992: Success in sight, a darkening sky

> Among the calamities of war may be jointly numbered the diminution of the love of truth, by the falsehoods which interest dictates and credulity encourages.
>
> —*Dr. Samuel Johnson,* The Idler, *No. 30, 1758*

Success in Sight, a Darkening Sky

Vision well articulated, policy broadly set, and launch of The Monitor Channel accomplished in rare good form, the Monitor's entrepreneurial leadership and their 400 or so television employees in Boston, Greenwich, New York, Washington, Denver, Los Angeles, London, Paris, Moscow, Tokyo, Manila, Santiago, and way points, hurtled through the summer of 1991. There were long hours, hard work, plenty of quickwitted improvisation, and a normal complement of mid-level differences of opinion and competition for resources among colleagues. But in their cleanly focused state, management and those employees working in television—and in radio and at the new magazine—accomplished more than any objective review of the human and material resources at their disposal would suggest was possible: much of the new organization was "in the flow."

Watching from every corner of the public communications market were ever more numerous and knowledgeable pairs of eyes—would-be employees, likely clients, potential partners, and rivals.

Breaking News: Covering the Soviet Coup

As coverage of the Gulf War gave way to coverage of the dramatic end of seventy-five years of Communist Party dominion over Soviet lands, the muffled competition grew sharper between the *World Monitor News* half-hour airing each weeknight on The Discovery Channel and the *Monitor News* hour-plus airing seven days a week and as needed on The Monitor Channel. In terms of budget, *Monitor News* anchored by Gail Harris still played second string to *World Monitor News* with John Hart. The *Monitor News* team was scrappy, though, polite but playing hard. Management was encouraging them, and they were gaining.[1]

Like any other smart, talented team players, TV newspeople are never so fully alive as when, adrenaline coursing through their veins, they strive for ambitious goals and reach them—in this context, the goal was to deliver high-quality, accurate, fair communications on a shoestring or two—or three. Who can say "no" to extra satellite time, with one of the biggest stories of the century playing itself out? That incremental shoestring may cost dear, but there is nothing in the news business as seductive as covering a big story while it breaks. With Danny Wilson and Rod MacLeish, the *Rodina* crew and a correspondent in Russia, and with Dave Cook, Bill Chesleigh, and Netty Douglass at *World Monitor News* in Boston, decision after decision was made to do whatever it took to deliver the best, added costs notwithstanding.[2]

Distribution, Distribution, Distribution

Sid Topol and others worked to define and articulate The Monitor Channel's niche more precisely for the three or four distinct audiences any fledgling cable network had to play to: viewers, advertisers, hard-bargaining cable operators, and the scarce investors of the early 1990s. Topol was preoccupied with differentiating The Monitor Channel's franchise clearly from CNN's.[3]

Barbara Bellafiore Sanden commissioned an astutely worded survey of cable operators, which would govern her choice of tactics in the critical months to follow. Does, she asked, an aggressive sell help a new cable network's chances of getting carriage, or hurt? The big operators answered that on balance aggressive tactics are a distinct plus—in that Darwinian market, a new service has to be "top of mind" to get carried. That was all she needed to hear, *so aggressive it would be!*[4]

By mid-August, Sanden and a consultant had worked out a highly differentiated rate card of the sort common in the cable industry—per-month subscriber rates graduated annually, with low costs in early years, charter rates for early launch, rate breaks for operators who carried The Monitor Channel on most or all of their systems, and "super-volume discounts" for cable giants.[5]

Four months after launch, signed commitments were in hand from 242 cable systems with 3.5 million households in forty-five states, but did this mean the glass was half empty or half full? A "high-concept service" like The Monitor Channel could be expected to achieve carriage in 30 to 35 million homes, or about half the cable universe, eventually. Fifteen million subscribing households was the threshold at which the most coveted national advertisers could begin to justify routine buys.[6]

A fresh set of Fleet Bank projections pulled together for potential equity partners showed The Monitor Channel reaching this all-important 15 million households in about the fall of 1993. As of the fall of 1991 and through the winter, affiliate sales would remain on target. Never far from anyone's mind was the knowledge that with any significant expansion in channel availability, signing up affiliates would accelerate dramatically.

The Monitor Channel's prices for cable operators were set to make sales happen. The standard "launch partner rate card" for years one to six was the lowest in the industry at the time: the first year free, one cent each month per subscriber in the second year, two cents in the third year, and so forth to year six. A separate in-house study—done by Monitor Television's Fleet-supplied, Harvard Business School-educated chief financial officer at Don Bowersock's request—determined that although the rates offered those signing on and launching in at least one system by December 1 were low, the Monitor's discounted rates for the big cable players were comparable to Discovery's, and the Monitor's standard rate card beyond the early years set The Monitor Channel's prices at or slightly above industry norms.[7]

A Fast Game of Leaks and Spin

News of the Church's decision to publish Bliss Knapp's controversial book and thus receive the $100 million Knapp bequest began to get out. On July 31, an anonymous letter made the rounds, sounding the opposition alarm that the Publishing Society would include the book portraying Mrs. Eddy as in some ways more than human in a forthcoming series. The next day, Netty Douglass circulated the facts in a routinely worded memo to twenty or so top managers in the Publishing Society, and the day after that, a letter enclosing Douglass's memo went out to Christian Science teachers around the world from the Church's board of education.[8]

For the next eight months, both in the Knapp affair and in disclosures

about Church finances generally, Church Directors and the Monitor's entrepreneurial leadership found themselves perpetually off balance, trapped in
round after round of an embarrassing game of catch-up. Sometimes the
entrepreneurial leadership's in-house opposition stole documents and published them directly or leaked them to sympathizers at the *Boston Globe.*
Information circulated—sometimes new, but often not—would be given a
sensational spin. The Church and the Publishing Society were then obliged
to confirm the basic accuracy of these breathless reports, at the same time
trying without much success to put their own, often quite reasonable construction on matters that had been made sensational by dint of the fact that
the information had been stolen and the way it was reported.

Hoagland, Douglass, Hal Friesen, Don Bowersock, and Harvey Wood
were mentally prepared for increased resistance. For his part, Hoagland had
long since absorbed Peter Drucker's insights on reforming non-profits, including the broad rule of thumb that the closer to success innovators come,
the stiffer the opposition from the old guard will be.[9]

The Industry Interface

On the eve of its third anniversary broadcast in mid-September, *World Monitor News* won an Emmy for its outstanding Soviet coverage. Hoagland, by
then understanding the value (and the cost) of the programming that was
being exhibited on someone else's network, again sought more money for
World Monitor News from the Discovery Channel, a demand he had made
successfully a year earlier. Discovery at first acquiesced, then refused. The
Discovery team had not built its success by paying top dollar for programming, and furthermore the fact that The Monitor Channel, a potential rival
for scarce channel space, was underselling them did not amuse them.[10]

On weekday afternoons and weekend mornings, *News for Kids* replaced
the usual half-hourly news breaks, and *After School,* with movies and features suitable for teens, debuted. With the start of the new school year,
Monitor World Classroom, with a vastly improved fifteen-minute daily
format, gave young people background and perspective on the news with
younger-looking, mixed-race male and female hosts, and won endorsements
from the American Federation of Teachers, the National Education Association, the National Association of Secondary School Principals, the National School Boards Association, and the National Association of School
Superintendents. Talks were under way with a major textbook publisher to
establish a joint venture that would repackage the Publishing Society's print
and broadcast products to create multimedia educational materials, including a video atlas.[11]

A daily roundup of international business and economic news moved toward launch.[12]

A new positioning statement was issued under the headline, "The Monitor Channel: The Journalism of Ideas." The themes were familiar—reporting that is clear, accurate, factual, calm; subject matter that includes news, education, entertainment, and in-depth looks at a broad range of topical and cultural subjects. The global view was emphasized, and the potential audience was described as the "interested, committed, demanding citizen of the 1990s," both "mature and youthful," who wants something "challenging and exciting" from television.[13]

The focus was getting sharper. But would audiences, advertisers, the cable world, and investors get it, and would they buy in?

Internal Quarrels Go National Yet Again

It was reminiscent of 1988.

On September 18, the *Boston Globe* took the Knapp controversy public with an attack on Jack Hoagland: a column on the first page of the business section sided with the Christian Science opposition's theological objections to publishing the book, comparing Hoagland to Judas Iscariot and including Hoagland's picture, should anyone miss the point. The writer took the position—an outlandish one, on the face of it, for a business columnist and a stranger to the faith—that to publish this particular book was an intrinsically unethical act and, furthermore, that the Publishing Society had no business dedicating the $100 million or so it stood to receive as a result to electronic publication of its editorial product. Perhaps mindful of legal jeopardy, the editor of the business page gave Hoagland verbal assurances that the reference to Judas was "nothing personal."[14]

Hoagland in turn wrote the *Globe*'s editor a restrained letter de-emphasizing the attack on himself and noting that the business issues in question touched the *Globe,* as well:

> All major news enterprises are faced with important challenges in the 1990s. Because of our editorial character and distribution patterns we began facing ours a decade earlier than most publishers. The *Globe* itself is faced with challenges in the months and years ahead, including a steep decline in revenues and the possibility of changes in ownership. We believe that the *Globe* has both the right and the obligation to meet these challenges with all the talents and resources available to it, and we wish it success in doing so. And yet, for at least the last five years, our own efforts to set a course into the next century for this worthy enterprise, in which we believe deeply, have been

assailed repeatedly by the doubt, scorn, and ridicule of the *Boston Globe*. . . .
We read little in your pages about the *Globe*'s adjustments to meet the future
and a great deal about our smallest changes.[15]

A few days later, freshly printed copies of Bliss Knapp's book, *The
Destiny of the Mother Church,* complete with the Publishing Society's imprimatur as required by the will, began to be distributed to Christian Science reading rooms. On September 25, a second column on the first page of
the *Globe*'s business section by the same writer, again accompanied by a
picture of Hoagland, mockingly reported that he had objected to the previous week's insult.[16]

Shortly after these columns appeared, a note threatening the lives of Lyn
Chamberlin's two grade-school-aged children—and making it clear that the
writer or writers knew where they lived—was placed after hours on her
desk at the Publishing Society. Chamberlin was then separated from her
husband, and Netty Douglass quickly and quietly had a sophisticated alarm
system installed at the Publishing Society's expense in Chamberlin's Cambridge home. At about this time, Douglass's car was defaced again, now
with deep gouges down the length of the driver's side.[17]

No one considered turning back. The first show in the *Mort Sahl Live!*
series was taped during the Atlantic City Cable Show with an apprecia-
tive audience of industry executives and employees, the mayor of Atlantic City, half the City Council, and other notables from among the city's
black leadership—and the trade press loved it. A Boston-based reporter
from the *Philadelphia Inquirer* who had been befriended by the opposition was there, preoccupied by minutiae that bore on religious issues;
what about the location of the reception (on the top floor of a hotel that
housed a casino on the ground floor) and what about the refreshments
(no alcohol, although the reporter seemed to have a difficult time believing that this was really so).[18]

Hoagland, by then taking calls nonstop from *Time, Newsweek,* the *New
York Times,* and others, about the decision to publish the Knapp book could
scarcely concentrate on the all-important meetings with cable operators that
had been set up for him. Shortly after Atlantic City, Sanden and her team
were given higher monthly goals for cable sign-ons, but larger bonuses if
they managed to exceed those targets.[19]

On Sunday, October 13, the *Globe*'s religion writer, a consistent critic
of the Christian Science establishment and its new publishing activities,
came out with a 1600–word piece from the opposition viewpoint, detailing
the Knapp controversy and the likely use of the bequest to fund broadcast
operations.[20]

A Collision of Inevitabilities

At the same time, John Hart was preparing to resign in style. After the October 31 broadcast, Hart submitted his resignation to Douglass and Cook. Saying he felt he had done all he could to help launch *World Monitor News* and that it was now time to move on, he allowed Hoagland, Douglass, and Cook to announce that he was "on leave" while they scrambled to limit the damage.

Hoagland was frantic. A clause in the Monitor's 1988 agreement gave Discovery the right to discontinue carriage of *World Monitor News* if the nature of the programming changed, or if the anchor were not John Hart or someone comparable. Working with Bill Chesleigh, it took Hoagland less than twenty-four hours to line up NBC veteran John Palmer to fill Hart's slot. Then, and only then, he placed a call to Discovery's president Ruth Otte, who remained his best contact there. Otte reassured him that from Discovery's point of view, Palmer would be an eminently acceptable replacement.[21]

Unbeknownst to his employers and his colleagues at *World Monitor News,* Hart had been working for many weeks with a freelance writer on a long article, essentially a self-portrait originally intended for publication in *Boston Magazine,* then accepted by the *Globe,* and in queue for publication in the *Globe Sunday Magazine* on November 10. A full-page color picture accompanying the 3,500–word article had Hart in casual dress, sitting in pensive profile at the foot of a huge old tree, amid the beauty of the New England autumn.[22]

On Thursday, November 7, an advance copy of the *Globe* article on Hart found its way into Netty Douglass's hands. On Sunday, the article hit the doorsteps and newsstands of New England: Hart was depicted as intense, difficult, given to dark moods, and known for his great integrity as a journalist. Nowhere, Hart made it clear, including at the Monitor, was television news being done in a way he found acceptable; everywhere, the owners' agendas intruded. The following Tuesday, the *Globe* put out an article questioning the Monitor's increasingly transparent fib that Hart was only on leave.[23]

Hart also spelled out the shift in the Monitor's organizational priorities that had left him feeling betrayed. Clearly, the Monitor's resources were now being put, not into the *World Monitor News* nightly half-hour, which he anchored, but into The Monitor Channel's twenty-four-hour clock. Three days later, on the following Wednesday, Hart's resignation and John Palmer's appointment were announced.

On November 15, an Associated Press story—which the Monitor's Washington bureau immediately traced back to Discovery CEO John Hendricks—suggested that the Discovery Channel might drop *World Monitor News* in the wake of the Hart resignation, after all. After dodging Hoagland's calls for two days, Hendricks finally confirmed that Discovery now intended to drop *World Monitor News*. The wording of the public announcement was worked out in a tense session at the San Antonio Cable Show a few days later, and made official in a joint press release on November 27, just as the cable industry's huge annual Western Show got under way in Anaheim, outside Los Angeles.[24]

Plainly, for both John Hart and for Discovery's executives, the association with Monitor Television had gradually ceased to make good business sense. As the Publishing Society moved from the old broadcast model exemplified by the *World Monitor News* nightly half-hour newscast to a twenty-four-hour-a-day cable model, everything about John Hart except his fine mind had become anachronistic. His inaccessible, network-star demeanor on air was irritating even to Discovery's executives, and, sadly, he was unwilling or unable to see a plus in the Monitor's emerging institutional imperatives, and to actively join Gail Harris, Peter Kent, Rod MacLeish, Doreen Kayes, and others in breaking the new ground that lay ahead, delivering in-depth news and thoughtful features around the clock—perhaps earning a bit less and no longer dominating center stage—as part of a cable-style team.[25]

If the evolution of Monitor television from the fall of 1990 to the fall of 1991 had made John Hart, as an old-fashioned anchor, seem a professional anachronism in these changing circumstances, it had also placed The Monitor Channel in direct competition with Hoagland's and Douglass's former protectors and guides at Discovery. It was not just that the Monitor people had asked forcefully for two years running that Discovery pay more than the original contract stipulated for their programming, nor even that *World Monitor News* viewers did not stay on for Discovery's prime time offerings in the numbers everyone had hoped for. These were bright red flags signaling a bigger trouble ahead: the two organizations had evolved into natural rivals, competing for the same scarce cable distribution, for advertisers looking at not-so-very-different upscale demographics, and, if the cable industry's "beauty contests" were giving accurate information, soon, surely, for audiences.

Noting that *World Monitor News* was in the running for three cable ACE awards, *Multichannel News*'s November 9 take on the parting of the ways with Discovery was commonsensical: the programming fit was not there for either party. For the Monitor, as the writer observed, "The show was an expensive piece of programming that was attractive to advertisers, viewers, and critics, but sitting on another network's schedule."[26]

The Monitor's parting of the ways with Hart and Discovery was inevitable. All Hoagland could have done—all Hart or Hendricks could have done, for that matter—was to have recognized the inevitable earlier and accommodated it more gracefully.

Why, then, was Jack Hoagland blindsided?

Part of the answer lay in over-centralization common to high-powered entrepreneurial start-ups. Hoagland, who had wooed and won Hart himself in the beginning, had not had time for many months for the long intellectual chats both men had enjoyed. Only Hoagland and Douglass themselves were assigned to maintaining a good working relationship with Discovery, and by 1991 they each had, week in and week out, a dozen more urgent priorities on their agendas than John Hart or even the Discovery connection.

Amplifying this, in the judgment of several observers including David Cook, Danny Wilson, and Ruth Otte herself, was a certain tendency to avoid conflict. Hoagland and Douglass never sat down in the course of 1991 to thrash out their increasingly obvious differences either with Hart or with Discovery, and because the task was not specifically delegated to anyone else, those differences piled up.[27]

Perhaps, also, with the additional distraction of attacks from the Christian Science opposition and the *Boston Globe,* it was too much like trying to win at World Cup tennis, when someone in the stands you cannot quite see has a gun—and, from time to time, is using it. Your concentration suffers, you miss some important returns.

The Cable Industry Continues Its Slow Salute

To the cable industry, The Monitor Channel was still looking like a winner. The November 18 issue of *Multichannel News* reported that cable operators were being extremely conservative about adding new services, and that new channels might be offered only on condition that viewers pay a surcharge to see them—a nightmarish prospect for new networks because it was sure to depress viewership and so depress ad sales. Harsh business climate notwithstanding, in a survey of operators The Monitor Channel was named the new service they were most likely to launch, with Court TV and the SciFi Channel in second place. In the course of the preceding year, the Monitor's sales and marketing people had planned and executed one of the most sophisticated and visually beautiful campaigns the industry had ever seen, and by November 1991, it was clear that they had succeeded: the Monitor Channel was, as the trades put it, "top of mind."[28]

Sanden's tactics were ruffling some feathers, but, just as her survey earlier in the year predicted, on balance they were paying off. By November, the package The Monitor Channel was offering included a long list of "value-added benefits" amounting to de facto price cuts: free customized direct mail pieces targeting *World Monitor Magazine* and *Christian Science Monitor* subscribers in a given operator's franchise who did not yet have cable; free one-year subscriptions to *World Monitor Magazine* for first-time cable customers; free spots for local cable operators on MonitoRadio and The Monitor Channel; free newspaper ads and slicks; free cross-promotion throughout the Monitor's newspaper and the magazine; and a one-time local scholarship through *Monitor World Classroom.* Monitor Television's Executive Vice President and former Washington bureau chief, Scott Goodfellow, undertook a high-level campaign to get senators and representatives who appeared on *Congress This Week,* the Monitor's Washington-based weekly talk show, to write cable operators back home, urging them to carry The Monitor Channel.[29]

A flap developed with one large operator over whether the Monitor would control the narrow electronic space known as the vertical blanking interval, or VBI, which exists, invisible to viewers, in the margin of the transmitted cable television signal. Technology buffs had long predicted that VBIs would one day have a significant value in the market place, perhaps delivering alpha-numeric information business to business: but because cable evolved as an almost exclusively home-delivered, consumer-oriented service, the value of the VBI had always remained hypothetical.[30]

To Jack Hoagland, however, the importance of the VBI was anything but hypothetical: he had long anticipated that The Monitor Channel's cable VBI might be the medium for home delivery of an electronic newspaper product—the *Christian Science Monitor* of the future—as soon as tomorrow arrived. He had Sanden back off, but told her to instruct her team to hold on to VBI rights for The Monitor Channel whenever possible.[31]

Despite the tight market for cable "shelf space," the Western Show in Anaheim in the last days of November was a huge success for the Monitor Channel. Smaller and more sedate than the enormous displays of established services and the cable industry's biggest hardware suppliers, yet more important than the booths of any of the other new services, the Monitor Channel's 3,000–square-foot, white-on-white exhibit and the printed literature that went with it were handsome.

The twenty-five-person Monitor presence was up to full speed—meeting with interested operators in an enclosed room created at the middle of the exhibit or in reserved conference rooms upstairs, greeting the steady stream of foot traffic, chatting up decision makers wherever they were to be found. A member of the Monitor Channel news team delivered news on the hour from a set in the middle of the Monitor booth—she was believable, classy, and a big favorite with the trade show crowd. A representative from "Monitor World Classroom" was at the ready to pitch interested operators. And, as he had in Atlantic City, the inimitable Mort Sahl demonstrated his own peculiar brand of worldly-wise idealism to a delighted audience of several hundred high- and mid-level cable executives and suppliers' reps.[32]

John Hart had quit and Discovery had dropped *World Monitor News* less than two weeks earlier, but those who counted in the sophisticated crowd took it all in stride. Events that had seemed devastating in Boston were clearly of only marginal interest in Los Angeles. Letters of understanding were in hand from a growing list of the cable giants: Time Warner, Viacom, Jones Intercable, Continental, Cox, ATC. Now the secondary sell to regional and local operators could begin. A number of small and mid-sized owners also stepped forward to kick the tires, and some bought. For those who had capacity, it came down to variations on a single straightforward question—What can The Monitor Channel do for me in my community, that the services I already carry are not doing?[33]

Collecting the Knapp Bequest Gets More Complicated

For two days during the Western Show in Anaheim, Jack Hoagland was nowhere to be found: Only Netty Douglass knew that, on the first day, he flew to San Francisco, leaving at the crack of dawn and returning that same night. He picked up both his secretary and Knapp estate trustee Heidi Holbrook, who had flown in together from Boston the night before, and drove them to Palo Alto, where they had breakfast until it was time to meet with Stanford's lawyer and her assistant.

The purpose of the meeting was to convince the lawyer that Stanford's status as alternative beneficiary would not be relevant, because the Church and the Knapp trustees were united, the book published as required, and the deal done. The meeting lasted for three hours and was cordial enough, but the Stanford attorney's politely probing questions showed great sophistication regarding internal Church matters. Ultimately, it became clear Stanford had had the benefit of detailed conversations with the Church opposition. Stanford's counsel, for her part, believed on the basis of that interview that Hoagland and Holbrook knew their case might not be airtight. Thus coached on the divisions within the Church, Stanford was considering whether to argue that the Knapp fortune should be awarded to it. One hundred million dollars was, after all, a lot of money.

The same issues arose the next day when Hoagland and Mrs. Holbrook met in Los Angeles with representatives of the Los Angeles County Museum, which, like Stanford, was an alternative beneficiary. There, however, the meeting was anything but cordial. Clearly, the opponents of the Church's right to the Knapp bequest had presented their views successfully, and the gloves were off. The nub of the argument was that the Church could not guarantee that Knapp's book would be displayed and sold as required in "substantially all" Christian Science reading rooms, because these were self-governing bodies and, in an unknown number of cases, might choose not to do so. The elegant, elderly Mrs. Holbrook was thoroughly disgusted.

The Church opposition had indeed contacted Stanford University and the Los Angeles Museum some weeks earlier. They were urging them to mount a challenge to the Church's right to the $100 million bequest, despite the fact that the Knapp trustees were in unanimous agreement that the terms of the trust had been met and the disbursement of the funds to the Church should proceed.[34]

December's Programming: A Healthy Feast, but Hold Those Desserts!

December 8, 1991, brought *Fifty Years Ago Today*'s program schedule to Japan's surprise attack on Pearl Harbor. The event was marked by a two-hour special that included broadcast of *The Hunt for the Pearl Harbor Files,* a controversial film by a British historian and former BBC-TV producer that attempted to reconstruct Western intelligence failures in the months leading up to the attack. Host and ex-Navy man Professor Lincoln Bloomfield was in his element.[35]

December 14 gave the Monitor's audiences two special treats. *Inner City Beat,* by then being hosted by Harvard's Professor Charles Willie, carried an exclusive interview with Nelson Mandela by a first-rate African-American woman correspondent: the subject was South Africa's long-anticipated but yet to be scheduled first free election. On the same day, Peter Kent hosted "Power to the People," an hour-long special on the U.S. Bill of Rights, beginning with historical background, then wading straight into some of the big questions: abortion (women's rights versus the rights of the fetus), free press versus fair trial, and affirmative action. Both programs were rerun periodically throughout the month.[36]

Between Christmas and New Year's, The Monitor Channel aired Horton Foote's *The Texas Trilogy,* three powerful vignettes depicting what the author calls the "moral development" of his characters, and an unforgettable portrait of life in small-town Texas early in this century.[37]

Eyebrows flew up and jaws dropped among loyal staffers, however, when Netty Douglass announced that a new monthly show called *Lifestyles* was in development—and not just because the air was beginning to thicken with rumors about money. The host, the very same *Globe* celebrity journalist who had been drafted by Tom Winship to profile Kay Fanning two years earlier, would offer viewers "an exciting look at the 'triumphs and setbacks' of well-known celebrities, as well as fashion and lifestyle features, and glimpses into the worlds of theater, music, and art." To many who were giving their hearts and their minds to building The Monitor Channel, the *Lifestyles* concept was embarrassing. In the end, most swallowed hard and let it go: the Channel was a work in progress, after all, and the new show seemed unlikely to survive the test of time.[38]

The top news staff united to challenge a second program in development, which would have brought the former owner of the New England Patriots on as host of a program covering sports as business. The concept was first-rate, the man was terrific on camera and generally a good person, but he and his father were entangled in a lawsuit with the NFL. Instead, the would-be host was used as an occasional commentator.[39]

Another note threatening the well-being of her children if she continued at the Monitor was left on Lyn Chamberlin's desk, and Netty Douglass' car was savagely defaced in the dead of night for a fourth or fifth time.[40]

Money, Money Everywhere, But Not a Dime to Spare

Don Bowersock was uneasy about the level of spending at Monitor Television by then, especially the climbing ad hoc costs of Barbara Bellafiore Sanden's operation. These were generic concerns, he acknowledged, in a sense built into the situation.

He could extrapolate in a meaningful way from his own considerable business experience in the high-tech world to the peculiar world of cable television only up to a point. Reporting relationships and overlapping responsibilities among the top people on the Monitor's entrepreneurial team were complicated, and a certain amount of forbearance combined with skill at bureaucratic arm-wrestling went with the territory.[41]

Over the years, Bowersock had supplemented the information he received from his good friend Jack Hoagland and from Netty Douglass, to their considerable irritation, with a system of formal and informal channels that had included the former head of the Syndicate (then WQTV and short-wave, and ad sales for electronic media) and—ongoing—at the heart of operations at the Publishing Society, a comptroller who reported to him. Hoagland, Dick Nenneman, and others accepted the fact that unless and until the Publishing Society could pay its own bills, oversight of this sort, sometimes annoying, could hardly be avoided—and no one better to exercise it than an ally like Bowersock. Douglass was by temperament less tolerant of the Treasurer's habit of intervening in operational decisions at the Publishing Society through the Comptroller and, worse, recruiting informants from among some of the top-level employees who reported to her.[42]

By early December 1991, a confluence of unrelated developments abruptly left the Church with somewhat higher ongoing expenses and considerably less ready money than expected. Don Bowersock now faced a concern that was not generic: a dangerously tight cash flow.

The nationwide recession in ad sales had not eased as predicted but deepened, and revenues were far below projected levels at newspapers, magazines, and radio and TV stations everywhere. Those like WQTV, with a natural ad base in New England, suffered most acutely, and the combined shortfall in revenues at *World Monitor Magazine* and at WQTV came to $1 million below budget. The dissolution of the Discovery partnership meant that an additional $1 million or so was lost for the current fiscal year and about $6.5 million more, for the fiscal year starting in May. Talks with the Providence Journal and others about investment in The Monitor Channel were inching along, and while some of the attention was flattering, any deal or deals would take time to close, and the $6 to 10 million a year that could be expected from new partners might not kick in for another six to twelve months. Against this background, when the Hoagland and Holbrook meetings at Stanford and at the Los Angeles Museum made it clear that disbursements from the Knapp bequest might be delayed by a court challenge, matters took a serious turn.[43]

An obvious way to save money was to combine the Monitor's two parallel TV operations into one. When Discovery made its exit in November, Don Bowersock had indeed asked Jack Hoagland to disband *World Monitor News* as a separate operation and combine its staff with The Monitor Channel. Only part of the total annual cost of $24 million for *World Monitor News* could be saved by such a tactic, because much of its footage was already being recycled onto the channel and would still need to be produced under any new arrangement. Without layoffs, combining the two operations might save $1 or 2 million in the current fiscal year and maybe $4 million annually thereafter. With layoffs, the savings could be greater. Hoagland refused, and announced a no-layoffs policy. Bowersock did not push him.

Both Hoagland and Bowersock later regretted their failure to act decisively to combine the Monitor's two television operations at that juncture. Netty Douglass agreed that combined operations were desirable, and she expected that all top managers except perhaps Bill Chesleigh, the executive producer of *World Monitor,* would support a move in that direction. In retrospect, Hoagland would see his insistence that *World Monitor News* remain a separate operation as a turning point: a precious opportunity lost, not simply to economize, but to reassure Bowersock and the directors that he was prepared to work with them to get through the near-term crisis that was building.

The Church remained in control of vast debt-free fixed assets that, for a conventional business operation, would have provided considerable room to maneuver through a temporary cash shortage. These kinds of alternatives were probably even less appealing to Don Bowersock and the Church Directors in December 1991 than they had been a year earlier, when he first outlined them. Any move that incurred debt, such as taking out a mortgage on real estate holdings, would be met with howls of protest by the opposition when they became public and would, no doubt, be reported as evidence of insolvency or irresponsibility or both by friends of the opposition at the *Boston Globe* and elsewhere. Hoagland and Bowersock both feared that more publicity emphasizing internal divisions would scare cable players away from entering into equity partnerships with Monitor Television and in turn that blocking these all-important symbolic partnerships would jeopardize their securing the most important currency of all in the cable world: distribution.[44]

A sale and lease-back of the shortwave stations in Maine and South Carolina or of The Monitor Channel's satellite transponder might be less controversial, if only because these actions would be less easily understood as debt. A bond offering through a quasi-public corporation such as the Massachusetts Industrial Finance Agency might require sharing detailed information on finances that would include income from membership dues and thus data on membership, traditionally treated as a matter of strictest confidence. Perhaps, too, in the wake of the Twitchell trial, an alliance with the Commonwealth of Massachusetts would be distasteful to most members, including many among the entrepreneurial leadership itself. More could be borrowed against the pension fund in the short run, and that might be all that would be needed, but who could tell?

On December 5, just days after Hoagland had reported back on the disturbing meetings he and Mrs. Holbrook had had with the Stanford lawyers and representatives of the Los Angeles County Museum, Don Bowersock sent a handwritten memo with year-to-date estimates and the size of the expected shortfall to Netty Douglass: he emphasized that he had consulted no one else in putting it together. "My concern," he wrote, "is 'the system' will not give us what we need in a timely fashion." He asked if she could manage a reduction in spending of about $2 million over the remaining four and a half months of the fiscal year.[45]

She could: An operational challenge, even an unpleasant one, was exactly what Netty Douglass excelled at and she quickly drew up plans for selective cutbacks. Some initial blows of the ax would fall at MonitoRadio, some at the magazine, and some in television production. Shows like *The Children's Room* and *The Good Green Earth* were in effect "evergreen" products, and they could go into reruns immediately. The use of part-timers and free-lancers could be cut back, and travel could be reduced.[46]

For the first time, Jack Hoagland put a specific dollar limit on The Monitor Channel's affiliate sales and marketing group. Within ten days, Barbara Sanden responded with a detailed plan for reaching the 4.75 million subscriber goal by the April 30 end of the fiscal year within the new budget guidelines.[47]

On December 20, Harvey Wood was on Church business in Australia; Don Bowersock had said he would be out of the office until after Christmas; and Jack Hoagland was skiing with his family in Vermont. Late that afternoon, Dave Cook was sitting with Netty Douglass in the Managers' eighth-floor office at the Publishing Society, reporting on meetings that he, Bill Chesleigh, and John Palmer had had in London over the previous two days to reassure the gathered correspondents and staff about life after the Discovery Channel. Two Church Directors rarely seen at the Publishing Society put their heads in the door. Douglass was expecting them; Cook quickly excused himself and left.[48]

The Directors had come to talk money, and the meeting lasted about twenty minutes. They were there to insist that cuts in current operations be made. Douglass informed them of the steps already taken, and added that she would propose a hiring and salary freeze. This pre-Christmas visit to the Manager of the Publishing Society in Harvey Wood's absence was the first clear signal that his policies might no longer have the same unconditional backing at the Directors' level they had enjoyed for at least a decade.

Don Bowersock, hard at work from his home near the ocean, circulated a long memo dated December 23, which gave an overview of revenues and expenditures—budget, actuals, and variance—for all radio and television activities for the first seven months of the fiscal year. Distribution went out to individual Directors. Copies were sent to Hoagland, Douglass, the Christian Science Publishing Society's Comptroller, and Monitor Television's Chief Financial Officer as well as to two top members of Bowersock's own staff.[49]

The total variance from budget for radio and television, reflecting the combined effects of lower revenues and higher expenses than expected for the period from May through November, came to just under 10 percent, or $4.3 million. On the expense side, not surprisingly, television programming and related operations accounted for the lion's share of the overspending. Of this, much had gone to two specific projects: some, to mounting *Mort Sahl Live* shows at cable conventions in New York, Atlantic City, and Anaheim as part of the campaign to market The Monitor Channel to the movers and shakers of the cable industry, and most of the rest, to the prize-winning coverage of the Soviet coup.

Scaling Back

On Thursday, December 26, Douglass telephoned her managers in television programming and operations, instructing them to prepare to contribute beginning immediately to a $500,000–a-month reduction in programming costs, for a saving of $2 million in the remaining four months of the fiscal year. At lunch on Monday, December 30, Hoagland, Douglass, and Wood agreed to stand by the no-layoff policy announced when *World Monitor News* was dropped by Discovery. At lunch on Thursday, January 2, the same group plus Don Bowersock decided to prepare an "asset report," to spell out what the market value of the Monitor's current television operations might be, for the Publishing Society trustees and the Church Directors.

On Friday, January 3, Netty Douglass presided over an emotional, daylong budget retreat in Monitor Television's small conference room at Soldiers Field Road. Jack Hoagland began the day with a twenty-minute pep talk about "The Journalism of Ideas." Present in addition were five top technical operations people, plus Cook, Chesleigh, Chamberlin, and King for programming. The goal was to push expenses down from $3.7 million a month to $3.2 million, and, looking forward, to plan a total television budget for the fiscal year beginning in May that would come in at $35 million for programming and operations combined, down 21 percent from an expected $44.4 million tally for the current year.

Chamberlin came in with clear nuts-and-bolts suggestions for substantial savings: cut back on remote shoots; do without weekly visits of the Washington-based talent coach; maybe cut the sassy, state-of-the-art continuity segments that were providing transitions between shows. The two operations men who had been Bowersock's unofficial sources for the past two years gave what another manager present described as a "bizarre, zen-like presentation," cooperating fully yet seeming disconnected from the task at hand. King came prepared with a concept for a four- to six-hour programming wheel that went well beyond the cuts Hoagland and Douglass had asked for, and at one point angrily demanded that the no-layoffs policy announced in November be rescinded, lest the same personnel levels be folded into reduced programming and undermine any chance for real savings. At 371, the actual number of employees in television was already lower that the 410 provided for in the budget, and was even down from the 396 on board at the start of the fiscal year. Hoagland refused flat out to roll back the no-layoffs policy.[50]

All concerned pulled together: cuts that met the levels requested were agreed upon and put in force. Meetings of television managers and their respective staffs to fine-tune the responses followed. The Asset Report covering all media was presented to a combined meeting of trustees and directors on January 15.[51]

Meetings, lunches, phone calls, meetings. In back-to-back sessions on January 22 and 23, Don Bowersock, Netty Douglass, and the three Publishing Society Trustees (of whom Hal Friesen was one) wrestled with the immediate crisis, with secondary issues such as cross-charges, with their vision of the future, and with each other. Neither bond issues nor mortgages on real estate appeared on a list of potential new sources of funds compiled for the January 22 meeting, but included were transponder lease-back ($15 million), equity partners ($6 million), a major bequest ($90–100 million), and ABB ($35–50 million). ABB, (Asea Brown Boveri), the Swiss-based conglomerate that had provided the shortwave transmitters in Maine, South Carolina, and Saipan, had already indicated it was open to a sale/lease-back arrangement.[52]

On February 7 the news that insiders had been dreading for eight weeks finally came: Stanford University and the Los Angeles County Museum would join forces in legal action to contest the Church's right to the Bliss Knapp bequest. On February 9, Don Bowersock sent a memo to all employees, and the one-year hiring and salary freeze that management had already agreed to in principal became official.[53]

Cable Successes Roll On

Barbara Sanden had started the new year with a volley of letters, notes, and memos: some congratulated colleagues throughout the industry whose career moves had been noted in the trades, some thanked Church members who had written to ask when The Monitor Channel would be on their local cable systems and whether they could help, others were advisories and exhortations to her sales and marketing team. Invitations and follow-ups to invitations for Mort Sahl's January 8 and February 8 tapings went out to cable executives, ad agency people, and potential advertisers. Letters of agreement dated December 29, 30, and 31 came in from Viacom and some mid-sized cable operators, getting them in under the wire for charter rates for five years going forward, and these were acknowledged and forwarded to the lawyers. Another competitive preview—a beauty contest—was set up in Cablevision's important Long Island systems, this time pitting The Monitor Channel against Comedy Central, Black Entertainment Television, the Country Music Channel, and Mind Extension University. And there were two dozen thank-you notes—always personal, often witty—for an assortment of corporate Christmas gifts and messages.

On January 9 the systems Sanden and her team listed as likely to launch by the April 30 close of the fiscal year added up to 4.4 million viewers, still just shy of the 4.75 million goal Hoagland had set. By mid-January, general agreements were in hand for twenty-two of the twenty-five biggest cable operators, enabling the affiliate sales team to fan out on a regional basis. National subscriber lists for the newspaper and the magazine had been sorted by zip code and were being used to generate interest and support for The Monitor Channel in a sophisticated system-by-system campaign.

A more accurate indicator than the beauty contests of The Monitor Channel's prospects as of January 1992 were two industry surveys. Myers Marketing and Research found that cable operators who planned to add a new service placed The Monitor Channel fifth on their list, behind Comedy Central, American Movie Classics, Encore, and the SciFi Channel. Beta Research found that 18 percent of viewers were interested in The Monitor Channel, which also put it in fifth place in a nine-service field. These data support the level of expectations in Fleet's projections for distribution. The task outlined in the business plan Fleet had prepared was not easy, but it could be done.

Comcast came on board, and Viacom gave the Western sales team a boost by allowing them to run the Channel in the executive offices of an important California system. In an exhaustive, 130–page report on January 31, Sanden could list agreements in hand from all twenty-five top cable operators: eight signed contracts, seven contracts pending, nine executed letters of agreement, and one signed letter. Agreements with forty-one of the top fifty were in hand. The best coverage in terms of percentage of subscribers reached was, in order, in Washington, D.C.; Minneapolis; San Francisco; Miami–Fort Lauderdale; Chicago; Portland, Oregon; Raleigh–Durham; and New York.

Working from her Greenwich office, racing against time, Sanden geared up a grass-roots marketing campaign. Individual letters went out to *Christian Science Monitor* and *World Monitor Magazine* subscribers in twenty targeted systems, telling them that The Monitor Channel was being considered for carriage in their home communities. A thick binder of responses was soon in hand, with strong support from Church members, educators, and notables including elected officials. February's goal for new subscribers was very nearly reached by mid-month.[54]

In mid-January, the Monitor's cordial, wide-ranging, year-long talks with the Providence Journal bore fruit of sorts. A document setting forth terms for the sale of convertible preferred stock in the Monitor Channel, contingent on the participation of a second and possibly a third cable investor, was initialed. The sums anticipated, up to $30 million over three years, were modest—in effect, a proposed helping hand and a look-see—

and had been scaled back and hedged in part, Providence Journal executives admitted later, as a result of the publicity surrounding the Knapp bequest in the preceding six months. But it was a beginning.[55]

The Globe's Part: Was There a Corporate Motive?

On February 25 the Los Angeles Superior Court granted a three-month delay to Stanford University and the Los Angeles County Museum to allow them time to prepare their challenge to the Knapp trustees and the Church. That same day, four editors from the Publishing Society's religious periodicals resigned, giving as their reason the publication of the Knapp book four months earlier. Although few in Greater Boston had even heard of these tiny, highly specialized publications, the editors' resignations were page-one news the next morning at the *Globe*.[56]

With this, the *Globe*'s coverage of the Monitor's entrepreneurs began to move beyond calculated discourtesies to something qualitatively different: an unrelenting campaign involving nearly daily coverage and, frequently, loud overinterpretation of obscure events that might have been comical, except for what was at stake.

By way of comparison, that same year two Boston-area high-tech giants collapsed, sending further shock waves through the region's battered economy and throwing tens of thousands of breadwinners out of work. The fall of Digital Equipment Corporation was covered by the *Globe* in some ninety-two stories totaling 48,200 words, and the end of Wang Computer, in thirty-four stories totaling 25,600 words. Raytheon, a third major regional high-tech employer, stumbled, downsized by 5,000 jobs and was buffeted by scandals that included graphic mafia-style death threats and accusations of cheating in the fulfillment of government contracts, and these dramatic events warranted twenty stories totaling 15,700 words. Numbers like these reflect editorial judgments about the enormous importance of these stories: the New England economy had been on its knees for three years by then, and with the crumbling of DEC, Wang, and Raytheon, the region's hope to be a strong contender in the global high-tech economy in the 1990s was dealt a near-mortal blow.[57]

By this measure, for the *Globe*'s higher-ups, events at the Monitor were even more important: the upheaval at the Monitor merited a volume of coverage that, except for elections, was unmatched by any other regional story in the entire preceding five years. In the course of 1992, the *Globe* ran an apparently unprecedented eighty-five stories totalling 81,500 words, just slightly less than the coverage of DEC, Wang, and Raytheon *combined*. Almost all of this coverage was packed into the four critical months from the end of February to the middle of June.[58]

The *Globe*'s coverage became a factor in The Monitor Channel's collapse. As story followed story, anguish and confusion became the order of the day at the Publishing Society. The young and idealistic among the Monitor's employees, especially, felt the barrage of claims and innuendo spread across the *Globe*'s pages week after week must be true, because if not, why did not Jack Hoagland and his allies find some way to fight back directly? Others more in the know cited the long friendship between Fanning and Winship, and believed they saw, not institutional policy, so much as personal revenge behind the stories that began on February 26 and continued into June. Still others dismissed "conspiracy theories" and explained the excesses as nothing more culpable than a zealous dedication to selling newspapers.[59]

The most potentially damaging speculation was that the *Globe*'s owners and top managers might have an overriding corporate interest in bringing down the Monitor's ventures into new media. The facts were these: Affiliated Publications, the *Globe*'s parent, was in a serious predicament itself in the winter of 1992 and the financial interests of all major shareholders hung in the balance. Though Affiliated stock was publicly traded, majority ownership rested with two large trusts representing 110 widely scattered heirs, and these trusts were set to dissolve in 1996. To avoid the kind of costly pandemonium that had brought down the Binghams of the *Louisville Courier-Journal*, a sale, perhaps to a group of insiders, needed to be arranged. By late 1991, it was reported that the *Globe* was being actively, albeit discretely, shopped around.[60]

It was not an auspicious time for this particular newspaper to be looking for buyers, however. Profits had fallen in 1989 and again in 1990 as the recession took hold; in 1991, for the first time in its 119–year history, the *Boston Globe* lost money—a whopping $67 million. Whether or not buyers included current owners or managers, large sums of outside money had to be found, in an inhospitable investment climate and on an uncomfortably tight deadline. The *Globe*'s asking price was reported to be $1 billion, or two times cash flow. This figure was high although not exorbitant for a publication that had accounted for well over half the Greater Boston area's advertising income for many years. But the timing was very bad.[61]

Any buyers and any lenders underwriting buyers would make a number of strategically important educated guesses: given the long, gradual weakening of the newspaper business nationwide, could the *Globe,* if it remained a newspaper only, really prosper? Could newspaper publishers as a guild hold onto the de facto monopoly on classified ads that was their economic lifeblood, or would these be carried by electronic media—telephone lines, cable TV, the Internet—in the future? If diversification became necessary, would the *Globe*'s management have what it takes to stay ahead of the process and continue to dominate the competition? Forty-eight months remained to put the *Globe*'s house in order, and management's bargaining position would weaken as it approached.

Retired Editor Tom Winship was said to be one of the principals in the process of lining up a buyer or buyers. When in late January, a tiny notice on a back page reported the nomination of Winship's old friend Kay Fanning to the Affiliated Board, Boston's busy *Globe*-watchers speculated that this was in some way related to the difficult transition that the newspaper had to negotiate.[62]

According to the corporate imperative line of reasoning, once the Monitor's talks with the Providence Journal became known, a highly volatile ingredient was added to an already dangerous mix for those trying to arrange the sale of the *Boston Globe*. Danny Wilson, a wise old observer of media wars, does not mince words: as he saw it, when the *Globe*'s most active stakeholders found out that the Providence Journal and the Monitor were on the verge of concluding a strategic alliance, *"They ... went ... berserk!"*[63]

The reason, Wilson and others argue, is that a strong, well-financed Monitor–Pro Jo partnership could be expected to claim a modest piece of the national communications market, but a somewhat larger slice of the regional market—taking a direct bite out of the *Globe*'s franchise. Such added uncertainty would provoke consternation among potential investors or buyers, drive down the newspaper's price and make any sale far more difficult to pull off. According to this school of thought, *Globe* higher-ups understood all this only too well, and in most cases their own personal fortunes were also at stake.

Was the *Globe*'s assault on the struggling Monitor operation across town in the winter and spring of 1992 yet another undeclared media war—never reported to the public—of the sort that has characterized so much of the history of public communications in this century? Affiliated Publication's inner councils were no more visible to the public than those of their chosen adversaries at the Christian Science Church. In any case, as the prediction goes in conventional warfare, an early casualty was the truth.

Chapter 8

Collapse

*February–June 1992: From tactical
maneuver to strategic retreat and collapse*

> We took our resources to the edge, because we believed in what
> we were doing.
>
> —*Don Bowersock, 1994*

February 27–March 8: A Bold Tactical Maneuver

To underwrite the launch of The Monitor Channel and to meet ongoing
costs at the Publishing Society, including the continuing deficit at the
newspaper, Church Directors had been fully prepared to spend down the
substantial cash reserves in hand at the end of the 1980s. However,
expenses were higher, revenues lower, and the time line for attracting
outside partners longer than expected. It was conceivable that any major
purchase of equity in The Monitor Channel might not close until after
the presidential election in November 1992 gave the cable industry a
better sense of what the regulatory climate might be in the future. So far,
internal borrowing had bridged the gap, but now the Knapp money—a
done deal, it had seemed, well into the previous fall—would be tied up
in court for the foreseeable future. Netty Douglass and her managers had
cut back expenses as asked, but another round of tough decisions still
had to be made.

On Thursday, February 27, Don Bowersock circulated the monthly
"Treasurer's Narrative," covering the first three quarters of fiscal year

1992. This two-page overview put the value of the Church's restricted and unrestricted funds on hand at $65 million. For the first nine months of the fiscal year, income from all sources, estimated at $47.2 million, had come in at $52.3 million, but total expenses including both the Church and the Publishing Society, at $107 million, were now 12 percent over budget. About half of the spending over budget was attributable to the combined costs of television production and marketing.[1]

Stamped confidential as always, the monthly report was distributed to the usual short list: the five Church Directors, four members of Bowersock's own staff, four members of the Church Finance Committee, and to Netty Douglass, as Manager of the Publishing Society. By the next day, a Friday, the "Treasurer's Narrative" and other internal financial documents were in the hands of *Globe* reporter, Jim Franklin.[2]

Franklin's Saturday morning story on the first page of the Metro section gave the clear impression that the Church had been caught engaging in secret, highly irregular, and possibly fraudulent practices, flouting the terms of two separate trusts and putting the pensions of elderly retirees at risk. The numbers were accurate, and it was certainly true, as the headline put it, that the Church was digging deep for cash. But the air of sensational discovery ignored (among other things) that the same reporter had noted ongoing internal borrowings himself four and a half months earlier.[3]

Jack Hoagland rushed back from a family ski weekend in Vermont to meet with Netty Douglass and the badly shaken top managers in the Publishing Society boardroom to draft a response titled, "Staying the Course." Don Bowersock began to draft an accompanying financial memo that attempted to answer the accusations implicit in what had appeared in the *Globe*. "Staying the Course" and the Bowersock memo were intended as background, as perspective, and as a statement of resolve—for employees, for members of the press, for the Christian Science Field, for anyone who would listen.[4]

The next day, Sunday, Franklin repackaged the same story in a second long article under the headline, "Christian Science Borrowing Stirs Alarm." The article began with three damaging opinions, two from anonymous sources and a third from Kay Fanning's colleague, David Anable, and again suggested that the financial security of retirees had been thrown into jeopardy. On Monday, March 2, Franklin rewrote the same story for a third day, with the headline "Pension Fund of Church Has Fallen Too Low, Says Member."[5]

None of these stories offered a context for balanced judgment. There was, for example, no summary of the federal law by which for-profit businesses were bound in running pension funds, with which the Church had complied voluntarily for many years. There was no general discussion of the common practice and standard terms of borrowing against pension funds in business. There was no hint that, while not required to do so, the Treasurer had in fact always notified members and retirees in writing of such activities in the past and on that basis could have been expected to do so in this instance as well.

The Office of the Massachusetts Attorney General, prompted by the *Globe*'s reports of crisis and irregularity, began to make inquiries—and then the fact that inquiries were being made was also reported. Both the *Globe* reporter and his most energetic collaborator among the Church's former employees, the former Church publicist, made visits to the Attorney General's office in person.[6]

Two weeks and the informal exchange of considerable documentation later, the Attorney General's office would conclude that there had been no wrongdoing. The Church's fully cooperative officials had been engaged in legitimate behavior. The pension funds were part of a general fund that could be used at the Church's discretion, and even so the internal transfers had been set up as loans with prime or prime-plus interest rates attached. The terms of the two trusts had likewise been respected, with Church officials themselves calling the investigators' attention to a matter of subtle legal interpretation that had been discussed pro and con internally for years, and which was then addressed promptly in a mutually agreeable way. The Church's substantial annual income and wholly unencumbered real estate holdings suggested that as a practical matter there could be considerable flexibility in meeting the current difficulties.[7]

On Tuesday, the *Globe* ran a fourth long article retelling the original story, again suggesting that retirees should fear for their security and quoting three sources to that effect: the former archivist, another employee who had also been let go, and an anonymous source. By then, the national press had begun to run with the story.[8]

That day the *Globe* also carried a front-page story reporting—incorrectly—that "technical problems" had kept The Monitor Channel from nationwide distribution for several hours on Monday. The *Globe*'s error would be noted briefly in the next day's paper: the short-lived problem was only with a cable at the locally broadcast UHF, WQTV, after all, and The Monitor Channel had been beamed up to the Galaxy V satellite in the preceding days without interruption.[9]

However, the reporter, new to the Monitor story and apparently sent out to do a simple piece about technical matters that he (and his editors) did not quite understand, had also gone the extra mile, checking Monitor Television's reputation with cable industry sources. In the second half of his story, important industry figures were quoted characterizing The Monitor Channel as "high quality," a "serious option" for operators with space, and "already a major player" in the cable programming world. Except for one article coauthored with Franklin the following week, this enterprising writer was never assigned to the Monitor story again.[10]

On Tuesday, the Monitor's entrepreneurs released "Staying the Course," seven pages long, signed by Jack Hoagland and Netty Douglass but authored in several drafts over two days with the participation of their four or five top managers, and reviewed by the Publishing Society Trustees and at the Church. Given the *Globe*'s assertions of scandal and malfeasance, "Staying the Course" seemed a curious communication to those unfamiliar with the self-imposed restraints of Monitor journalism. No attempt was made to spell out any possible personal or corporate motives for the *Globe*'s attack, much less to answer slander with slander. Three sentences toward the beginning said, simply:

> At the moment, we are witnessing an all-out assault on the television activities of the Monitor, the purposes of which are not entirely clear, but which, admittedly, makes our work harder. Spurious reports questioning our financial stability and future prospects are being run as page-one stories. We know these are as disturbing to you as they are to us.

The rest of the document stubbornly emphasized the positive, reviewing the enormous achievements to date, looking forward at what remained to be accomplished and at the importance of the journalistic values at stake. A brief cover letter from Harvey Wood declared, "Our resolve is unwavering." Attached also was Don Bowersock's patient two-and-a-half-page summary detailing for the public record the intricacies of the internal borrowing.[11]

To some of the 250 or so non-Church employees at the Monitor in 1992 and to those outside the organization not familiar with the traditional scruples and habits of mind at work, including many in the mainstream press, such a high-minded response seemed weak. But fighting back would have meant talking about personalities—the Fanning–Winship connection, among others—and confronting *Globe* management publicly on their questionable journalistic standards in covering events at the Publishing Society and the Church, as well as their possible corporate interest in seeing Monitor Television fail. Generations of Monitor professionals had been taught to abhor personal attack and direct confrontation, however, and instead of gearing up for battle, the Monitor's entrepreneurs instinctively hunkered down.

The next day, Wednesday, the *Globe*'s Franklin reported on "Staying the

Course" as a continuation—now for the fifth day in a row—of the sensational series on the Monitor's borrowings.[12]

Meanwhile, the story of The Monitor Channel's year-long talks with the Providence Journal broke. *Inside Media* quoted Pro Jo President Trygvie Myhren praising the quality of the Monitor's television efforts, and the *Boston Globe,* the *Boston Herald,* and the *Wall Street Journal* picked up the story from advance copies. For the next two weeks, a *Globe* business writer (and Winship protégé) reportedly called Providence Journal execs constantly, sometimes several times a day, demanding whenever he reached anyone to know whether they were aware of the Monitor's financial problems and the extraordinary measures taken to meet them, and whether under the circumstances Providence Journal was really prepared to step up to the table with an investment.[13]

That same morning—Wednesday—Federal Express delivered a formal "Complaint" from a Church member to the Church directors, seeking the resignations of Harvey Wood, Hal Friesen, Jack Hoagland, and Netty Douglass. The main document was 112 pages long, accompanied by 203 pages of appended materials.[14]

The petitioner herself, well known to all concerned, was not considered a critic of particular stature but the rarely used process put in motion in her name—lodging a formal complaint with two witnesses—was among the most solemn available under the Church's governing *Manual.* The thick binder of materials, meticulously prepared, summarized the opposition's arguments against the policies of the incumbent leadership. Over the next two days, the possibility that the complaint might be published privately and circulated to the Field figured prominently in internal discussions.[15]

Harvey Wood was the Complaint's main target. By then in his fifteenth year on the Board, he stood for all the policies that had inflamed the opposition: the introduction of modern management techniques within the Church administration and the resulting staff reductions and disruption of routine; gradually bringing semiautonomous fiefdoms, notably at the Church archives, the external information department, and the Publishing Society's religious periodicals, under central control; the gradual move toward an open shelf of Christian Science literature, representing an expanded range of opinion and experience, accompanied by an implied tolerance of a wider range of opinion about Mary Baker Eddy's ministry; the interest in Third World membership; other directors' private dialogues with secular students of mental healing, such as Dr. Herbert Benson, or practitioners from other traditions, such as ayurvedic doctor Deepak Chopra; refusal to expand the traditional powers of the Church Finance Committee to include oversight of Publishing Society policies; diminished support for the much-loved but increasingly anachronistic daily paper and heavy investment in the move into new media; the adoption of EEOC standards in hiring in radio and television; the partial demystification of the Monitor's journalistic standards, the emphasis on efficient results, and the dramatically increased presence of journalists, managers, and technicians who respected the Monitor tradition but were not Church members.

At several junctures in the stormy years since the move into television, Harvey Wood, Jack Hoagland, Hal Friesen, Don Bowersock, and Netty Douglass had discussed the possibility of deflecting criticism and buying time with the tactical resignation of one or more of their number. On Friday, March 6, first at lunch, then at a long meeting later that afternoon, these same players revisited their options and decided on a bold move: Wood was to resign. At that meeting the Church board decided to take an action under discussion for some time, returning to closer integration of board members into operations under a form of governance known as the "cabinet system," a system that had been in effect until the court battle of 1917. Hoagland and Douglass would assume lower profiles. Bowersock said The Monitor Channel could be funded without the Knapp bequest or outside investors through September, at which time they could look forward and make decisions about the coming two years. Another meeting of the full Board was called for the next morning.

On Saturday morning, March 7, the full five-member board plus Hal Friesen (then one of three Publishing Society trustees), Netty Douglass, and Jack Hoagland met in the relative privacy of the small, utilitarian conference room at WQTV on the outskirts of Boston. A detailed review was made of expenses, income, available funds, the status of the Knapp bequest, and alternative sources of working capital for the next few months. Likewise reviewed were the intensification of opposition activity, including the *Globe*'s punishing campaign on behalf of the opposition and the probable damage that would do to staff morale and the search for cable partners.

Shutting The Monitor Channel down was discussed as a contingency. Because of the bleak New England job market, giving staff a year's severance in that eventuality was agreed to in principle.

The move to the old arrangement integrating the Church Board into day-to-day operations—the cabinet system—was endorsed. Douglass, Hoagland, and Bowersock were to resign and Directors would assume their positions. Douglass would be Executive Producer for radio and television, Bowersock would become Managing Treasurer. Hoagland, Douglass, and Bowersock would continue to run Monitor Television and The Monitor

Channel with their old titles intact, as Chairman and CEO, President, and Treasurer, respectively.

That afternoon a closed meeting of the Board concluded with Wood's resignation. Back at the Publishing Society, Hoagland, Douglass, and Friesen drafted letters of resignation, while the four remaining Board members elected Wood's replacement. No one minimized the formidable obstacles ahead, but at the end of the day on Saturday, the majority of the Board still expected to move forward with the work of the past five years, including most prominently The Monitor Channel. A meeting to prepare an announcement of the changes was set for 10:00 A.M.

On Sunday, after a three-day silence, the *Globe*'s assault was renewed, now on even more serious terms. The message the Monitor's entrepreneurs and the newly constituted Church board found early that morning in the Sunday paper materially changed the terms of the internal debate, and before the day was out, the consensus had shifted by ninety degrees. The Monitor's reformers had been operating on the assumption that their basic challenge was simply a matter of juggling money and time in the short term—that their core task was still to contain costs and build distribution and revenues at The Monitor Channel, funding operations by whatever means available, until an investor group was lined up. What they read in the *Globe* that morning snuffed out that simplifying assumption.

Using the usual quotes from anonymous sources and ex-employees, Franklin's Sunday article raised important new issues, two of which were understood to be fatal to The Monitor Channel's prospects in the long run. The *Globe*'s writer and his informants asserted the following:

- The Monitor's move into new media threatened Christian Science religious practices (though just why was not clear);
- Governance procedures at the Church were unsatisfactory;
- Members should cut off donations to the Church;
- The covert purpose of all Monitor media is to proselytize, or, alternatively—and this point was made with a quote from Kay Fanning—that insofar as Monitor media is not serving a specifically missionary purpose, it should be;
- No outside investor aware of these facts should want to put money into any Monitor undertaking, and any who might try would find they had a fight on their hands.[16]

If the aim was to damage the Monitor's diversification in general and its prospects for partnership with the Providence Journal in particular, the last two points had found their mark. The assertion that Monitor journalism was not really a public service, not disinterested truthtelling after all, but somehow concealed an aggressive religious agenda was shocking. Supported by the Fanning quote, it was also seen as a shocking personal betrayal on the part of the newspaper's former editor of the *Monitor*'s largely successful eighty-year struggle for credibility. Calling Monitor journalism a missionary activity was designed to confirm any skeptic's worst fears; it was tantamount to saying that Monitor journalism could not be trusted.

Moreover, Church decision makers and many others at the Publishing Society and at Monitor Television understood the final point as a clear threat both from the opposition and from the *Boston Globe* to make normal business life difficult indeed for any outside investor so foolish as to step forward.

Finally, the article had taken aim at the very foundation of Church governance: not only was the Monitor's right to be a respected member of the journalistic community disputed, the current Directors' legitimate right to conduct the business of the Church as they traditionally had done was obliquely but sharply called into question.

When Jack Hoagland, Netty Douglass, and Hal Friesen met in the Manager's office early that morning, it was Hoagland who forced himself and his two colleagues to read the handwriting on the wall. Given the movement's internal divisions and the *Globe*'s clear resolve to destroy the challenge in their backyard, he argued, there was no way out. The channel would have to be sold outright—perhaps with the Publishing Society continuing to supply most of the programming—or shut down. Douglass phoned Don Bowersock at home to tell him what they were thinking, and the Treasurer tried to dissuade them; he could, he repeated, keep everything funded at least until September, at which time they could all take stock anew.[17]

The 10:00 A.M. meeting in the Directors' informal conference room began with a defiant acknowledgement by a member of the new Board that the stakes had been abruptly raised by the Globe's article that morning, but that he, for one, was inclined to fight on. Hoagland cut discussion short, and quietly, logically, laid out the options, ending with his recommendation that The Monitor Channel be sold, if possible, or shut down. At one point, Hoagland remembers, he was in tears, nose bleeding, and had to leave the room to compose himself. The Board's most fiscally conservative member, Richard Bergenheim, stood quietly by him until he could return to the meeting and continue.[18]

The 10:00 A.M. meeting ended, and the five Directors continued with discussion and prayer among themselves. By 3:00 P.M., the Board sent word that it would—with extreme reluctance—accept Hoagland's and the Trustees' recommendation to sell The Monitor Channel, or close it. They set the deadline at June 15.[19]

Dave Cook remembers that he was at home watching *60 Minutes* that Sunday evening when Netty Douglass called to tell him about the changes under way. Cook drove into town from the western suburb where he lives, and found Douglass across from the Broadcast Center in the snack bar at the Sheraton Hotel with Hal Friesen, Gail Pierson, and Al Carnesciali, the dedicated California practitioner and teacher who had just been named to replace both Harvey Wood on the Board and Douglass herself as Manager of the Publishing Society. Eventually Cook and Douglass drove in their separate cars out to WQTV to meet Jack Hoagland, and reviewed the statements the Directors would put out for employees and the press the next morning, changing a word or two. It must have been nearly midnight when the three said goodnight under the sodium vapor streetlights in the deserted parking lot.[20]

March 9–April 15: Can the Channel Be Saved?

As Monitor Television employees arrived at work after the weekend, they found e-mail and voicemail messages summoning them to the Broadcast Center's spacious second floor newsroom. Many assumed Jack Hoagland and Netty Douglass had called the Monday morning meeting to fight back with yet another eloquent exhortation to "stay the course." But Hoagland, tall, gray, tailored, was announcing his resignation. Douglass, his tough, indefatigable executive right hand, was also stepping down. That morning, she stood behind him and to the side, alternately scanning the crowd of nearly 200 employees and looking down. An audio link carried the meeting live to employees gathered in the Monitor's bureaus in Washington, London, and Tokyo.

Half reading from a prepared statement and half extemporaneously, Hoagland struggled through what he had to say:

> We've had a lot of happy meetings in this room, but getting through this announcement is about all I can accomplish today. . . . An onslaught of negative publicity has made a key part of the work extremely difficult. . . . The

editorial quality in television is superb, a major achievement; it has raised the quality of television journalism. . . . We also want to thank our affiliate sales group, which has represented us so successfully and has won so much respect among cable operators in the country. . . . I wish we could have performed at the same level. . . . The Board of Directors is announcing changes. . . . Several sources of funding and equity participation in The Monitor Channel . . . part of our planning from the start, were taking shape . . . of those potential outside partners, one here in New England, as the onslaught hit, it became very difficult to keep those negotiations in place; alliances are a vital necessity (in the cable world) . . . yesterday's press coverage, quoting unnamed members of our church . . . signaled a determined opposition to the principle of partnerships in this enterprise. . . . We will be taking every step to complete an outright sale of The Monitor Channel. . . . The time limit is June 15. . . . If there are any layoffs, six months salary up front, with another six months for those who don't find a position; there will be 12 full months of coverage. . . . Keep up the quality, stay here and show them what we're capable of. You've done a wonderful job. . . .

Hoagland turned to give up the microphone to Douglass. She shook her head slightly and said, "I can't."[21]

Immediately afterward, at a packed all-employee meeting in the tiny original church, all five directors (two women and three men) took the stage. Most of the outsiders who had been hired in the build-up of television had never seen them before; Harvey Wood's successor as chairman, Virginia Harris, blond, attractive, intense, spoke for the group. Praise was conferred on The Monitor Channel and admiration expressed for the professionals who had put it together. Later that day, without naming the *Boston Globe,* the Publishing Society's new Trustees and Manager issued a statement giving the leadership's view of what had forced their hand:

> Our potential partners experienced a barrage of attention which was disturbing to them and detrimental to orderly negotiation; and senior industry figures have told us of press interviews that, in their view, became heated in the effort to elicit negative statements about The Monitor Channel.
>
> Yesterday's press coverage, quoting unnamed members of our Church, raises further challenges for us in two ways: by trying to reinterpret the very purpose of the *Christian Science Monitor* that was so clearly established in 1908—to be an independent, unbiased source of the most objective, in-depth journalism—thus raising doubts about our greatest asset, our journalistic integrity; and by signaling a determined opposition to the principle of partnerships in this enterprise—an opposition which has already proved capable, on occasion, of disrupting our normal business operations. . . . Given the prospects of continuing opposition within our Church ranks, we must now face

the necessity of an outright sale of The Monitor Channel to an outside party, no later than June 15, 1992.[22]

The next morning, the *Globe* ran 3,270 words of copy in five separate articles on the upheavals at the Monitor—two page-one stories and three others, also in the first section of the paper. Chock-full of quotes from the opposition, about half of which were anonymous, Jim Franklin's two stories set out the opposition's terms: Harvey Wood may be gone, but Hoagland and Douglass only relinquished their titles but kept their jobs, and The Monitor Channel is not dead yet. One anonymous member saluted "these first steps." A prominent female Church member (unnamed) declared, "We have shifted the furniture but not the scenery." The former publicist, by then on record as advising Stanford in its legal battle with the Church over rights to the $100 million bequest, though this important detail was omitted in the *Globe* story, suggested withdrawing the Knapp book "as a gesture of good faith."[23]

On a WGBH-TV talk show that evening, Robert Bergenheim, a local publisher, former Church member, and the father of Church Director Richard Bergenheim, sharply criticized Kay Fanning for her supposed behind-the-scenes machinations. Other participants on the show, including the *Globe*'s Franklin and the woman who had written the long farewell article on John Hart for the *Globe* in October, were subdued, as if they were not quite sure themselves what was happening.[24]

Now that there was the smell of blood in the water, as one industry observer put it, given the difficult business climate and given that The Monitor Channel had launched nationally less than a year earlier, finding buyers would be no mean feat. Before the end of the week, the scramble to do just that against all odds was on.[25]

Sid Topol placed calls throughout the cable world. Jack Hoagland worked his international connections. Fleet and others briefly considered, then dropped, the idea of underwriting an initial public offering. Some cast about even more broadly.

Peter Ackerman, former Milken associate at Drexel Burnham, a respected member of the Church and a friend of Virginia Harris's, arrived from London for the first of several trips to advise the Board, and he, in turn, consulted with a senior analyst specializing in communications properties at Donaldson, Lufkin, Jenrette in New York. Netty Douglass worked on an even leaner new business plan, with Topol and others scrutinizing every line.[26]

What was The Monitor Channel worth? Mature cable networks are usually valued with the help of two formulas, either cash flow times 13–15 or subscribing households times $7–9. Then intangibles—likely potential for growth, quality of the competition, quality of incumbent management, likely appeal to cable operators, viewers and advertisers, political plusses and minuses at both the local and the national level, opportunity costs of all sorts—move the hard numbers around. Given the Monitor's impressive performance in the first ten months following launch, the channel might have fetched about $40 million in an orderly sale that spring and much more, of course, in subsequent years. But there were two ugly flies in the ointment: the industry's uncertain regulatory climate, for one, and the air of scandal and doubt surrounding the Publishing Society, calling into question its ability to continue as a supplier of the channel's programming.

The Pro Jo team, with cash a-plenty from the October 1990 sale of cellular telephone properties, was in the happy position of buyer in a buyer's market. They had great respect for what Hoagland and Douglass had accomplished and liked them personally. The fit was good in theory for many reasons, including the commitment of all concerned to quality and their mutual interest in pursuing joint ventures in the regional market. But if they and other cable operators invested and eventually became managing partners, could the Publishing Society now be counted on to be a reliable supplier of content? Reluctantly, Pro Jo's executives began to distance themselves from the agreement in principle they had arrived at with the Monitor in January.[27]

The indefatigable Barbara Bellafiore Sanden and her highly motivated affiliate sales team continued to sign up new cable subscribers through March and into April. Sanden supplied cable trade publications with good news to counter the bad news that had by then been picked up in the national press: testimonial letters from viewers who did not want to lose The Monitor Channel, survey results showing more than respectable audiences by cable standards.[28]

Potential buyers—real, unreal, and surreal—appeared, took a tour of the Monitor's state-of-the-art Broadcast Center and dropped out or were politely shown the door. One exasperated participant, resorting to hyperbole (and mixed metaphor) to capture the flavor of the experience, said afterward, "At one point, everybody and their mother was making calls to other people, some of it authorized, some of it not authorized. . . . The inmates were running the asylum, the ship was adrift and dead in the water, people were jumping overboard and blowing up the boiler room, and when Jack and Netty had stepped aside, the place was left to the wolves."

A colorful multimillionaire from Texas revealed over dinner with Netty Douglass and an associate that he had a gambling channel in mind, exclaiming again and again, "That's pretty hot skillet!" A New York investment banker presented the Trustees and the Board with a proposal to underwrite a sale and help find a buyer. The *Globe*'s eager investigative reporters wrote about prospects no one remembers hearing of or talking to. Three separate individuals, each either with sufficient personal net worth or with associates making him a qualified potential buyer, came forward and, eventually, were directly or indirectly discouraged from pursuing a purchase by the Church Board itself.[29]

As March moved toward April, the *Globe* continued to play megaphone to the opposition's cheerleaders, citing four former employees, three anonymous sources, and one highly eccentric perennial amateur litigator to report that "Church members demand accounting," coupled with suggestions that the administrative reforms of the 1980s be rolled back. Two sentences buried deep in that story note that in effect the Attorney General had found no wrongdoing in the Church's use of funds. A sarcastic, super-hip article by the *Globe*'s television critic made programming suggestions for a future buyer. A nostalgic article wondered if the old newspaper could ever regain its former glory. A solemn piece by a religious scholar whose credentials were not made clear hoped for change of exactly the sort the opposition favored. The *Globe* shared the outrage of the former editors of the Publishing Society's religious periodicals who found to their surprise that, having resigned and publicly attacked their employers' policies, they were not welcome to continue to frequent their old offices. Then, more on the Church's internal borrowing and, finally, continuing the opposition drumbeat, "Many in church begin open critique of policy." The *Globe*'s coverage of the crisis at the Monitor in March alone came to twenty articles, totaling just under 20,000 words.[30]

On March 31, Peter Ackerman advised the Board that there was little chance of finding a suitable buyer by June 15. Jack Hoagland, back from London following leads of his own, headed for Tokyo where a friend of his at Japanese National Broadcasting (NHK) had set up a presentation to Sony, in Sony's main downtown offices. Hiro Oka, Takashi's enterprising wife, served as translator. The presentation went well, but all parties acknowledged that the time for putting a deal together was uncomfortably short.[31]

While Hoagland was in mid-air on the return trip, the Directors told Netty Douglass that they had decided to move the closing date up to April 15. A letter of intent was faxed in from a private buyer. The new date was announced, then rescinded. After meeting with Douglass and others, Ackerman advised the Board that unlikely as they were to find a buyer within the time frame set, it still made sense to keep the Channel up in reruns, its high-quality product visible, through June 15.

On Friday, April 10, the board swallowed Jack Hoagland's poison pill, and termination notices were handed out to most of the Monitor's 400 broadcast employees. Netty Douglass finalized the programming schedule to continue broadcasting the Channel in automated reruns until the end of June. That Sunday, April 12, Hoagland and Douglass resigned from their positions at The Monitor Channel, although Douglass would continue full-time well into June helping her successor get a handle on operations at the Publishing Society. On Wednesday, April 15, the Hoagland and Douglass resignations were announced and The Monitor Channel went into automated reruns. Dave Cook was named Editor of a newly created division within the Publishing Society, Monitor Broadcasting. Sid Topol still had one or two slender leads to pursue in the cable world.

April 15–June 28: Prospects Dim, and the Channel Goes Dark

Through April, May, and June, The Monitor Channel's embryonic cable network of just under 5 million subscribers remained intact; despite attractive offers dangled by rivals like Court TV and VISN, not a single cable operator defected, and several new systems even came on line. On April 16, Barbara Sanden was able to put out a press release that included lengthy and warm remarks about The Monitor Channel by executives representing nine large and medium-sized cable operators around the country. Even as news of the Channel's problems spread, 10,000 viewers nationwide wrote in for monthly Monitor TV programming guides.

Meantime, Sid Topol drew on the immense respect he commanded throughout the industry to pull together one final meeting of big operators who might somehow be persuaded in the eleventh hour to form a consortium to buy and manage The Monitor Channel. Pro Jo's Trygvie Myhren worked with him. That meeting was first fixed for the National Cable Television Association's Dallas Convention in early May, then moved to the Manhattan offices of an investment banker. Comcast's Brian Roberts was present, and perhaps Cox—memories of those weeks became a blur. Topol and the Monitor Channel CFO who worked closely with him during this period made their presentation, then left the room. The conversation turned on reregulation, on CNN, on costs, and eventually the answer was no.[32]

Contacts with Crown Cable, a subsidiary of Hallmark Cards created a flurry of excitement—like Pro Jo, Hallmark had cash and a corporate culture the Monitor felt comfortable with—but a last meeting in a conference room at Boston's Logan Airport, which had seemed to go well, led nowhere.[33]

The *Globe* pursued the Monitor's leadership with one major article almost every day, using minor events such as the receipt of a lawyer's letter in some obscure Church matter, the leaking of a document containing no important new information, a disingenuous interpretation of an accountant's end-of-year advice, or a restatement of the preferences of those who agreed with Kay Fanning, as pegs on which to hang stories filled with innuendo and alarm.

Most were written by Jim Franklin, and most of the time, the sense of moral condemnation conveyed depended on unstated, thus unexamined, assumptions about who decides, beyond the requirements of custom and the law, just how a small private organization should conduct its business or just who can belong to the exclusive club of serious journalists or just what the cost of entry into the television news business should be. Nevertheless, the drumbeat rolled on, and on, and on. In May, Franklin's articles began to suggest that there might be trouble at the Church's June 8 annual meeting.[34]

On May 20, Kay Fanning officially joined the board of the *Globe*'s parent company, Affiliated Publications, apparently acquiring some 7,400 shares of Affiliated stock in the process.[35]

For the exhausted remnants of The Monitor Channel team, hoping against hope for a last-minute reprieve, the cable convention in Dallas proved an anticlimax. The Monitor's prime space in the exhibit hall had long since been paid for, and the big, beautiful white-on-white booth was set up. At the Monitor's invitation-only breakfast event, Rod MacLeish gave graceful and authoritative remarks on filming the vast wealth of the Hermitage Museum in St. Petersburg the previous spring and summer amid the maelstrom of the Soviet coup to forty or fifty cable executives and their associates. But no deal came together.[36]

⁓⁓⁓

Five or six credible potential buyers outside cable remained. Every proposed deal was different, each put forward with a different degree of clarity. A key question for the Monitor was, would those most qualified financially guarantee, as the big cable players had been prepared to, that the Publishing Society would have clear and complete editorial control, stretching forward indefinitely into the future? The Monitor imprimatur was the Publishing Society's greatest treasure. The more the Church Directors listened to those who were out looking for buyers on their behalf and to the would-be buyers themselves, the more uncomfortable they became. In the absence of an established corporate partner with a known corporate culture the Directors could feel comfortable with, what would protect the Monitor name in years to come? Money as such seemed less and less an issue.[37]

By the first week of June, closure on the matter of The Monitor Channel was what the Directors felt they needed more urgently than almost anything else. The annual meeting would be held in eight days. Even the most attractive offers represented complications. One interested player proposed an intricate arrangement for joint ownership, and a second, a Salt Lake City man with certifiably vast amounts of money and a possible Mormon connection, put in a strong bid. A group of well-to-do young Church members calling themselves The Affinity Group tried to convince the Directors to let them sell shares to other Church members, thus passing ownership of The Monitor Channel to a closely-held corporation of those who supported diversification into television.[38]

On June 4, declining to meet with two remaining groups, the Directors cut off all talks and announced their decision not to sell. That same day, Don Bowersock announced that the satellite transponder had been sold off, which meant there was now, in fact, nothing left to discuss: without distribution, there could be no Monitor Channel.[39]

⁓⁓⁓

On the eve of the annual meeting, the *Globe*'s Jim Franklin published a 2,000 word repetition of the themes of the previous three months, quoting sources who called for the resignation of the unrepentant Church Board, still deliberately keeping themselves on record as in favor of the move to television. The next morning, Franklin's 1,400–word article, published hours before the annual meeting was set to begin, took a softer tack, sounding now like a call from the opposition for negotiations.[40]

~~~

On Monday, June 8, 4,000 of the faithful gathered under the capacious dome of the Church for their annual meeting. Eight or ten representatives of the press, allowed to attend for the first time in the history of the Church, sat together in a balcony behind and above the proceedings, primed for high drama. Twice muffled calls came from the floor questioning the publication of the Knapp book, from individuals who concealed their identities by shouting from their seats without rising or gesturing, but the gathering, while tense, was otherwise uneventful. Hymns were sung. The director who had stepped in as treasurer presented the financial report. In the course of that warm afternoon punctuated by thunderstorms, The Monitor Channel was pronounced dead and generously eulogized.[41]

The *Globe*'s Franklin published a long article the next day and another a few days later, expressing his sources' continuing dissatisfaction with Church governance and finances. On June 28, broadcast reruns ended, and The Monitor Channel went dark.[42]

Chapter 9

Perspective

The Monitor Channel in industry perspective

What ultimately counts is the soul of the owner.

—Bill Moyers, 1992

The Monitor Channel in Industry Perspective

The future came first to the *Monitor,* as Jack Hoagland was fond of saying. Now that future is tearing at the bloody heels of the rest of the news business in the United States.

The old relationships that subsidized news and public information throughout the nineteenth and twentieth centuries—the historic ties between newspapers and advertisers, and between television news and the entertainment business—are coming unbundled. Especially in video-based formats but also in print, quality news and public information is an exceedingly expensive commodity to produce. When done right, the news will rarely be a break-even business proposition as a stand-alone on the open market. The proverbial rational actors making individual choices in any given day or week, whether they are owners or consumers, are very unlikely to support the real costs of quality news and public information on economic grounds as such. Even mediocre news and public information often represents a foolish deployment of resources for rational actors in the short term.

Three peculiarly American habits of thought have obscured a clear view of the dangerous pass we as a society are approaching. The first is the media's institutionalized unwillingness to describe and analyze itself as a

167

business with candor. The second is government's reluctance to champion forcefully the clear public interest in having abundant, high-quality information and analysis disseminated broadly throughout the population in compelling formats on a daily basis. And third, a pernicious, almost magical assumption abroad in our culture holds that markets and new technologies will create good outcomes eventually on their own, and these forces are believed to replace the need for responsible human judgment or direct action.

It is sobering to review how we have done as well as we have for so long.

By the Mid-1980s . . .

William Paley and David Sarnoff probably never put it so bluntly in public, but by 1985, the television networks' news operations had been subsidized by their enormously profitable entertainment divisions for over a generation. Only because the larger-than-life founders of these fabulously profitable twentieth-century empires dominated their boards and controlled huge blocks of their companies' stock could they indulge their own uneconomic impulses—such as personal pride or public service—if they so chose.

In the mid-1980s, the truth about the costs of television news—nowhere to be found in corporate reports—had begun to dawn on a new generation of owners. Communicating balanced or complex information in the glamorous new medium had never been easy, but under cost-conscious new owners, even such tentative professional standards as had evolved began subtly and not-so-subtly to be eroded by the realities of the marketplace.

Overseas bureaus were cut back. Seasoned staff moved aside for less expensive junior colleagues. Technically less demanding and more predictable indoor work replaced field shoots. More stories set up by government officials and other public figures were covered for want of time and other resources. More video grabs were taken off satellites from free-lancers not under any network's editorial direction. More sensational presentations were favored—especially of disasters—to attract somewhat larger audience share and ensure somewhat greater advertiser dollars.[1]

Historically, the federal government had been a shortsighted and unpredictable owner. By 1985, the Corporation for Public Broadcasting had come under direct assault from the Reagan administration and had lost significant funding. Congress and the executive branch together functioned as self-absorbed majority owners, concerned above all to protect and increase their own political capital. As structured, public television could not produce either a broad, credible nightly broadcast nor even an independent-minded weekly news review, nor could it deliver compelling public affairs documentaries in important amounts on a freely chosen range of topics.

The *MacNeil/Lehrer News Hour*—owned by the on-camera anchors, sub-sidized by public-spirited corporations, and produced within the constraints of a modest budget—was short on field reporting and long on white male talking heads and Washington-insider topics. By limiting its scope, *Mac-Neil/Lehrer* was able to afford a thoughtful view of the world from a van-tage point close to the pinnacles of power in Washington, DC, and Manhattan, and that was about all.[2]

In 1985, only Ted Turner's CNN, internationalist in impulse but not known for in-depth coverage, had a formula for making comprehensive television journalism into a robust business. Although the cost structure at CNN was rational and the news operation was growing and although a powerful founder with a vision insulated the venture from shareholder de-mands, the pressure to perform well in the market was still very much there. And the same mix of people under the same kinds of professional pressures inevitably made for a certain sameness in editorial product.

Enter the Monitor, bringing two attributes to the television news playing field, which, in combination, no other owners in the mid-1980s could match: a coherent and distinctive philosophy of journalistic excellence and a will-ingness to be patient with the marketplace. A few years later, they were out. What happened?

The Logic of a Twenty-Four-Hour Cable Television Channel

By the mid-1980s, repositioning the Monitor's journalistic enterprise was long overdue. Historic changes far beyond the control of any Monitor editor or Publishing Society manager had reduced the *Christian Science Monitor* to the status of an aging mascot in the troubled and testy world of print journalism. Newspaper after newspaper closed and surviving independents were increasingly swallowed up by chains, yet the evidence in the press of the day suggests that few editors or publishers anywhere grasped just how harsh the equation was. In 1985, Jack Hoagland was an exception.

Over several years of internal discussion among a close-knit team at the top, a new corporate vision was articulated at the Boston-based Publishing Society. The old product line—Monitor journalism—would be produced in more compelling formats, the better to fulfill the organization's original mandate. Not surprisingly, television quickly became the Monitor's vehicle of choice, for by the mid-1980s, television was where the public from all walks of life—and the national advertisers—were to be found. Hoagland understood as early as 1986 that if costs and revenues were spread across media, the Monitor could afford to publish a first-rate electronically deliv-ered daily print product, although perhaps not a newspaper in the old sense.

The three years between 1984 and 1987, during which were produced first a monthly, then a weekly television news analysis show, were exhilarating for those who could tolerate long hours, abrupt changes in tactics, stretched resources, the steep path straight up the learning curve, and the forceful, goal-oriented focus that were the entrepreneurial operational style.

But those years also held a clear lesson in the realities of distribution for those at the top of the organization. If a television news product did not secure a visible spot "on the shelf," viewers did not find it, and though the Monitor's news commentaries might contain all the truth, beauty, and sweet reason in the world, if they were not seen, they served no one. Nor was there the remotest chance of meeting a significant percentage of the costs in cash or in kind by patching together an ad hoc network of small televison outlets that would display Monitor programming at favorable times, and pay for it.

World Monitor News with John Hart was outstanding television journalism that emphasized exactly the sorts of serious international coverage the networks were being forced to abandon, and it was produced at a small fraction of the three networks' scaled-back news budgets. But as a stand-alone nightly news show, *World Monitor News* only re-created the network dilemma in cameo: nightly news with global scope generated costs that, however successfully contained, could not be met by selling the six or seven minutes of ad space available.

In the early days of 1989, the Monitor's entrepreneurs identified the winning strategy—The Monitor Channel—based on a twenty-four-hour cable format. With this format, and this format only, for the same reasons that allowed CNN eventually to prosper while the old network news divisions languished, break-even at the Monitor's television operations became possible.

The Quality of the Monitor's Entrepreneurial Management

The quality of the Monitor's core team was high: at the top were nearly a dozen broadly sophisticated executives—smart, flexible people capable of absorbing new information about product development, technology and markets with great speed, men and women who were wholly dedicated and tireless. They had articulated a coherent vision, which they shared with employees and other stakeholders.

Both budgeting and tracking procedures at the operational level were more than adequate by conventional standards, and key information was circulated routinely and in a timely fashion within the core group. Moreover, the Monitor's entrepreneurs consciously and systematically recruited the best people available to them nationally as advisers, colleagues, and employees.

If their revenue projections were chronically overoptimistic, the Monitor's entrepreneurs were hardly alone. The business climate of 1989–1991 was widely misjudged, with economists at first denying that the recession pounding the ad-supported media even existed, then predicting it would end years before it finally did. And building a business without a time-tested model—the essence of the entrepreneurial challenge—inevitably involves repeated revised calculations, whether you are a Turner, a Neuharth, or Hoagland and Douglass.

Is it true, as one observer surmised, that the Monitor's reformers took on too many media projects simultaneously? Was it a good strategy simultaneously to publish a daily paper, start an international shortwave radio service, produce programming for public radio, and create an important new magazine, as well as undertake to program a twenty-four-hour cable news and public information channel? The answer is not obvious, for it depends on whether editorial synergy across media can work—whether a group of journalists, working alternatively as individuals or as a loosely integrated team, can produce pieces suitable for print, radio, and television simultaneously. The answer to this key question still eludes management at many a media conglomerate today and will be answered definitively where news is concerned, perhaps, only by a new generation of journalists trained in a truly multimedia work environment. If synergy can work—as it seemed to sporadically at the Monitor during the excitement of covering the Soviet coup—then establishing multiple outlets simultaneously, as Hoagland and Douglass did, was exactly the right move.[3]

Some questions about centralization and decentralization at the Monitor's television operations are impossible to separate from the particular exigencies of a high-energy start-up. What works in a period of consolidation or gradual expansion will not necessarily work while rapid innovation is under way. The Hoagland–Douglass style, which dominated operations between 1985 and 1992, created some confusion and ruffled many feathers. By industry standards as measured by two key objective criteria, however—efficient use of resources and the quality of the end product—management's performance at the Monitor was consistently high.

The Use of Resources Was Efficient

The Monitor produced high-quality news and public affairs programming for a fraction of the cost of competing products.

The widely hailed *World Monitor News* nightly half-hour produced 260 shows a year for $24 million, while the big three networks produced 365 shows a year with annual budgets of upwards of $400 million. Refining the data might move the network numbers up or down some, but the fact would remain that the Monitor's budget for a first-rate nightly newscast was less than 10 percent that of the competition.[4]

The costs for the full twenty-four-hour Monitor Channel also compare well with the costs incurred in CNN's famously lean 'n' mean start-up. The best way to demonstrate this point (because the least favorable to the Monitor) is to set the Monitor's combined television programming costs when they were at their highest beside CNN's 1982 operating costs not including capital expenses, marketing, ad sales, or distribution costs, converted into constant dollars. For the Monitor, annualized costs were created using the first seven months of fiscal year 1991–1992, before any scaling back began.

By this measure, then, at its top run-rate, Monitor Television's total programming costs—including the nightly news—came to about $53 million a year. CNN's operating costs for 1982 were $66 million, or in 1992 dollars, a little over $90 million. Again, refining the numbers could change the percentages a little, but roughly Monitor Television's costs for programming The Monitor Channel came in at just under 60 percent of CNN's comparably calculated costs in its second year of operation. By the early 1990s, CNN's costs came to about $360 million a year. In the industry context, then, Monitor Television was a strikingly thrifty operation.

Did the Monitor Channel Have a Workable Plan?

Revenues were depressed and would have grown slowly, more slowly than anticipated in the Monitor's various business plans for several reasons, none of them mysterious. For one thing, the world had changed between CNN's 1980 start-up and 1991, when The Monitor Channel went to market: revenues everywhere were abysmal, empty cable channels were scarce, and new programming services were many. To compete for channel space in the buyers' market of 1991, The Monitor Channel responded rationally and aggressively by slashing prices then giving add-ons to the basic deal, to the point where revenues would not really start coming in from operators until year three, and at only a fraction of the fees CNN was commanding.

The Monitor Channel's early 1991 business plan, put together by a cable-wise former member of Discovery's original board and Fleet Financial working with Don Bowersock and Netty Douglass, predicted operating break-even in year seven, with total costs in that period at about $250 million, revenues at $150 million, thus total investment to break-even at about $100 million.

Using a substantially higher but still modest annual number for news and public affairs programming—$75 million—and taking advantage both of hindsight and of better comparative data, one might estimate The Monitor Channel's probable net investment to break-even at something in the neighborhood of $400 or $500 million, with break-even likely pushed out to the ninth or tenth year following the May 1991 launch. The expense side resembles CNN's early years; the revenue side grows more slowly.[5]

In electronic media, unlike print, there are no additional materials or labor costs for each additional consumer reached. Costs do not need to go up significantly as a network expands, so after break-even, additional revenues can either be reinvested or distributed as profit. If a television product is compelling, for example, and if the market is neither a de facto monopoly nor saturated with similar products, once break-even is achieved even high initial investments can be recouped.

What Is Acceptable Risk?

Is a hypothetical investment of $500 million over ten years to launch an individual news vehicle high—or is it low? What do the communications industry's standards seem to be for risk, investment, and patience in specialized content such as news and public affairs? The answers to some questions are ultimately subjective.

Given knowledge and forethought, few mainstream business people would undertake a project that needs as long and expensive a development period as The Monitor Channel. However—and this is a fundamentally important consideration for purposes of this study—many of the most important communications vehicles available to the American public today have survived miscalculations that pushed costs into multiples of what was originally anticipated, and the years to break-even well beyond the endurance of any boards representing a broad base of shareholders. Parameters on the order of ten years and hundreds of millions of dollars are not unheard of. *Sports Illustrated* was in the red for a decade before it broke even in 1964, and *USA Today,* slowed down by recession, exacted ten years and $700 million in losses from its founder before beginning to break even in 1993. *Fortune* magazine took eleven years to break even. The *New Yorker* still loses money. Neither *Harper's* nor the *Atlantic Monthly* is profitable.[6]

Officially, CNN broke even in 1985, its fifth full year of operation, but major expenses, such as satellite transponder costs, cost of ad sales and cost of cable affiliate sales and marketing seem to have been absorbed by its parent, TBS. Actual break-even more likely came in 1987 or early 1988. Programming costs had topped $100 million annually in 1992 dollars from 1983 on, climbing steadily as better and better news and public information programming was produced.[7]

The three networks each probably sell a little over $400 million in advertising spots into their half-hour newscasts every year and that may barely cover costs. Rupert Murdoch has announced that NewsCorps will spend about $80 million a year programming a news channel, with cost of sales and distribution coming to at least another $15 million and probably more; if this new venture moves forward, it will be subsidized by the parent company for many, many years to come.[8]

Who Are the Risk-Takers?

An interesting common thread runs through many of these stories, does it not? Many of the most important sources of news and public information in the United States today, some of which are also commercial successes as mature businesses and some not, would not exist at all, if the market as commonly used to gauge investment and risk were the only arbiter of events.

Often, only a strong-willed founder or owner with considerable autonomy and lots of money ensures eventual success of the properties that prove among the most attractive, financially and in terms of their contribution to public communications, in the long run. Someone—a William Paley, David Sarnoff, Ted Turner, Henry Luce, Allen Neuharth, Rupert Murdoch, or the brothers Newhouse—has to be willing and able to take unpleasant surprises in stride in the pursuit of goals that do not meet conventional standards for economic rationality or make for good telling in early annual reports.

Sometimes, as in the networks' news operations, important communications vehicles are developed and continue to exist for a mix of considerations having little to do with the nuts and bolts of running a real business. The motives have been diverse and mixed: government pressure or fear of government pressure, or patriotism, or ego, or love of sports, or ideas, or the arts.

This is the mold the Monitor's entrepreneurs fit, and in their case, the non-economic motivation was public service.

The Quality of the Product Was High

In February 1992 ten months after national launch, The Monitor Channel as a news and public information programming service was uneven—running the gamut from faintly embarrassing to downright brilliant—and improving fast.

From the earliest "TV: Special Programming" days, Hoagland and Douglass had cheerfully demanded that new programming go on air long before the desperate production team and talent rushing it through development considered themselves ready. However awkward some of the first weeks' and months' results were, one team after another found terror was an efficient teacher: those who could stand the heat, stayed and began turning out creditable to excellent work long before there was any objective reason to believe they could. Industry awards were abundant from the start because programmers naturally submit their best efforts for consideration, and this swelling stream of accolades was a legitimate indicator of the quality likely to mark the whole in another two or three years.

Danny Wilson, Sid Topol, and others foresaw—albeit for different reasons—an evolution toward less emphasis on breaking news, with more time given over to in-depth features and documentaries that could be rebroadcast periodically as "evergreen" materials. Such a shift would have kept costs down some, and refined The Monitor Channel's market niche, particularly vis-à-vis CNN.[9]

Joint production agreements were already in place for specific projects with Germany's Beta and the BBC, as well as the enthusiastic young group producing *Rodina* throughout the Russian-speaking portions of the former Soviet lands. Thanks to the Monitor's special relationship with Japanese National Broadcasting (NHK) in Tokyo and the good offices of Hiro and Takashi Oka, a strong Japanese connection was also assured. Danny Wilson and Jack Hoagland both expected substantial amounts of Monitor Channel programming to be produced through such production and distribution agreements around the world, building initially on their own lifelong personal connections. Production-based internationalism of this sort would be part of Monitor Television's signature, they believed, and would give a distinctive cosmopolitan flavor to The Monitor Channel as broadcast to U.S. audiences.

Given Monitor Television's accomplishments between 1988 and 1992, rich, thoughtful high-quality communications were assured. That was not all: clearly, the new channel's programming was well on its way to being fundamentally different—far more internationalist in perspective, than anything seen on American television before or since.

Would Viewers Watch the Monitor Channel's Kind of Quality?

Could a single channel build audience loyalty on a mix of programming based on the sections of the old paper—straight news and public affairs programming, plus minority-produced programs like *El Monitor de Hoy* and *Inner-City Beat,* plus softer features like gardening and ecology, and two or three hours a day of semi-educational fare for children and young people?

The Monitor Channel's untimely demise left open the intriguing issue of psychographic versus demographic, which separated most old Monitor hands including Hoagland and Douglass from many of the industry pros they recruited. Very preliminary data gathered even as the channel was going down suggest that two or three different audiences might eventually have developed, and that separating them clearly on the programming clock—with children's programming after school and Saturday and Sunday mornings, for example—might have sufficed to build Monitor "brand loyalty" on a household-by-household basis.

There was stronger though still preliminary evidence—partly anecdotal, partly based on surveys—of considerable interest in the more sharply focused Monitor speciality, in-depth social and political reporting with an international flavor.

The Internal Opposition

Opposition activities seriously encumbered the efforts of the Monitor's entrepreneurial leadership. Had the internal opposition not been aided and abetted by the *Boston Globe,* however, it seems unlikely to this observer that their objections to the duly constituted Board and its policies would have prevailed in the long run.

Some opposition represented the leading edge of an industry-wide anger among print journalists as they began to grasp that the end of an era they cherished was at hand. The intense unease mixed with contempt that had dominated the *Monitor* newsroom since the 1970s came to characterize relations between the editorial staff and the business side at many a newspaper nationwide in the eighties, as the juggernaut of changing technologies and popular tastes slowly rolled over them.

Equally important, as events unfolded, was a diffuse sense of ownership peculiar to a certain kind of nonprofit corporation. Virtually everyone in the organization identified personally with its lofty humanitarian mission. Everyone knew that the more talented members of the community could make better money elsewhere, and there was an assumption of shared privilege and sacrifice. From management to writers and editors to support staff, every employee, and usually the members of an employee's family, were proud stakeholders. Very much like other successful nonprofits, everyone involved directly or indirectly with the Monitor was psychologically in effect a part owner. In the Monitor's case, this sense of proprietary right sometimes extended well beyond those working in the organization's publishing activities, to local Church members far and wide.

This diffuse sense of psychological ownership leads under pressure, not to grace, but to a sort of willful anarchy. Ted Turner could bushwhack across the electronic frontier without a map, parlaying the fortune his father made in the billboard business to found a global television news empire, yelling, *"Lead, follow, or get out of the way!"* to those around him. However hare-brained his plans seemed to others, he was the boss and could implement his policies unchallenged. Mrs. Eddy's own distinctively entrepreneurial style notwithstanding, Jack Hoagland, Harvey Wood, even the Directors and Trustees as a collective body of legally-constituted decision makers, found their authority to act decisively on behalf of the Monitor's journalistic enterprise challenged at every turn.

Weighing Three Outside Factors

Three outside factors contributed in varying degree to the collapse of The Monitor Channel: the recession of 1988–1992, the severely constrained cable environment of the early 1990s, and the assault mounted on the Monitor's leadership from the fall of 1991 through the winter and spring of 1992 by the *Boston Globe*.

Of these, the recession—punishing as it was, especially in the Northeast—did the least direct damage to The Monitor Channel's prospects, but the Channel was hurt indirectly. Slower than expected ad sales at Discovery cut into resources available to promote *World Monitor News,* with the predictable feedback effect on audience-building efforts and ad sales, increasing friction all around.

The acute shortage of unprogrammed channel space in the early 1990s favored established programming services and new services with the ability to hang tough and expand slowly. From this angle, the early 1990s was not such a bad competitive setting for The Monitor Channel. And indeed, the Monitor's scrappy affiliate sales operation held its own quite well, given the givens, meeting plan in subscriber levels by cutting prices to operators, staying top-of-mind through a strong presence at cable shows, aggressive ad campaigns in the trades, and talking quality, quality, quality.

More damaging for The Monitor Channel was the highly ambivalent investment climate within the cable industry. Because debt loads were heavy and ad sales depressed, ready money was in short supply. Technical breakthroughs in cable's delivery systems were much slower in coming than expected, and when and exactly how future competition from the telephone companies might hit was unclear. For this reason and because in 1991 and early 1992 there was no way to predict the next federal administration's intentions regarding reregulation, cable's future flexibility in setting prices was also uncertain. Then, too, The Monitor Channel would end up positioning itself vis-à-vis CNN, of which several big cable operators already owned a part.

Still, there was interest, and open and generous praise from cable operators for the quality of the Monitor's programming. Chances were strong that a consortium of industry partners could have been put in place in another year or two. It was the suddenness with which the need for cash at the Monitor became apparent and the disorder surrounding those events that made a partnership impossible.

Did the *Boston Globe*'s attack contribute materially to bringing down the Monitor's weakened leadership? Little attention to the *Globe*'s allegations was paid in the cable industry as a whole. As one exasperated cable professional based in the West put it in the spring of 1992, "The *Boston Globe* does not mean squat in Denver. The *Boston Globe* does not mean squat in Dallas. Why are they folding?!"

The *Globe*'s readership is indeed confined to central New England, but that still gave ample scope for mischief-making. Close attention was paid at the Providence Journal, already intending to become an investor, committed to help bring in others, and one of the few cable players with substantial cash in hand in 1991 and 1992 for new programming ventures. Even more damaging was the *Globe*'s loud alliance with those in the Publishing Society and the Church who wanted the Monitor's diversification into new media to end. Pro Jo might be replaced with another investor, but the opposition, speaking through the *Globe,* vowed to block them, each and every one. To this end, it became clear, the opposition camp was even prepared if need be, to undermine the Monitor's hard-won reputation for unbiased journalism.

The Monitor Channel as a Business Proposition: Summing Up

Viewed in an industry setting, The Monitor Channel was neither a conservative gambit nor was it a fool's errand. It was innovative and involved risk, but the objective level of risk was no higher than that frequently seen in the communications industry in the early years of developing an important new vehicle.

Overall, The Monitor Channel and its television production arm at the Publishing Society were a well-run, high-energy start-up. If self-imposed targets were often unrealistic, achievements were nonetheless impressive by industry standards. Break-even was probably three years beyond what had been anticipated in the last complete business plan, but it was there. Cable industry response had been favorable, and there is no reason to doubt that industry partners would eventually have stepped forward for The Monitor Channel, as they had since the mid-1980s for virtually every other programming service that showed merit.

Still in development, the quality of the Monitor's television product was by and large good, and, more and more frequently, it was breathtakingly good. The Monitor Channel held promise, not just for general excellence in public affairs programming, but for its dedication to bringing far greater breadth and diversity of perspective than is now available in the American communications market.

Findings Beyond Profit and Loss

The media are not merely businesses like other businesses, of course, because their products—public communications—directly and ubiquitously shape our mental and moral capacities, and those of our neighbors. Everyone has a legitimate interest in what constitutes good quality in public communications and in understanding what the conditions are that produce a desirable result.

The Monitor Channel story yields five interesting rules of thumb, both about the television news business in particular and about the news and public affairs business in general.

1. *Although television programming has been the single most influential source of news and public information in our society for two generations, television news is not an especially lucrative business.*

2. *Because of the high costs and low profit margins intrinsic in producing and distributing quality news and public affairs programming with global scope for television (or for other video-based media), only owners with strong noneconomic motives will produce such communications with any regularity.*

3. *The general worldview and specific motives behind the Monitor's decision to launch a top-quality news and public affairs television channel biased their communications in ways that seem useful from the public's perspective.*

All media have owners, and all these owners operate within some sort of conceptual framework that directly influences the way they do business, including the kinds of communications products they put on the market. So it was at The Monitor Channel. From society's point of view, the interesting question with respect to media becomes, what conceptual frameworks promote quality news and public information in that video-based medium—television—which the public at large has for forty years now used as its primary source of information?

Several assumptions made by The Monitor Channel's owners biased their communications products consistently toward quality. These include:

• *Thought itself is the most important single variable operating in human affairs.*

From this assumption, much follows. Because of its unique ability to affect the quality of public thought broadly, directly, and daily, journalism as a vocation is of central importance in human affairs and carries with it a commensurately great responsibility. Good journalism's general goal is to improve the quality of thought in those it reaches, by leaving its public well informed, unafraid, optimistic about the long run, and ready to take positive action. Good journalism's methods include supplying a wealth of meticulously accurate information and sound analyses, and noting pragmatic solutions when possible. The general tone of communications should be calm and respectful, and should de-emphasize crisis, not by ignoring it, but by describing a larger historical context within which today's events, however disturbing, become intelligible. Images of disaster and destruction are used sparingly, lest the communication leave the viewer enervated and fearful.

• *All human beings are worthy of respect, and the world is fundamentally a good place.*

A democratic, internationalist bias is front and center in all Monitor journalism, and the common man or woman worldwide is seen as a natural potential source of principled insight and effective initiative. The beauty of the natural world is a constant subject of comment and celebration. And facts matter: accurate facts are a reflection of the fundamentally good world, as well as a pragmatic tool for improving the human condition. Journalists in the Monitor tradition, therefore, have tended to be curious and well informed to the point of being learned in their chosen areas of expertise. Finally, optimism in the long run is warranted, and so informed action is meaningful. Monitor journalism, therefore, carries within it a bias for identifying solutions and noting pragmatic actions. (Conversely, degrading or intrusive images of fellow human beings are avoided, as are facile explanations using villains and scapegoats.)

4. *A somewhat larger public may be available for quality news and public affairs programming on television (and possibly in other video formats) than is generally assumed among communications industry professionals.*

Fully supported conclusions based on public response to The Monitor Channel lay a year or two in the future, but early indications were very positive where the Monitor's traditional niche—in-depth, globally oriented news analysis—was concerned.

Some objective evidence came from the ten or twelve local cable competitions the channel's affiliate sales group entered around the country, in which The Monitor Channel consistently did well. Research in the Boston market suggested that channel's most likely viewers were not heavy users of television, that they therefore became aware of the channel very gradually, and that they skewed toward well-educated and upscale viewers, with an important admixture of "doers" from across all economic and ethnic groups.

Choosing news and public information sources may be something like making a considered purchase of a car or a house, or deciding to change political parties. Lifelong habits and attitudes come into play, and change may involve a shift in self-image. This sort of decision typically involves a long lead time or "buy cycle" before a commitment is made. Sellers of quality news and public information must make themselves easy to find and be prepared to be skillful and patient. The upshot is, though, that there may be a market for quality news and public information in video format of at least modest size that has, as yet, to be tapped.

5. *Communications industry management will voluntarily promote quality and diversity in national and international news and public affairs communications—if, in doing so, they can still honor their prior obligation to owners/shareholders to maximize profits in the short and middle term.*

As a high-end news and public information service, The Monitor Channel benefited from much spontaneous goodwill on the part of individuals and corporations in the cable industry. The trade press led the welcome, and local and regional operators, short on channels though they were, came to the Monitor booth at trade shows or received the Monitor's sales team in their home offices. First they talked price, and then they talked quality.

This positive response was not identifiably regional. Interest in the full range of the Monitor Channel's programming was high among cable operators living and doing business in every corner of the American heartland.

Public Communications as the Environment of the Public Mind

To applaud Monitor journalism, one need not share the owners' assumptions about the primacy of thought or about the innate goodness of humankind and the world. Even someone who remains unconvinced about whether optimism is warranted in the matter of human survival in the long run can still acknowledge the great value of the Monitor's informed, wholesome, and pragmatic bias, geared as it is to empower its consumers for intelligent action.

To assert that the loss of a Monitor Channel will somehow be compensated for in some vaguely automatic way through the evolution of new technologies for delivery or through the actions of the market alone is to indulge in wildly optimistic thinking. Cable television's vaunted ability to deliver 500, or 1,000, or 5,000 channels is in and of itself irrelevant. Multiplying that capacity with the entry of telephone companies into the market would not automatically add to the quality of content. Similarly, the Internet's dramatic arrival in the mainstream, linking the population with 1,000 times 1,000 games and specialized chat rooms and database access, or even personalized menus of replays of what has appeared on radio or television, will have little bearing on the intransigent facts of cost and return in the news business, and no bearing at all on issues of news judgment.

Public communications is a part of the human environment just as surely as are the air and the water we cycle through our bodies each day. Like air and water, public communications affects both mental and physical well-being, for good and for ill; the effects are intimate as well as general, immediate as well as incremental.[10]

Common sense increasingly warns us not to hope for an acceptable level of protection from traditional sources: not from the energetic, relatively free, ultimately disappointing public communications market, not from the tightly circumscribed benefits of the First Amendment, not from the waffled concept of public trust written into the Communications Act of 1934 and its subsequent reworkings, nor from the unraveling conscience of the journalists' guild or the preferences of their employers, given the structural constraints they all face.

Even the most privileged, their families, and their friends are vulnerable to the consequences of a public communications system that contains enormous amounts of compromised factual information; a systematic bias toward trivialization and disrespect, constant instruction in violence, greed, narcissism, and fear; and a pervasive and enervating message—wholly unintended by anyone involved—that at the end of the day, neither individuals nor community can act effectively in most truly important matters.

If, then, public communications is the environment of the public mind, what would that environment look like if it were life-giving and life-sustaining? The answer may be deceptively simple: A healthy mental environment may be one that nourishes the ability of the individual and of society to adapt over time. This in turn would mean providing abundant, diverse, appropriate information in a timely fashion about all aspects of social reality and the natural world from a multiplicity of viewpoints. Indeed, if such a discussion were joined, international experts, industry leaders and ordinary citizens alike might suggest criteria not so very different from the standards and practices that evolved gradually under the aegis of Monitor journalism in the course of the twentieth century.

The loss of The Monitor Channel, imperfect as it was and would likely always have been, was a tragic event. Whatever its shortcomings might have turned out to be, The Monitor Channel would on balance have been an exceptionally healthy element in the environment of the public mind. Its presence would also have provoked a better-informed and livelier debate, pro and con, about what constitutes a healthy mental ecosystem.

Perhaps the story of The Monitor Channel's promising launch and tragic collapse can help point toward a serious, empirically grounded discussion within and about the global communications industry, concerning where that industry might try to go from here.

Chapter 10

Epilogue Notes

What we learn and ultimately know about our struggles to improve ourselves is profoundly shaped by television. . . . I believe the norms and habits of TV news now threaten to undermine our collective ability to respond as a nation to the most serious problems we face.

—Alfred C. Sikes, Chair,
Federal Communications Commission, March 1992[1]

When The Monitor Channel went dark in June of 1992, like many employees, I was angry—but at whom or at what, I didn't know. I understood the business side of cable television well enough to know that there was no obvious simple explanation for why Monitor Television's shining promise, so clearly within reach, so solid at the level of operations, so badly needed in the world of public communications, had suddenly vanished.

My initial intention was to write an account narrowly analyzing the business realities behind the story, looking only for a clear answer to one central question: Can high-quality, global news and public information for television (or other video-based media) be produced and distributed as a viable for-profit business proposition in today's information marketplace?

What are the full costs of high-end television journalism? If the Monitor's entrepreneurial leadership foundered and sank because they slammed into some hard business reality I had not seen, does that mean no one else can be successful in such an enterprise? Does it mean that the imperatives of information markets will inevitably, inexorably deprive citizens of quality news in their medium of choice?

As a manager, I saw only the budgets I put together myself for my own small division, but I had been in and around cable television long enough to know Monitor Television's undertaking was remarkably efficient at the operational level. It was clear, too, that money poured with such seeming abandon into securing cable "shelf space" was the key strategic move in the entrepreneurs' gambit, for without distribution, there was no channel.

At first, all questions beyond the hypothetical feasibility of quality news and public affairs programming for television seemed peripheral. Did the Church really run out of money? When I began this project, I was only mildly curious. Was the internal opposition large or small, principled, self-interested, or insane? I didn't care. Was there, as the *Globe*'s coverage seemed to imply, some systematic violation of the law about to be revealed or some dark personal or professional scandal about to break concerning Hoagland and Douglass or the Directors of the Church? Could a happenstance like the Winship–Fanning friendship account for the *Globe*'s punishing campaign? These particulars paled beside the general: the narrowing prospects for quality news and public information in the sorts of audio-visual formats that a broad public would accept.

Although the book's focus gradually expanded, issues of feasibility, competence, and industry norms remained central. For me, the pivotal empirical question soon became how the Monitor's expenses compared to those of the only other business it resembled, Ted Turner's Cable Network News. This comparison would in turn lend a sense of proportion one way or another to every other aspect of the story. I began to call Atlanta. The half-dozen top executives I contacted at CNN were courteous—but no one was willing to interrupt current agendas in 1992 to dig up internal data from CNN's start-up years a decade earlier. Week followed week, finally I stopped calling. Without CNN's numbers as an empirical baseline, the Monitor book would make little sense.

At the same time, my view of the questions at hand became more nuanced. The more I worked on the project, the more it seemed important to describe and analyze the Monitor's traditional commitment to quality journalism in all its complexity, so readers not familiar with the Church could form an opinion about the nature and the magnitude of the loss. This in turn meant listening carefully to the arguments of Church members who had so stubbornly opposed the Monitor's entrepreneurs. In addition, the weeks I spent researching the evolution of electronic journalism convinced me that behind-the-scenes rivalry among media was not a footnote, but a core issue. This meant that a careful review of the *Globe*'s coverage of the Monitor's diversification and perhaps even an inquiry into whether there was a possible corporate interest in seeing the Monitor fail was in order.

With the shift in emphasis to include the internal opposition and the *Globe* came fear: fear of the highly charged feelings that surrounded every aspect of the expanded topic, fear that willingness to destroy projects and reputations would ultimately find me, and fear based on the threats of physical violence, which, I learned, had been part of the daily lives of at least some at the Monitor's entrepreneurial team from the moment it seemed they would succeed.

At about this time a somewhat tattered package arrived by first-class mail at my home office—a little larger than a car battery but not quite so heavy. There was no return address. I carried this ominous object up from the building's small public area, gingerly set it on my dining room table and put the cat outdoors. I opened the package to find that inside were complete copies of CNN's early corporate reports, the missing half of the book's empirical foundation. Excited by the clarity that the comparison with CNN's early expenditures would bring to The Monitor Channel story, I resumed the project in earnest.

After the Fall: The Monitor's Entrepreneurial Leadership

After leaving the Monitor Channel, Jack Hoagland and Netty Douglass quickly turned their energies to new enterprises as partners in a holding company called the J-NET Group.

Under Ecology Communications, Inc., in partnership with some former executives of the Discovery Channel and environmental organizations, they have produced handsome cable television programming on the environment available as of the winter of 1998 to over 6 million homes on local origination channels and 10 million on Outdoor Life Network; ad sales is now their principal hurdle. They have also started a profitable technical support service company for CD-ROM and online publishers, and consult for a number of traditional print publishers and communications companies seeking to diversify into new media. In February 1998, Cable Network Services, an umbrella company owned by cable MSOs Comcast, Cox, MediaOne, and Fox, entered into an agreement to acquire a minority position in the J-NET Group/Ecology Communications. The agreement includes a multiyear contract to purchase programming.

Hoagland serves as an active director of the nonprofit International Media Fund, whose mission is to encourage development of independent journalism in Eastern Europe through funding resource centers, sponsoring university programs, fostering international contacts, ensuring that equipment is available, and offering consultations. He is also on the board of the American Air Museum in Britain Campaign of the Imperial War Museum.

Using hands-on technical expertise acquired during her years at the Monitor, Netty Douglass has become a frequent consultant to publishers in American and Europe. She is a member of the Research and Engineering

Council of the Graphic Arts Industry, Inc., an active member of several other trade associations, and is in demand as an industry speaker on the uses of new media.

Harvey Wood, still a highly regarded Christian Science practitioner and a popular teacher, lives in a Chicago suburb. Don Bowersock worked closely with the new Church Board as Managing Treasurer until January 1995 when he retired to California; he died a few months later.

Barbara Bellafiore Sanden was with Prodigy for two years, then returned to run her own media consulting firm, Bell Media. Lyn Chamberlin became director of the Office of Communications for Radcliffe College. Gail Pierson is an independent technical consultant contracting her services through J-NET. Gail Harris's considerable talents were employed by WQTV's successor, WABU-TV.

David Cook, Managing Editor of *World Monitor News* when The Monitor Channel went dark in 1992, was subsequently named Editor of Monitor Broadcasting and charged with overseeing the remaining shortwave and public radio operations. In 1994, he became Editor of the *Christian Science Monitor* as well.

The Opposition

In April 1992, with The Monitor Channel in reruns and weeks away from going dark, a story—possibly apocryphal—made the rounds at the Publishing Society. A short piece using the public-domain musical theme "Hooray for Hollywood!" was being rerun around the clock. One day, so the story went, the telephone rang in the office of one of the Church's directors, and an elderly Church member indignantly demanded to know why "Hooray for Harvey Wood!" was being played over and over on the channel: "I thought we got rid of him!"

Perhaps: but not all the opposition were reclusive elders, and neither Harvey Wood, Jack Hoagland, Netty Douglass, nor the Church Directors were rid of those who had opposed them when The Monitor Channel went dark. Two major law suits wended their tortuous way through the courts, and personal reputations, large sums of money, and Church governance remained in question for another five years.

Katherine Fanning taught an occasional course in ethics at the Boston University School for Public Communications and continued to serve on a number of highly visible boards and professional committees. In the summer of 1997, David Anable left the Boston University School for Public Communications to become director of the International Center for Foreign Journalists in Washington, D.C., where the chairman is the *Globe*'s powerful retired editor and staunch Fanning supporter, Tom Winship. Winship also writes a monthly column for *Editor and Publisher* magazine.

Steven Gottschalk, the former Church employee who coordinated mailings to Church membership worldwide and who acted as an unpaid consultant to Stanford University in their challenge to the Knapp estate trustees, continues his opposition and works on a book from his pleasant home in a Boston suburb. The New York judge who worked with him, Thomas Griesa, continues patiently tracking Church expenses and reporting procedures, as he has for the better part of twenty years.

John Hart did not return to the television news business. According to a professional friend, in 1994 Hart permitted himself to wonder out loud whether he had made a mistake in leaving *World Monitor News* after all.[2]

The *Boston Globe* Sells Its Assets for $1 Billion

Corporate chaos was avoided and individual fortunes were secured forever at the *Boston Globe* when the *New York Times* stepped in and bought the paper for $1 billion in a deal announced in June 1993, one short year after The Monitor Channel went dark. Under the agreement, editorial control and management reside in Boston with the family who has owned the paper for over a century. In September 1997, Ben Taylor, following his father and his grandfather before him, was named publisher.[3]

The *Globe*'s coverage of the Monitor is now low key, though perhaps not entirely devoid of ulterior agendas. Jim Franklin, the reporter who covered the Monitor's attempt to diversity into television renewed coverage briefly with several long summary articles at the end of 1992, preparing to submit the *Globe*'s unprecedented 80,000–word campaign against Monitor television for a Pulitzer. In the next two years his byline rarely appeared at all beyond occasional updates on the opposition's continuing legal challenges to the Church.

In April 1994, Franklin wrote "The Monitor Channel Is Missed"—a short piece, courteous in tone and seemingly disconnected from anything happening in the present. Aside from pleasant reminiscences, the thrust of the article was to assert that The Monitor Channel had been a valuable service, which, regrettably, went down because of "fiscal mismanagement."[4]

Two weeks later, Franklin's peculiar article made more sense: the *Boston Globe* revealed that it would be going into cable television itself. On May 9, 1994, *Around the Globe* was launched on Hearst's New England Cable News TV. Just like the old *Today's Monitor, Around the Globe* used its own writers as on-air talent and its own newsroom as a backdrop.[5]

In the five years following Monitor Television's collapse, other *Globe* reporters did more or less routine articles chronicling the inevitable after-shocks of the fall of The Monitor Channel: the sale of WQTV, the discontinuation of *World Monitor Magazine,* the dismantling of the international shortwave capability, the shutdown of MonitoRadio, the continued decline in circulation and continuing deficits in the $16 to $18 million range at the newspaper.

In August 1997 another decidedly peculiar piece appeared, this time a long one by the paper's outgoing ombudsman. Pictures of Mary Baker Eddy and Katherine Fanning were juxtaposed, and hope was held out that the *Christian Science Monitor*—still losing circulation and still running a large deficit—might somehow be revived. Reminiscent of the denials of the shift in media realities common in the print world of the mid-1980s, this article appeared to some Monitor insiders to be yet another attempt by Fanning's friends at the *Globe* to promote her for the job as the *Monitor*'s editor some nine years after she had resigned.[6]

The Providence Journal's Assets Bring Just Under $3 Billion

When the Providence Journal's top management backed off from the partnership with The Monitor Channel, they continued to shop for appropriate cable programming to invest in. In January 1993 they and four other mid-sized communications industry players announced plans for the Food Channel, valued at $60 million before it launched and long before it was scheduled to turn profitable in year five. The Food Channel began broadcast on Thanksgiving Day, 1993.

In November 1995, the Providence Journal Company sold its cable systems to Continental for $1.4 billion. In the first half of 1996, Pro Jo bought out its partners in the Food Channel, and sold stock in the parent company to pay down debt. Its holdings consolidated, relatively debt-free, and superbly managed, the company was given a coveted "outperform" rating by brokerage firm Donaldson, Lufkin, and Jenrette in August. One month later, The Providence Journal Company was acquired by Dallas-based A.H. Belo Corporation, a low-profile owner of newspapers and television stations nationwide, for a little over $1.5 billion.[7]

While respected as a newspaper, the *Providence Journal* had only a fraction of the *Globe*'s concentrated regional political clout. On the other hand, economically, Providence Journal was the stronger company; its assets were spread from New England to the West Coast and included print, cable systems, and cable programming. When these assets were sold, the combined price was almost triple what the *Boston Globe* had fetched two years earlier. Had Providence Journal backed The Monitor Channel, the combination might well have been an important multimedia challenge to the *Globe*'s primacy in New England.

Fear or Favor?

In the spring of 1997, Bill Kovach, Curator of Harvard's prestigious Nieman Foundation, suggested on the strength of a recommendation from a mutual acquaintance in New York that I excerpt a chapter from the Monitor book for the summer 1997 issue of *The Nieman Reports*. I proposed instead a general piece focusing not on the Monitor, but on the likely impact of ownership changes at ABC, CBS, CNN, and NBC on television journalism.

Kay Fanning soon telephoned me to say her "great friend Bill Kovach" had told her he had read the book manuscript and enjoyed it. She warned me sternly not to attribute anything to her on the basis of our two interviews.

The Nieman Report's editor, Bob Phelps, a retired *Globe* man of high reputation, read the completed article carefully, pronounced it "strong," and asked for one revision, which I promptly supplied. A four-sentence aside on Monitor Television was not mentioned.

A few weeks later, galleys were faxed to my home office with a note from Phelps's secretary saying authors were to check for typos. It seemed perfunctory, I was swamped with work, enervated by the death of a beloved brother, and almost did not bother. The pleasure of seeing my piece all set up for print in such a high-quality publication was too much to resist, though, and I began to read it through, noting small changes in sub-heads, in punctuation, a word or phrase here and there.

Three-quarters of the way through, though, in the brief mention of The Monitor Channel, the summary sentence had been deleted; a different sentence with an opposite meaning had been inserted in its place. The original words were,

> Monitor TV was brought down by internal resistance to television as a medium, combined with a tendentious campaign in the *Boston Globe,* which together made it impossible for Monitor TV's far-sighted management to forge the strategic partnerships needed to move forward.

The new sentence stated, "Monitor TV, however, could not make it in the marketplace."

I was incredulous. Within hours, I hand-delivered a memo to Phelps's office at the Nieman Foundation, respectfully asking that my sentence be put back in place of his and offering to support what I had written with whatever documentation might be needed.

Having failed to get his version of the Monitor story inserted under my name, Phelps then threatened to pull the whole story if that one sentence were not removed. I offered to omit the word "tendentious," omit mention of the Globe, and refer only to "the regional press." Phelps said that still was not good enough: "Everyone will know you mean the Globe. I'm going to pull the story." The Foundation's Curator was fully informed, but did not intervene. I could not find it within myself to bend, and the story was killed.

This anecdote again illustrates the highly sensitive nature of the Monitor story in the Boston market. Others have asked me whether it is not also symptomatic of a corporate culture which—while indeed dedicated to truth-telling—makes it extremely difficult for all concerned to proceed without fear or favor when their own corporate interest or their heroic self-image as truth tellers is at stake.

Monitor Journalism without The Monitor Channel

World Monitor Magazine's last issue was published in May 1993. WQTV was sold for $3.8 million in June 1993, and shortwave operations began to be scaled back later than summer. MonitoRadio continued to broadcast on public radio stations until June 1997. In April 1996, the *Christian Science Monitor* got its first Pulitzer Prize in almost twenty years for stories written by David Rohde, a brave young reporter who risked his life to get evidence of Serb-run death camps in Bosnia. Rohde, not a member of the Church, was promptly hired away by the *New York Times.* By 1997, the *Christian Science Monitor*'s paid circulation had dropped to 77,000, and its losses stabilized at about $17 million a year, a level of subsidy that the Church can easily afford.

Without the twenty-four-hour television channel to amortize the costs of an independent global newsgathering capability and to attract national and international advertising dollars, the plain truth is that Monitor communications could not, cannot, and will not ever approach break-even. An independent source of world news on radio and a newspaper with circulation spread thinly over many markets can contribute editorial depth and help draw educated audiences, but as a business proposition, an independent global news operation that does not dominate any one regional market must move forward in the slipstream of something resembling a mass-audience vehicle. Now and for the foreseeable future, such a mass-market vehicle means television.

In the winter of 1998, the Church finds itself in a strong position both financially and legally. Income in recent years has exceeded total expenditures by $12 to $20 million annually, and the Church, in sound financial health by any reasonable measure, is now embarking on a $55 million restoration of its Back Bay campus.

Hours of depositions, months and years of distraction, and millions of dollars in expenses later, legal action supported by the opposition and aimed at preventing the Church from receiving the Knapp bequest has been settled to the Church's satisfaction. This challenge was settled out of court, with the Church receiving 53 percent or about $53 million of the Knapp bequest in 1996. A second suit, this one challenging the Church Directors' right to govern, prompted a unanimous ruling in favor of the Church in state court. The Massachusetts Supreme Judicial Court affirmed the Directors' right to have conducted their affairs as they did in the 1988–1992 efforts to diversify into television under Harvey Wood's and Jack Hoagland's entrepreneurial leadership. The Monitor Channel is long gone, but the Directors and their supporters can enjoy the bittersweet satisfaction of having been supported in their defense by a broad-based, friend-of-the-court brief submitted on behalf of eighteen Protestant, Jewish, and Catholic organizations in their insistence that traditional modes of governance be upheld. The opposition's request that the U.S. Supreme Court hear the case was turned down.

How best to honor the Monitor's traditional journalistic vocation going forward remains a vexed question both at the Church and at the Publishing Society.[8]

National Television News: A Third Generation of Owners Takes Over

Jack Hoagland grasped Ted Turner's business equation early on. Others eventually understood: however much a thirty-minute national and international news operation is stripped and downsized, however much its stories are recycled into low-budget breakfast shows and news magazines, the revenues will just not add up to a solid profit center. Only a full channel selling ads twenty-four hours a day had a fighting chance.

In 1995, three years after The Monitor Channel's collapse, a veritable stampede to create twenty-four-hour news channels began. First, Rupert Murdoch's Fox TV, then ABC/Cap Cities, then GE's NBC announced their plans. No sooner had these plans moved into development, however, than the ground under the television news business suddenly shifted again, as a third generation of owners took over.

Westinghouse's announcement that it would buy CBS was accompanied by more ritual vows to slash costs and boost cash flow. Disney, excited by virtually unlimited opportunities to market its entertainment brands on a major network, bought ABC and soon pulled it out of the running for a full news channel. CNN and entertainment giant Time Warner declared their intention to merge. Before the end of 1995, GE's NBC and software titan Microsoft entered into a joint venture to spin off a twenty-four-hour news service for cable and the Internet, the idea being that NBC news and its local affiliates around the country would supply much of the video copy and the stories. In the spring of 1996, Fox added muscle to its on-again, off-again attempts to mount its own twenty-four-hour news channel, offering cable operators an unprecedented $11 bonus per household to carry it. Westinghouse/CBS eventually unveiled their plans for a news-and-entertainment channel, too.

With these changes, the importance of the news divisions to the corporations that own them was still further diminished. The surviving news divisions of these vast global entertainment conglomerates represent an ever-smaller fraction of the parent companies' business. The new corporate owners of our country's television news and public information services gross between $6 billion a year (Westinghouse) and $80 billion a year (GE and Microsoft combined), and their U.S. news divisions account for roughly 7 percent to well under 1 percent of their corporate budgets. Not only are these vast media empires not making much money in the TV news business, in many cases in most years, they run at a net loss. Every one of them (CNN always excepted) could make a much better return if they just plowed the resources they now devote to national and international news back into entertainment. One might hazard an educated guess that there is room for no more than one more profitable news channel in addition to CNN and predict that the rest will continue to scale back and further cheapen their product and that some will fold their news operations entirely within five years.

The ultimate owners of electronic media in the United States today are a shifting cast of mutual funds, pension funds, professional speculators, and other corporations, few with a mission even remotely connected—either practically, legally, or sentimentally—with news and public information. The news is nobody's corporate mission, indeed decision makers are almost all governed by fiduciary responsibilities that directly conflict with delivering quality news and public information. To break even is not enough, and such glamor as still attaches to the news will not guarantee anything in this competitive environment. The technology has yet to be imagined that will allow factually rich, historically grounded, and well-analyzed information to be as good an investment as entertainment or sports or piles of data detached from real-world meaning.

The general public persists in its strong preference for getting its information from television, yet the structure of the market inevitably keeps the quality of the product low and forces it lower. As public preferences shift, they move toward other video-based media where, unfortunately, the same constraints exist, futurist fantasies to the contrary notwithstanding.

Facing Forward

The Monitor Channel provided an imperfect and fleeting glimpse of the kind of quality news and public information our citizens deserve to have available on TV and the other video-based media they so strongly prefer.

Ownership of electronic media is now almost completely detached from authorship of news and public information, and authorship is increasingly detached from any clear, mature, comprehensive concept of truth. While some players at the top of the new media conglomerates are more attractive figures than others, it is important to understand that the larger communications industry story, deeply disturbing as it is, is not dominated by villains. The forces that have created the current grave crisis in the quality of news and public information our general population receives are rooted in the structure of the markets.

Solutions, by contrast, must involve individual action beginning at the highest levels: urgently needed are a few genuine heroes.

Organizational Chart: The Christian Science Publishing Society and Monitor Television, Inc.

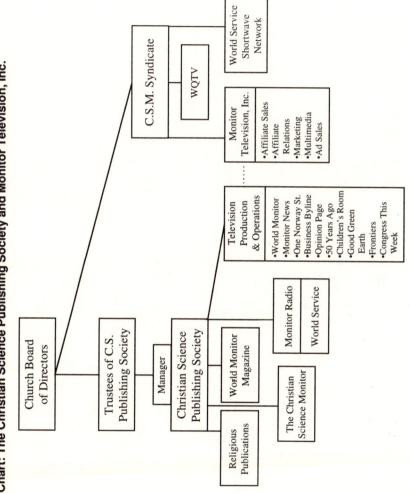

Notes

Chapter 1. The Changing Business of News

1. E.B. White, upon seeing a prototype television set at the 1938 World's Fair; quoted in Fred W. Friendly, *Due to Circumstances Beyond Our Control* (New York: Vintage Books, 1967).

2. Shifts charted by the Roper Organization's annual "America's Watching: Public Attitudes Toward Television," commissioned by the National Television Association and the National Association of Broadcasters. Annual since 1948.

3.

Table 1.1

The *Christian Science Monitor*'s Operating Losses, 1980–1985 (in millions of dollars)

1980	1981	1982	1983	1984	1985
8.7	7.7	8.0	9.9	14.3	17.3

Source: The Christian Science Publishing Society.

4. Erik Barnouw, *A Tower of Babel: A History of Broadcasting in the United States to 1933* (New York: Oxford University Press, 1966), pp. 211 ff.; Barnouw, *The Golden Web: A History of Broadcasting in the United States, 1933–1953* (New York: Oxford University Press, 1968), pp. 22–23.

5. House of Representatives, *Compilation of the Communications Act of 1934 and Related Provisions of the Law: Including Communications Act of 1934, Communications Satellite Act of 1962, Selected Provisions from the United States Code* (Washington, DC: GPO, 1989).

6. See Sydney W. Head and Christopher H. Sterling, *Broadcasting in America: A Survey of Electronic Media,* 5th ed. (Boston: Houghton Mifflin, 1987), pp. 73–74; Robert L. Hilliard and Michael C. Keith, *The Broadcast Century: A Biography of American Broadcasting* (Stoneham, MA: Butterworth Heinemann, 1992), pp. 67–70; Christopher H. Sterling and John M. Kitross, *Stay Tuned: A Concise History of American Broadcasting,* 2d ed. (Belmont, CA: Wadsworth, 1990), pp. 122–123.

7. Barnouw, *The Golden Web,* pp. 20–23; Head and Sterling, *Broadcasting in Amer-*

ica, p. 74; Hilliard and Keith, *The Broadcast Century,* pp. 67–69; Sterling and Kitross, *Stay Tuned,* pp. 123, 175, 178; see also Sally Bedell Smith, *In All His Glory: The Life & Times of William S. Paley: The Legendary Tycoon and His Brilliant Circle* (New York: Touchstone, 1990), pp. 165–166.

8. Barnouw, *The Golden Web,* pp. 145–215; Head and Sterling, *Broadcasting in America,* pp. 78–82; Hilliard and Keith, *The Broadcast Century,* pp. 92–102; Smith, *In All His Glory,* pp. 170–227.

9. Barnouw, *The Golden Web,* Chapter 4.

10. Barnouw, *The Golden Web,* pp. 227–236; Head and Sterling, *Broadcasting in America,* p. 512; Hilliard and Keith, *The Broadcast Century,* pp. 106–107; Smith, *In All His Glory,* pp. 293, 297; Sterling and Kitross, *Stay Tuned,* pp. 304–305.

11. Head and Sterling, *Broadcasting in America,* pp. 75–76; Hilliard and Keith, *The Broadcast Century,* pp. 53–68; Smith, *In All His Glory,* p.186.

12. Barnouw, *The Golden Web,* pp. 125–128; Hilliard and Keith, *The Broadcast Century,* p. 99; Sterling and Kitross, *Stay Tuned,* pp. 208–210; Smith, *In All His Glory,* pp. 171–177.

13. Erik Barnouw, *Tube of Plenty: The Evolution of American Television,* 2d rev. ed. (New York: Oxford University Press, 1990), pp. 95–96; Hilliard and Keith, *The Broadcast Century,* pp. 131, 144; Sterling and Kitross, *Stay Tuned,* pp. 210–211.

14. This is conservative; extrapolating from numbers in Head and Sterling's *Broadcasting in America* (pp. 258–259) almost doubles that again.

15. Like information on costs, data on profitability (or lack thereof) at various news operations is historically a closely guarded trade secret; as one observer noted, "The owners did not expect network news to earn a profit" (Ken Auletta, *Three Blind Mice: How the TV Networks Lost Their Way* [New York: Vintage Books, 1991]), p. 285.

16. Barnouw, *The Golden Web,* pp. 302–303; Erik Barnouw, *The Image Empire: A History of Broadcasting in the United States from 1953* (New York: Oxford University Press, 1970), pp. 42–55; Barnouw, *Tube of Plenty,* pp. 151–154; Head and Sterling, *Broadcasting in America,* pp. 99–101; Hilliard and Keith, *The Broadcast Century,* pp. 111–128, 146–148; Smith, *In All His Glory,* pp. 362–368.

17. See especially Barnouw, *The Image Empire;* Smith, *In All His Glory,* pp. 362–373.

18. Barnouw, *The Image Empire,* Chapter 2.

19. Smith, *In All His Glory,* Chapter 37; first a monthly, then a weekly, *CBS Reports* owed its existence to the need to draw the FCC's attention away from the quiz show scandal.

20. Barnouw, *The Golden Web,* Chapter 3; Smith, *In All His Glory,* Chapter 19.

21. Smith, *In All His Glory,* pp. 311, 376, 386; David Halberstam, *The Powers That Be* (New York: Alfred A. Knopf, 1979), p. 411.

22. Halberstam, *The Powers That Be,* pp. 437–441.

23. Friendly, *Due to Circumstances Beyond our Control.*

24. Hilliard and Keith, *The Broadcast Century,* p. 184.

25. Halberstam, *The Powers That Be,* pp. 733–734.

26. Barnouw, *The Image Empire,* pp. 154, 317, 325; Sterling and Kitross, *Stay Tuned,* pp. 355, 419.

27. Sterling and Kitross, *Stay Tuned,* Chapter 9; *Report of the President: Commission on the Causes and Prevention of Violence,* Milton S. Eisenhower, Chair, 1969.

28. Barnouw, *The Image Empire,* pp. 293–5; Hilliard and Keith, *The Broadcast Century,* p. 227; The Carnegie Commission, *A Public Trust: The Report of the Carnegie Commission on the Future of Broadcasting* (New York: Bantam, 1979).

29. Frank Pace of General Dynamics.

30. Note courtesy Robert Hilliard: "President Richard Nixon's dislike of the press was well known, and within a few months of his 1969 inauguration he sent Vice President Spiro Agnew and others to take them on. Network news was singled out and CBS, at least, responded by suspending their customary commentary following presidential news conferences for the better part of a year. Then the Nixon FCC hit the networks where it hurt the most, in their entertainment revenues, instituting rules that barred them from having a financial interest or syndication rights in the highly profitable TV rerun aftermarket. First Agnew was out, then Nixon was out, but the so-called "finsyn" rules barring broadcasters (but not cable) from owning much of their own programming, remained—a monument to how presidential displeasure with news operations could lead to retaliation in matters of great financial consequence for the networks, but not directly related to the news. President Ronald Reagan, like Nixon a man with no small dislike for network news and a Californian with loyalty to the LA-based entertainment industry, did not include finsyn in the sweeping deregulation overseen by his FCC Chairman, Mark Fowler."

31. Head and Sterling, *Broadcasting in America,* pp. 440, 539, 542.

32. Big cities would not be wired for cable until the 1980s.

33. Hilliard and Keith, *The Broadcast Century,* pp. 206–207.

34. Porter Bibb, *Ted Turner's Amazing Story: It Ain't As Easy As It Looks* (New York: Crown, 1993); Hank Whittemore, *CNN: The Inside Story: How a Band of Mavericks Changed the Face of Television News* (Boston: Little, Brown, 1990); Christian Williams, *Lead, Follow or Get Out of the Way: The Story of Ted Turner* (New York: Times Books, 1981).

35. Whittemore, *CNN: The Inside Story.*

36. Cable advertising alone increased from $53 million in 1980 to $1.8 billion in 1990.

37. Auletta, *Three Blind Mice;* Edward Bliss Jr., *Now the News: The Story of Broadcast Journalism* (New York: Columbia University Press, 1991); Peter J. Boyer, *Who Killed CBS? The Undoing of America's Number One News Network* (New York: St. Martin's Press, 1988); Reuven Frank, *Out of Thin Air: The Brief Wonderful Life of Network News* (New York: Simon and Schuster, 1991).

Additional sources:

Donaldson, Lufkin & Jenrette, "Current Trends in Broadcasting, Cable, Advertising, Publishing and Filmed Entertainment Industries," *DLJ Media & Entertainment,* no. 73 (November–December 1992).

National Television Association, "Trends in TV Network Ad Revenues Including Cable and Barter Syndication (1980–81)" and "Growth of TV Penetration (1950–92)," courtesy Steven Singer, senior vice president, director of research.

Sue Bomzer, "Cable Audience Report," PBS Research, February 3, 1992.

Twentieth Century Fund Task Force on Public Television, *Quality Time?* New York: The Twentieth Century Fund Press, 1993.

Chapter 2. Tradition Is Not Enough

1. Colonel Archibald McLellan as quoted in Erwin W. Canham, *Commitment to Freedom: The Story of the Christian Science Monitor* (Boston: Houghton Mifflin, 1958), p. 39.

2. Mary Baker Eddy's acquaintance, Bronson Alcott, and his earlier associates, the Boston-based transcendentalists, entertained such thoughts; on Eddy's contacts with

Alcott, see Robert Peel, *Christian Science: Its Encounter with American Culture* (New York: Henry Holt, 1958), Part II.

3. Robert Peel, *Mary Baker Eddy: The Years of Trial* (Boston: Christian Science Publishing Society, 1971), pp. 50–56.

4. Norman Beasley, *The Cross and the Crown: The History of Christian Science* (Boston: Little, Brown, 1952), pp. 396–398, 413, 415, 558; Mark Twain (Samuel L. Clemens), *Christian Science: With Notes Containing Corrections To Date* (New York: Harper and Brothers, 1899).

5. Beasley, *The Cross and the Crown,* pp. 422–476.

6. Ibid., Chapter 14.

7. Except where noted otherwise, the account of the newspaper's beginnings through the 1921 settlement of the Publishing Society's legal challenge to the Church depends for its factual base entirely on Canham's history, *Commitment to Freedom.*

8. Canham, *Commitment to Freedom,* p. 29.

9. Massachusetts Supreme Judicial Court, November 23, 1921.

10. Willis J. Abbot, *Watching the World Go By* (Boston: Little, Brown, 1934), Chapter 1.

11. Canham, *Commitment to Freedom,* p. 178.

12. Abbot, *Watching the World Go By,* p. 322.

13. Canham, *Commitment to Freedom,* p. 232.

14. Ibid., pp. 272–275.

15. Ibid., p. 269.

16. Ibid., p. 271; technically, Drummond's title was "executive editor."

17. Ibid., Chapter 34; Jack Hoagland interviews. Except where noted otherwise, the account of his father's tenure as manager of the Publishing Society is drawn from interviews with Jack Hoagland.

18. John H. Hoagland, "The *Christian Science Monitor:* Faster Delivery to Its Readers Everywhere; A Survey for the Board of Trustees of the Christian Science Publishing Society and for the Information of the Christian Science Board of Directors," Boston, October 1955, bound, typewritten manuscript.

19. *The* Christian Science Monitor: *Assignment: Mankind,* 1958, videotape copy of film original.

20. Jack Hoagland interview.

21. The *Monitor's* five Pulitzers are recorded in the Christian Science Publishing Society archive.

22. Jack Hoagland interview.

23. Netty Douglass interview.

24. Jack Hoagland interview.

25. Except as otherwise noted, the account of the 1970s is a composite story based on interviews with Don Bowersock, Netty Douglass, Jack Hoagland, Dick Nenneman, John Parrott, Gail Pierson, and Harvey Wood.

26. Richard C. Nenneman, "The Monitor and the Christian Science Movement," 1971 or 1972, typewritten manuscript.

27. "Big Back Bay Expansion Plan: Will Cost Christian Science Church $71 million," *Boston Traveler,* July 1, 1965; George M. Collins, "Christian Science Area Renewal Begins June 6," *Boston Globe,* February 24, 1966; George Forsythe, "Back Bay Plan Opposed," *Boston Traveler,* April 10, 1967; Bill Dooley and Burt Peretsky, "Black 'Crash' Science Church, Demand $100 M," *Boston Herald,* June 3, 1969; Tom Riley, "Residents' Suit Delays $60 M Development," *Boston Herald,* March 23, 1973; Paul Sullivan, "Christian Science Center Open," *Boston Herald,* May 31, 1973.

28. John Hughes, "Elimination of the Deficit," report to Board of Trustees, Christian Science Publishing Society, May 23, 1977.

29. Harvey Wood interview.

30. The famous accordion report was not found. This account is drawn from John Parrott and Harvey Wood interviews.

Additional sources:

Mary Baker Eddy. *Church Manual of the First Church of Christ, Scientist, in Boston, Mass.* Boston: The First Church of Christ, Scientist, 1895, including also Deed of Trust, 1892, and Deed Conveying Land for Church Purposes, 1903.

Stephen Gottschalk interview.

John H. Hoagland, "Consulting Activities for the Mother Church, December 1980–May 1981," compilation of documents.

Richard Nenneman interview.

Gail E. Pierson interview.

Chapter 3. Vision

1.

Table 3.1

The *Christian Science Monitor*'s Growing Deficit (in millions of dollars)

	1980	1981	1982
Expenses	23.0	23.9	25.5
Revenues	14.3	16.2	17.5
Profit (Loss)	(8.7)	(7.7)	(8.0)

Source: Numbers verified by Donald C. Bowersock, treasurer.

2. Canham, *Commitment to Freedom,* p. 102.

3. Ibid., p. 310; Jack Hoagland interview.

4. Jack Hoagland interview.

5. Documents that chart the early consideration of electronic media include: Bruce Payne & Associates, Inc., "Radio and Television Feasibility Study for the Board of Directors, the Mother Church of the First Church of Christ, Scientist," May 11, 1966; Communications Coordinating Committee, "Television as a Medium for the Presentation of Christian Science," April 15, 1969; Records and Research, Joan Lindsay (Supervisor), to John Hoagland, "TMC Use of TV as a Communications Medium, 1952–1978."

6. Communications Coordinating Committee, "Television as a Medium for the Presentation of Christian Science," May 11, 1969.

7. Harvey Wood interview; John Parrott interview; Jack Hoagland interview.

8. Hoagland, McLachlan & Co., Inc., materials.

9. John Hoagland, "The Mother Church's Use of TV as a Communications Medium, 1952–1978," September 14, 1984, compilation of documents.

10. Ibid.

11. Ibid.

12. Jack Hoagland interview.

13. Harvey Wood interview; Katherine Fanning interview.

14. Don Bowersock interview.

15. Dick Nenneman interview and written communication.

16. Katherine Fanning interview; also Katherine Fanning, "Katherine Woodruff Fanning," in *New Guardians of the Press: Selected Profiles of America's Woman Newspaper Editors.*

17. David Anable interview; John Parrott interview.

18. Jack Hoagland interview and written communication; John Parrott interview; Harvey Wood interview.

19. Jack Hoagland interviews; Harvey Wood interviews.

20. Harvey Wood interview.

21. Netty Douglass interview.

22. Harvey Wood interview.

23. John Hoagland, "The Christian Science Monitor—Its Mission for the Rest of the Century," Seventeenth Church of Christ, Scientist, Chicago, IL, December 11, 1983.

24. Don Bowersock interview.

25. "Transcript of Board Meeting, Friday, November 9, Re: Script for December 8 Meeting." 1984.

26. J.R.D., "Shake-Up Time," *Forbes* (August 1, 1983); William A. Henry III, "Giving Rebirth to the Monitor: A New Editor Brightens the Look and Style of Venerable Daily," *Time* (October 10, 1983); William M. Buckley, "Staid Christian Science Monitor Changing Its Look to Restore Readership and Profits," *Wall Street Journal,* October 3, 1983. See also, Alex Beam, "After a 10–Year Nap, the Christian Science Monitor Wakes Up: A New Editor and Publisher Finally Have Circulation and Ads on the Move," *Business Week* (May 27, 1985).

27. Harvey Wood interview; Directors to the Field, "Call to a meeting for all Christian Scientists," draft memo, probably September 1984; see also memos from Board Office to Hoagland, Bowersock, Whitfield, Talbot, Phinney, Selover, Nenneman, Parrott, Fanning, Robertson, Hand, Kendrick, and Waplington, "Re: Script for December 8 Meeting," November 9, 1984 and December 5, 1984.

28. Netty Douglass interview.

29. Jack Hoagland interview; Harvey Wood interviews.

30. Dick Nenneman interview; videotaped record of the teleconference, "To Live for All Mankind," December 8, 1984.

31. David Anable interview; Kay Fanning interview; Jack Hoagland interview; Jack Hoagland notes to trustees, "Principal Accomplishments, 1/83–12/84," undated; Kay Fanning to Newsroom staff, "Re: Five Year Plan," memo dated July 31, 1985; "A Five-Year Plan for the Christian Science Monitor, 1986–1991: Final Report," submitted to the board of trustees by the manager of the Christian Science Publishing Society, November 26, 1985; and Kay Fanning, memo to the Christian Science Board of Directors, "Re: The Five-Year Plan."

32. Memo dated November 5, 1984, from Kay Fanning to Harvey Wood, Jack Hoagland, Dick Nenneman, David Anable, Rob Nelson, Dick Cattani, Rush Kidder, "Re: Lunch with Boston Globe Editors"; memo dated November 11, 1984, to same list, "Re: Update on lunch with Boston Globe Editors, November 29, 1984," noting guests to include Bill Taylor, owner-publisher; Tom Winship, retiring editor; Mike Janeway, new

editor; Jack Driscoll, executive editor; Marty Nolan, editorial page editor, Helen Dono-
van, incoming assistant national editor; and David Greenway, national and international
news editor.

33. Netty Douglass interview.

34. John Parrott interview.

35. John Parrott interview.

36. John Parrott interview; Harvey Wood interview.

37. Jack Hoagland interviews; Netty Douglass interviews. Key among these early
attempts at introducing an instinct for profitability was the creation of a syndicate to handle
syndication and, eventually, ad sales. Memo from John Hoagland to all employees, "Creation
of The Christian Science Monitor Syndicate," November 11, 1984.

38. Personal observation; Lyn Chamberlin interview.

39. Netty Douglass, "Monitor Broadcasting: The First 24 Months," April 28, 1987,
three-page chronology; Jack Hoagland draft memo, December 31, 1984, apparently to
Publishing Society Trustees. Hoagland's memo noted: "Recently, in several different
ways, the concept of electronic publishing has pressed itself on us," and recommended
specific steps to explore opportunities for international radio broadcast.

40. Netty Douglass interview.

41. Jack Hoagland interview; John Parrott interview.

42. Netty Douglass "Monitor Broadcasting: The First 24 Months," annotated chronology, April 28, 1987; "Radio and Television Activities, 1985–1986," unsigned report,
Christian Science Publishing Society, January 25, 1985; see also, Manager's Office,
"Programs of the Christian Science Publishing Society for the *Christian Science Moni-
tor,* 1985 and Beyond," preliminary briefings for the Christian Science board of direc-
tors, the trustees of the Christian Science Publishing Society, the editor of the *Christian
Science Monitor,* the editor of the *Christian Science Journal, Sentinel,* and *Herald,*
February 20, 1985.

43. The issues were several (including standards for reporting illness and death, disaster,
prediction, and homosexuality) and typically involved *both* philosophical matters and matters
of taste; one of many intelligent communications intended for the Field was the letter from
the Christian Science Publishing Society board of trustees (then Donald C. Bowersock,
Chairman; Graves D. Hewitt; and Johannes Spanjard) and Manager Jack Hoagland, dated
August, 1986. The letter included the following eight summary points:

- [The Monitor] can be expected to expand and even multiply its usefulness
  to society. . . .
- . . . the Monitor must be viewed as a complete system of communication
  with the public, embracing the principal media through which people gain
  their perceptions of the world. . . .
- . . . this system must include radio and television broadcast editions as
  well as the daily and weekly print editions.
- . . . the core element of this complete system is . . . the daily newspaper
  established by our Leader. . . .
- The allocation of resources to the daily paper . . . has grown dramatically. . . .
- The price of the daily paper must continue to increase.
- The global outlook of the Monitor . . . must now be manifested more fully
  in its reach and audience. . . .
- . . . this wider service to all mankind will be provided by the availability of
  an improved international weekly product of the *Christian Science Monitor,*
  in addition to the launching of our international radio broadcasting service.

44. Jack Hoagland interview; Netty Douglass interview; Harvey Wood interview.

45. Personal observation.

46. John Parrott interview.

47. David Cook interview; Netty Douglass interview; William Bruce Dredge interview; Jack Hoagland interview. Gail Pierson, a dynamite worker and Principia graduate, saw it quite differently, however. From her perspective, Principians were as competent as any other group.

48. David Cook interview.

49. Netty Douglass interview; Gail Pierson interview.

50. Donald Bowersock and John Hoagland, memo to all employees, "Pending Acquisition of Broadcasting Properties," May 28, 1986.

51. See also Bart Ziegler, "Christian Science Monitor Buys TV Station, Plans Nightly Broadcast," Associated Press bulletin, May 28, 1986; Ed Siegel, "Monitor Agrees to Buy Ch. 68," *Boston Globe,* May 29, 1986; Lynn Kettleson, "Christian Science Monitor Buys WQTV," *Boston Herald,* May 29, 1986.

52. Jack Hoagland interview.

53.

Table 3.2

Newspaper Expenses, Revenues, and Profit (loss) (in millions of dollars)

	1983	1984	1985	1986	1987
Expenses	27.5	33.9	37.4	37.1	45.2
Revenues	17.6	19.6	20.1	21.1	22.8
Profit (Loss)	(9.9)	(14.3)	(17.3)	(16.0)	(22.4)

Source: Numbers verified by Donald C. Bowersock, treasurer.

---

54. Jack Hoagland interview; Don Bowersock interview; Kay Fanning interview; David Anable interview.

55. Some detailed preparatory work was done by Research Communications, Ltd., Chestnut Hill, MA, evaluating audience response to the CSPS weekly television programs. See "Christian Science Monitor Reports: Program, Hosts, and Correspondents," 2 vols., August 1987. The materials on which the meeting was based are contained in "Presentation to the Board of Trustees, the Christian Science Publishing Society, by the Manager's Office and Senior Managers," August 17, 1987. The report begins by tracing long-term trends in public communications, beginning with charts demonstrating the precipitous decline in the number of independent daily newspapers in the United States in the course of the twentieth century. The videotaped record of the actual proceedings is nearly eight hours long.

56. The newspaper's editor would not, as a matter of routine, attend meetings between the manager and the trustees. Accounts differ and feelings run high with respect to why it took so long for the import of this key meeting to come to Fanning's attention.

57. Videotaped record, cassettes one and two.

58. Ibid.

59. "Presentation to the Board of Trustees," August 17, 1987, page 89, column labeled "ALT 89/90."

60. Videotaped record, cassette three.

61. Videotaped record, cassette four.

62. Ibid.

63. Ibid.

64. Ibid.
65. Ibid.
66. Don Bowersock interview; Ruben J. Dunn and John Morris, *The Crash Put Simply: October, 1987* (New York: Praeger, 1988).

Chapter 4. Sharpened Focus

1. See especially videotaped record of the board of trustees meeting, August 17, 1987, David Morse report, cassette three.
2. John Parrott interview.
3. John Parrott interview.
4. Jack Hoagland interviews; Netty Douglass interviews; John Parrott interview' Harvey Wood interviews; personal observations 1989–1992, referring to this period.
5. Danny Wilson interview; Jack Hoagland interviews; Netty Douglass interviews.
6. See also discussion in Chapter Seven of this book, "Perspectives."
7. Jack Hoagland believes that at least one important defection among those who were making the transition from the newspaper to multiformat distribution was precipitated by his going outside for an anchor. True or not, the issue of who can and who cannot project credibility on television and why, and how malleable the public's perceptions are, is as fascinating as it is disturbing. In the 1960s, of course, television lore had it that women could never credibly deliver the news.
8. "The Christian Science Monitor Announces Nightly TV News Program, 'Monitor Newsworld,' to Be Anchored by John Hart: Will Feature Live Global Reports by Satellite," press release, April 7, 1988.
9. Sandy Socolow interview; Jack Hoagland interview.
10. Netty Douglass chronology, see Chapter 3, note 47.
11. Danny Wilson interview; Jack Hoagland interview.
12. The Discovery Channel contract was finally signed in July. John Parrott, memo to all employees, "Re: Press Announcement: World Monitor Television to Be Distributed by the Discovery Channel," July 5, 1988.
13. Malcolm Netburn interview; Frank McGill interview.
14. On Columbus Avenue, in Boston's South End; all concerned enjoyed the year or so start-up in these overcrowded, ramshackle quarters. Earl Foell interview; Malcolm Netburn and Frank McGill interview; Jack Hoagland interview.
15. See Chapter 5, note 29, for *World Monitor Magazine*'s impressive successes.
16. Personal observation.
17. Gail Pierson interview; personal observation.
18. Kay Fanning interview; David Anable interview; Jack Hoagland interview.
19. Gail Pierson interview.
20. John Parrott interview; conversation with writer who asked not to be named.
21. Jack Hoagland interview; Harvey Wood interview.
22. Jack Hoagland interviews; Netty Douglass interviews; Harvey Wood interviews; Canham, in *Commitment to Freedom,* recounts an earlier version of the same struggle in the 1920s.
23. The *Children of Darkness* series, which ran both in the newspaper and on radio, was a triumph of synergy. Sara Terry was one of two reporters who traveled to some of the worst hell-holes on earth from India to Latin America gathering material for this important series.
24. Videotaped record of the board of trustees meeting, August 17, 1987, cassette 4.
25. Abundant financial information was to be found among the cartons of papers made

available by Jack Hoagland and Netty Douglass; the formats and the distribution lists showed exactly which information was distributed, when, and to whom, both in putting together budgets and in tracking actual revenues as compared to budgeted revenues.

26. Kay Fanning interview. In September 21, 1987, memo to the Church directors, "Re: Final Recommendations to the Christian Science Board of Directors Pertaining to the Christian Science Publishing Society Manager's Presentation on August 17, 1987, and Including the Conclusions of the Trustees' Meetings with the Christian Science Board of Directors on September 14, 1987," the trustees declined Hoagland's August 17 request for a task force, feeling that the numbers spoke for themselves and that Hoagland, in recommending an emphasis on television in the United States and shortwave radio abroad, was on the right track. A September 24, 1987, memo, "Re: Your Memorandum of September 21, 1987," from the directors to the trustees, concurred. When Fanning became aware of the implications of the August presentation, she and Hoagland submitted a joint proposal to the trustees, reviving the task force and seeking a $500,000 budget to support its activities. See "DRAFT: The Future of The Christian Science Monitor Tuesday, November 17, 1987."

27. Alex Beam, "Christian Scientists Seeking Economic Cure: Monitor Can No Longer Afford to Write for Elite," *Boston Globe,* December 1, 1987.

28. Kay Fanning interview; John Parrott interview; Harvey Wood interview; Jack Hoagland interview; Netty Douglass interview. There were those among the *Monitor*'s journalists who were deeply offended ("staggered") by the scathing treatment accorded Hoagland in the newsroom confrontations, as several heartfelt and highly personal notes in his files attest. He also remembers that, just before one such meeting, held in a conference room in the Church Administration building, he was standing quite alone, half-turned toward a window as the angry print journalists filled the room, when he became aware that the newspaper's television critic had, without speaking, quietly come to stand beside him.

29. "Proposed Telegram to KQED and APR," undated draft prepared by John Parrott, reading in part:

> We are pleased to advise you that, in conformity with standard hiring practices of the broadcasting industry throughout the United States, the radio and television departments of The Christian Science Publishing Society and The Christian Science Monitor Syndicate, Inc., have adopted the following hiring policy as established by the Federal government's Model Equal Employment Opportunity Program and stated in FCC 391–A (page 4) of January, 1984: "It will be our policy to provide employment opportunity to all qualified individuals without regard to their race, color, religion, national origin or sex in all personnel actions including recruitment, evaluation, selection, promotion, compensation, training and termination.
>
> It will also be our policy to promote the realization of equal opportunity through a positive, continuing program of specific practices designed to ensure the full realization of equal employment opportunity without regard to race, color, religion, national origin or sex."

30. John Parrott interview.

31. John B. Padgett, "Furman Picked for Shortwave Radio," *Hampton County Guardian,* June 24, 1987; Bob Stuart, "Shortwave to Transmit from Hampton," *State/Columbia,* December 19, 1987; Martha Bee Anderson, "Ground Broken for Radio Station," *Hampton County Guardian,* December 30, 1987; Nancy Hemdon, "Children of a Split Community: Black Parents in Estill, S.C., Say They're Concerned About the

Quality of Education, Not with Integration—but in This District, the Two Are Linked," *Christian Science Monitor,* May 19, 1988; memo from Jack Hoagland to Kay Fanning, "Re: Some Thoughts on the Estill Episode," May 23, 1988; memo from David Anable to Kay Fanning, "Re: Story on Estill," May 25, 1988; memo from Kay Fanning to Jack Hoagland, "Re: Estill Memo of May 23," May 31, 1988.

32. Kay Fanning interview; David Anable interview; Jack Hoagland interview; Harvey Wood interview.

33. "The Story of the Moat," *Journal of Christian Science* (June 1988).

34. Robert Peel, *Health and Medicine in the Christian Science Tradition: Principle, Practice and Challenge* (New York: Crossroads, 1984), Chapter 10; memo from Jack Hoagland to Harvey Wood, "Re: Notes on Book Chapter," July 22, 1988.

35. Jack Hoagland interview; Harvey Wood interview; memo from the Christian Science board of directors to all employees, July 28, 1988; Peel, *Health and Medicine,* Chapter 10.

36. Jack Hoagland interview. The prototypes, one dated August 5, 1986, were intended to demonstrate the kind of daily print product that could be delivered electronically to the home using existing technology.

37. Jack Hoagland interview.

38. "World Monitor TV, dub of September 12, 1988," videotape record of the first broadcast; Jeremy Gerard, "Christian Science Publisher Expands into TV and a Magazine," *New York Times,* October 3, 1988; Leslie Helm, "The Church that Would Be a Media Mogul," *Business Week* (September 26, 1988); Joseph P. Kahn, "Television: All the News that Scans," *Boston Globe,* September 16, 1988, covering also the debut of USA's short-lived new show; Richard Zoglin, "A Mild Matron Goes Modern: The Christian Science Monitor Launches a TV Broadcast," *Time* (September 26, 1988).

39. Videotaped record, October 31, 1988, six tapes; the Task Force, sometimes referred to as "Kay and the Four Davids" included Katherine Fanning, Editor, who chaired it, David Anable, Managing Editor; David Els, Publishing Director; David Morse, President of Monitor Syndicate, and David Winder, Assistant Managing Editor.

40. Looseleaf binder with charts, "The Christian Science Monitor Daily Task Force Report, October 31, 1988."

41. Kay Fanning interview.

42. "Task Force Addendum," November 1, 1988.

43. Kay Fanning interview.

44. Kay Fanning interview; David Anable interview; Jack Hoagland interview; Harvey Wood interview.

45. Alex Beam, "Turmoil at the Monitor," *Boston Globe,* November 11, 1988.

46. Kay Fanning interview; David Anable interview; Harvey Wood interview.

47. Kay Fanning interviews; David Anable interview; Dick Nenneman interview; Harvey Wood interview. David Anable remembers that on that Monday morning Dick Nenneman offered him any overseas post he wanted if he would just stay on board; Dick Nenneman remembers that although he tried to reach Anable by phone to persuade him not to resign, he never did make the connection, and therefore did not have the chance to make such an offer.

48. Kay Fanning memo to directors setting forth "four minimal requirements for me to be able to remain in my position as Editor," November 14, 1988; David Anable letter of resignation, November 14, 1988; Kay Fanning letter of resignation, November 14, 1988; David Winder letter of resignation, November 14, 1988; "Statement to the Press from Katherine Fanning," November 14, 1988.

49. David Anable interview; Kay Fanning interview; Jack Hoagland interview.

50. Ibid.

51. Netty Douglass interview; John Parrott interview; Jack Hoagland interview; Harvey Wood interview.

52. David Anable interview.

53. Alex Beam, "Monitor Editor Resigns: Fanning, Two Deputies Leave in Protest of Planned Changes," *Boston Globe,* November 15, 1988; Bruce D. Butterfield, "Kay Fanning, a Risk-Taker: From Obscurity to Distinction, She Took Chances that Paid Off," *Boston Globe,* November 15, 1988.

54. "Question and Answer Period: Newsroom Staff and Representatives from Management Board of Directors, and Trustees," edited November 15, 1988; "Summary: Washington Bureau Staff Meeting with Church and CSPS Officials," November 16, 1988, transcript summary.

55. Alex Beam, "A Church Divided," *Boston Globe,* November 16, 1988; Sarah Snyder, "Changes Sadden, Embitter News Staff," *Boston Globe,* November 16, 1988; Frederic M. Biddle, "Christian Science Reaching Out: Church Will Continue to Spend Millions on 4 Media Ventures," *Boston Globe,* November 16, 1988; Alex Beam, "After the Fall," *Boston Globe,* November 18, 1988, part of the *Globe*'s TGIF column; editorial, "The Monitor's Reasoned Voice," *Boston Globe,* November 19, 1988; Frederic M. Biddle, "Television: Is It a Savior—Or a Fatal Mistake?" *Boston Globe,* November 20, 1988; see also Frederic M. Biddle and Alex Beam, "Walkout by Editors at Monitor Creates a Crisis for Church," *Boston Globe,* November 22, 1988.

56. Jonathan Alter, "Crisis of Faith at the Monitor: Sudden Resignations at a Venerable Newspaper," *Newsweek* (November 28, 1988); "Downsized: The Atlanta Constitution and Journal, the Christian Science Monitor," *The Nation,* December 5, 1988; Laurence Zuckerman, "Who's Running the Newsroom? Five Editors Quit Reflecting New Tensions with Publishers," *Time* (November 28, 1988); Marie Gendron, "Staid Monitor Takes a Radical Turn in News Biz," *Boston Business Journal* (November 21, 1988); Harriet Johnson Brackey and Anne Zidonis, "Two Editors Quit 'Science Monitor,'" *USA Today,* November 15, 1988; David Stipp, "Fanning and Two Other Top Editors Quit Christian Science Monitor in a Dispute," *Wall Street Journal,* November 15, 1988; Allan R. Gold, "Religious Views Cited in Monitor Resignations," *New York Times,* November 17, 1988; Allan R. Gold, "Editors of Monitor Resign Over Cuts," *New York Times,* November 29, 1988.

57. Harvey Wood interview.

58. David Anable interview.

Additional sources:

Memo from John Hoagland to group managers, editors, and department heads, "Re: Appointment of New Assistant Manager of the Publishing Society," January 29, 1987.

Earl W. Foell, Chair, with Bruce B. Clark, David E. Els, A. William Miller, and David E. Morse, for Donald Bowersock, John Hoagland, and Katherine Fanning, "Confidential: The Christian Science Publishing society Report of Weekly Edition Task Force," June 1987.

Letter from "Workers at the Mother Church" to "Beloved Teachers," September 26, 1987.

Christian Science board of directors, "The Pathfinding Mission of the *Christian Science Monitor,*" reprint from the *Christian Science Journal,* April 1988.

Memo from Dick Nenneman to Jack Hoagland and Hal Friesen, "Re: Some Thoughts on the Remaining Work of the Management Task Force on the Monitor," August 7, 1988.

Memo from Dick Nenneman to Kay Fanning, "Re: Manager's Office Work Regarding Task Force," August 30, 1988.

Memo to Paul Van Slambrouk and everyone in international news from Elizabeth Pond, November 15, 1988.

"Text from Two important Meetings," Church Center Bulletin, November 29, 1988.

"Figures Obtained by T. Griesa from D. Bowersock," December 2, 1988.

Letter to Church Board of Directors, signed by eighty-three *Monitor* employees, December 6, 1988.

Anonymous response to December 2 letter from John Lewis Selover, Chairman, board of directors, December 9, 1988.

Letter from Charlotte Saikowski to Richard Cattani, editor, the *Christian Science Monitor,* January 3, 1988.

Letter from Richard O'Regan, former editor of the weekly "Monitor Reports" to an unnamed senior editor at the *Monitor,* January 15, 1989.

Letter from Elizabeth Pond to Christian Science board of directors, February 15, 1989, with attached document, "Chronology of the *Christian Science Monitor,* 1988 Task Force and 1989 New *Monitor.*"

John Parrott, "The Christian Science Publishing Society: A Change in Direction, 1983 to 1989: One Participant's Recollections," March 30, 1989, and addendum, March 1992.

Chapter 5. Setting the Course

1. According to Christian Science Syndicate records, losses at WQTV were: $9.3 million in fiscal year 1988, $10.5 million in fiscal year 1989, $11.8 million in fiscal year 1990, and $8.0 million in fiscal year 1991.

2. Jack Hoagland interview; Netty Douglass interview.

3. In this the *Christian Science Monitor* has resembled large metropolitan dailies, with their thick specialized sections covering the arts, food, health, sports, and so forth, or to a lesser extent the omnibus programming of large local affiliates of the three broadcast networks; but it is precisely this kind of attempt to be many things to many people that provided radio and cable television the opportunity to capture the most dynamic segments of the consumer market with narrowcasting in the 1980s.

4. Faith Popcorn, *Popcorn Reports* (New York: Harper), irregular series to 1992.

5. Programming Director Lyn Chamberlin assumed at the time that the "TV: Special Programming" products she was developing were intended for the Boston market only; Lyn Chamberlin interview.

6. Netty Douglass interview; Lyn Chamberlin interview; personal observation.

7. *Today's Monitor* hosts were Clint Jones and Bill Mohler; the "One Norway Street" host was Schuyler Sackett; *El Monitor de Hoy* hosts were James Nelson Goodsell and Jacqueline Jordan.

8. The first host of *Inner-City Beat* was Luix Overbea. He was soon joined by Scott Mercer and Delores Handy Brown. The host of "Affairs of State" was George Merry.

9. Lyn Chamberlin interview.

10. Personal observation.

11. A partial exception to the general pattern was ESPN, owned by Cap Cities/ABC. Discovery's cable multi-system operators (MSO) owners were TCI/Liberty (49 percent), Newhouse (24.6 percent), Cox (20 percent). CNN's cable MSO owners were TCI (21 percent), Time Warner (18 percent), Continental (9 percent), and Comcast (9 percent). Ownership percentages are courtesy of John Higgins, then at *Multichannel News.*

12. Jack Hoagland interview; Netty Douglass interview; Ruth Otte interview; Greg Moyers interview.

13. Jack Hoagland interview; Netty Douglass interview.

14. Jack Hoagland interview.
15. *The Children's Room* hosts were Nona Scoville and George Capaccio.
16. John Parrott interview.
17.

Table 5.1

Profit and Loss Statement for the Fiscal Year Ending April 1990

	Costs	Losses
TV: Special Programming	$ 6.2	(6.2)
World Monitor News	22.6	(19.8)
WQTV	13.7	(11.8)
World Monitor Magazine	12.2	(7.2)
International shortwave facilities	4.3	(4.3)
MonitoRadio	6.9	(2.4)
Christian Science Monitor	26.9	(11.6)*
Religious periodicals	1.0	(1.4)
Other	5.2	(0.9)
Totals	112.0	(65.6)

*Reduced by half from a loss of $22.1 million in fiscal year 1989.

Figures shown in parentheses are losses.

Neither overall expenses nor the approximate breakdown by product is in dispute, although a combination of factors create some play in the numbers. For WQTV and for shortwave, eventually subsumed into a new entity, Monitor Television, Inc., d.b.a. The Monitor Channel, the fiscal year originally conformed to the calendar year. Within the Publishing Society, formula for allocating general and administrative expenses could vary. Determining a fair cost to The Monitor Channel for programming developed by the Publishing Society, reflected as non-cash transfers, would eventually add yet another accounting complication to the equations.

18. For CNN's costs from start-up through break-even, see chapter 6, note 32.

19. Earl Foell interview. *World Monitor Magazine*'s ad sales performance was good through 1990, despite the recession, but then fell off. See also *Monitor Month* (April 1990, September 1990, and April 1991).

20. *Monitor Month* (December 1989): 6.

21. Auletta, *Three Blind Mice;* Frank, *Out of Thin Air.*

22. David Cook interview.

23. Personal observation, 1989–1990.

24. In particular, Allen H. and Helen M. Taini, organized as "The 89th Edition," who later wrote Church directors regretting their actions and asking to be taken back into the fold. Sad to say, the systematic use of character assassination to gain purchase in disputes over other matters goes back to the 1970s, when for the better part of a decade, one Reginald Kerry, a consultant on real estate and security issues, wrote countless, sometimes highly fanciful letters about the alleged misdeeds of members of the Publishing Society and the Church administration, including the directors.

25. David Cook interview; Jack Hoagland interview. Hart interviewed President Bush on April 18, 1990. For a thoughtful discussion of news anchors subtly or not so subtly making themselves the subject of interviews, see James Fallows, *Breaking the News: How*

the Media Undermine American Democracy (New York: Pantheon Books, 1996).

26. Among these were John Yemma and, eventually, Paul Quinn-Judge.

27. Jack Hoagland interview; Dick Nenneman comment.

28. John Yemma, "Management by Fad" did run. The *Washington Journalism Review* ("Clippings: The Monitor Kills a Column" [January–February 1989]) reported that a story submitted November 22, 1988, by veteran columnist Joseph Harsch criticizing his employers was killed.

29. Earl Foell, the *Christian Science Monitor*'s editor from 1977 to 1982 and, before that, for many years the respected dean of the United Nations press corps, was *World Monitor Magazine*'s elegant guiding intellect. His close collaborators were New York–based publishing and circulation specialists, Malcolm Netburn and Frank McGill. The magazine's intended audience were leaders in government and industry.

Drawing on a lifetime of international contacts, Foell assembled a nonpareil roster of authors beyond the first issue's cover story by former presidents, Jimmy Carter and Gerald Ford, including Lincoln and Irirangi Bloomfield, Zbigniew Brzezinski, Harvey Cox, John Dessauer (on investing), Marshall I. and Merle Goldman, Elizabeth Janeway (on the child care crisis and on active aging), Eliot Janeway (on the economy), Jeffrey Sachs (on Polish capitalism), Ross Terril, Alvin and Heidi Toffler, Stansfield Turner, and "X" (on politics at the top in Deng's China). The range of topics was broad: from the dramatic transformation of the old Soviet Union, animal rights, a potential green revolution in sub-Saharan Africa, the creation of new materials from carbon, conflict in the Amazon basin, U.N. Secretary General Perez de Cuellar, global stock markets, the prospects for Mideast peace, the cost of automobile insurance, the international spread of African-based music, West European integration, and so forth. The magazine soon won a reputation for what Foell calls "crystal ball hits" for its uncanny ability, "whether by cleverness or luck" to spot the future before it arrived: the fall of the Berlin Wall, the threat represented by Saddam Hussein, the likelihood of a coup unseating Gorbachev, to name the most prominent. Husband–wife authors also seemed something of a specialty, including the Bloomfields, the Goldmans, the Janeways, and the Tofflers, as well as four or five others. Most saw, not luck, but the fine hand of the founding editor in the mix of top-level strategic analysis and homely topics *World Monitor Magazine* offered.

30. Florence Tambone interview.

31. Peter Steinfels, "Plan to Expand Church Media Reveals Christian Science Rift," *New York Times,* January 4, 1989; Thomas B. Rosenstiel, "Christian Science Rift: High-Tech Heresy at the Monitor?" *Los Angeles Times,* February 20, 1989; Stephen J. Simurda, "Can the Stripped-Down Monitor Stay Afloat? A Close Look at Why Katherine Fanning and Others Jumped Ship," *Columbia Journalism Review* (March–April 1989); see also J.l. Sheler, "Healing an Ailing Church," *U.S. News and World Report,* November 6, 1989.

32. The early activities of David Anable, Stephen Gottschalk (Church publicist), and Brooks Wilder (former general counsel for the Church) were said to be supported by a New York-based multimillionaire. Judge Thomas Griesa's persistent requests for more fiscal information than it was the Church's custom to publish began in the early 1980s. See also chapter 6, note 77 on the nature of some long-standing divisions within the Church.

33. Marian Christy, "Conversations: Kay Fanning's Staying Power," *Boston Globe,* December 21, 1989. There had been earlier direct efforts by Fanning supporters to broker such an invitation, even while the opposition was actively soliciting articles condemning the incumbents. One such effort came in the form of an unself-consciously insulting letter with chronology, some 32 pages in total, from the *Monitor*'s correspondent in Bonn, seeking reconciliation—on Fanning's and Anable's terms—and which read in part, "My proposal would therefore be that you invite the three editors—Kather-

ine Fanning, David Anable, and David Winder—to come talk with the board and see if it might be possible to reach a common understanding," dated February 15, 1989.

34. David Cook interview.

35. For a summary of the NBC–GE issues, see *EXTRA! The Magazine of FAIR* (1994).

36. This writer, a John Hart fan, found a close examination of his criticisms of Monitor Television's broadcast standards disappointing.

Hart's long article in the September–October 1992 *Columbia Journalism Review* named eight segments aired between September 1988 and July 1990 in which he claims the preferences of the Church as owner intervened in the journalistic process. It is unlikely that these key primary sources were available to the *Review*'s editors at the time of the decision to publish; they were certainly not available to the journal's influential readership—a systematic problem that goes with the territory in trying to evaluate media that are not only powerful but, at least for the time being, maddeningly ephemeral, too.

Of the seven which could be found, each one seems, on close and repeated re-viewing, to be good to excellent television journalism. The three most substantial are principally the work of other journalists, with Hart as anchor introducing them. Four of the seven pieces date from the period during which Sandy Socolow, whom Hart carefully does not criticize, was executive producer.

Socolow, who was on the Monitor Channel's editorial board from the summer of 1990 through the 1992 collapse, said in an interview for this book that at no time was there censorship in these matters. The debates that erupted while ex-NBC producer Bill Chesleigh was executive producer were regarding the following:

• The wording of an obituary for Sesame Street creator Jim Henson, who was raised a Christian Scientist—specifically, whether cause of death (pneumonia) was germane.

• Two long stories covering the Boston trial of the Twitchells, a Christian Science couple, whose two-year-old son had died in the care of a Christian Science practitioner of a problem that mainstream medicine probably could have cured. These two long, thorough pieces cover evenhandedly without fear or favor the horror of the child's death and the Church's role, and the host of unsettling questions about the legal status of children. Hart's condemnation here focuses on a suburban congregation's decision, first to allow, and then not to allow, a television crew inside their church to tape a service. Did the congregation have the perfect right to make that decision? Of course they did.

In summary, all the actual pieces reviewed were of high quality and were done under the supervision of highly professional executive producers who had held top positions at CBS or NBC.

Taken at face value, Hart's arguments tend toward a comical, if chilling, logical conclusion: that the *Monitor* should not be in the news business and never should have been; and that no other organization should be either. Far more salient in the specific pieces Hart puts at the center of his complaints are two other matters that, while less grand, are also important. First, what should the terms be on which authority over broadcast content is shared among anchor, executive producer, and editor? And second, what should the canon of broadcast journalism set as the range of acceptable guidelines in matters of news judgment, style, and good taste?

David Cook interview; Jack Hoagland interview; Sandford Socolow interview; Terry Ann Knopf, "An Anchor Adrift," *Boston Sunday Globe,* November 8, 1991; James L. Franklin, "Hart: Church Censored News," *Boston Globe,* August 17, 1992; John Hart, "The News for God's Sake: An Account of the Conflict Between a Church's Mission and a Journalist's Job," *Columbia Journalism Review* (September–October 1992); taped copies of broadcast segments: "Hurricane Gilbert," September 12, 1988; "Shushwap Indians" by Steve Delany, October 5, 1988; "Leprosy," September 21, 1988; "Strauss Obituary" and "Twitchell Trial," April 17, 1990; "Jim Henson Obituary," May 16, 1990. The piece on a dying elephant mentioned in the *Columbia Journalism Review* article was not found.

37. *Monitor Month* (May 1990).

38. Keith Botsford, "They Loved Their Child; They Also Loved God," *The Independent,* May 30, 1990. The allegations, unattributed and unsupported, included the following: that Hoagland had said privately that he joined the CIA in 1951 to avoid the Korean draft; that even in 1990 he might still be associated with the intelligence community, the implication being that the Monitor's move into television was somehow in the service of the U.S. intelligence community's covert operations. Hoagland's management style was called "ruthless," and it was alleged that he had used electronic surveillance internally at the *Monitor* against those who disagreed with his policies.

The possibility that Hoagland might still have been working for the CIA in some capacity was raised so regularly by some of Hoagland's bitter critics and denied so vehemently by Hoagland himself, that it seemed worth trying to establish the facts of the matter. Information obtained from the Agency and from retired Agency personnel as part of the research done for this book seems to indicate that these persistent charges have no basis in reality.

At age twenty-two, just out of college, Jack Hoagland went through a training course at the CIA for nine months from June 1951 to March 1952, after which he resigned from the Agency and enlisted voluntarily in the Navy. He went through officer training school at Newport, RI, received a commission as Ensign USNR, and was assigned to active duty with the naval detachment at the CIA until his honorable discharge in July 1955. From 1956 to 1961, Hoagland worked for the Agency from an office in downtown Boston as an overt intelligence officer known as a "Contact Specialist" in the Contact Division, later re-named the Domestic Contact Service and then the Domestic Contact Division. His job was to interview U.S. civilians, mainly academics and businessmen, who were willing to help the government gather and analyze information about Warsaw Pact defense capabilities. At the time he left the Agency, at age thirty-two, Hoagland's salary was $11,155, or about $50,800 in 1990 dollars. He then went on briefly to do some analysis for the Arms Control and Disarmament Agency, which the CIA tried, unsuccessfully, to block. In 1976, in a generally highly critical review of the Agency and its activities, Senator Frank Church singled out the Contact Division for praise, both for the quality of its fact-gathering and for having a clean record of respecting the rights of American citizens.

In the context of the 1950s, Hoagland's stint as a young man with the CIA seems unremarkable. He was recruited by his Shakespeare teacher in his senior year at Yale. Like many thoughtful people of his generation, Hoagland was a liberal cold warrior and an internationalist. His international outlook and his aptitude for technology made him useful to the CIA as well as to the Arms Control and Disarmament Agency, and also formed the basis for his subsequent successful career as a consultant to high-tech firms and others in the United States, Canada, Western Europe, and Japan.

Several individuals at the Monitor's broadcast operations or in the Church administration were asked to comment on the allegation that Hoagland used electronic surveillance against employees at the Publishing Society. Some of those questioned had supported Hoagland's policies and others had been relieved to see them suspended, but no one recalled any incident that could have led to a credible charge of the sort printed in *The Independent.* This accusation, potentially so damaging, was, like the others, apparently without basis in fact.

Jack Hoagland interviews; telephone interview and written communication from Jackson R. Horton, Hoagland's former supervisor at the Agency, June 20, 1995; document from Transactions and Records Division, CIA, August 11, 1995; written communication from Sara Newman, Employment Services Officer, CIA, August 11, 1995; correspondence with John H. Wright, Information and Privacy Coordinator, 1993–1995; "Report to the President by the Commission on CIA Activities within the United States," U.S. Senate, 1975, Chapter 15; "Final Report of the Select Committee to Study Governmental Operations with Respect to Intelligence Activities," Supplementary Detailed Staff Reports on Foreign and Military Intelligence, Book 4, U.S. Senate, 1976; Personnel Security Questionnaire, U.S. Atomic Energy Commission, 1966.

The *Independent* article further states that "between 60 and 75 percent of that once reputable newspaper's staff received golden handshakes," and that the Church was then $90 million in debt. Neither of these statements is even approximately true. The *Monitor*'s editorial staff had been reduced from 177 to 103, or by about 42 percent; the Church was entirely debt-free and had about $168 million cash in reserve at the time. "1989 Layoff Summary," data accompanying August 23, 1989, memo from Elizabeth Jenks; Church financial records.

39. *Monitor Month* and Monitor Channel marketing materials.

40. William Bruce Dredge interview; personal observation.

41. *Monitor Month* (January 1990 and July 1991).

42. *Monitor Month* (July 1990). Mandela has also noted that he drew great sustenance during his incarceration from the World Service of the BBC.

Chapter 6. Launch!

1. Cable in the Classroom, coordinated by energetic, politically adept Bobbi Kamil, moved from initial mindless boosterism toward delivering services actually useful to the schools.

2. One other woman, Zadie Hatfield, served briefly as manager of the Publishing Society in the 1970s.

3. Jack Hoagland interview; Netty Douglass interview; Barbara Bellafiore Sanden interview.

4. Estimate courtesy the late David Glickstein, president, Tendrel Associates.

5. Paul Kagan Associates, "Marketing New Media," report, January 20, 1992, p. 1.

6. Personal observations.

7. Scott Goodfellow, first as *World Monitor News* Washington bureau chief, then as Monitor Television's executive vice president, worked skillfully and with considerable success to patch together an embryonic global network carrying the Monitor's television products. Former Ambassador Gil Robinson, based in Washington, D.C., was also made a number of important introductions with respect to international distribution. Coopers & Lybrand's Advanced Technology Group was headed by Helen Ohja, Netty Douglass's whip-smart, hard-driving twin sister.

8. *Monitor Month* (August 1990).

9. *Monitor Month* (October 1991).

10. *Monitor Month* (October 1990 and January 1991).

11. Barbara Bellafiore Sanden presentation notes.

12. Padnos, Ink., positioning statement and strategic plan for the Monitor Channel. The ad agency that produced such brilliant work was Ahern and Hauser of New York.

13. Fleet Associates, Inc., and the Monitor Channel, Inc., Confidential Information Memorandum, February 1991.

14. *Monitor Month* (October 1990 and June 1991); Bruce McCabe telephone interview.

15. *Monitor Month* (November 1990).

16. Florence Tambone, a Boston-area publicist who worked with WQTV before it was purchased by the Church, stayed on to become a close Hoagland–Douglass associate, handling press and public relations for the Publishing Society during Douglass's tenure as manager. Tambone identified "The Silk Road" as a suitable property for the Monitor Channel and arranged for acquisition of its U.S. rights.

17. *Monitor Month* (October 1990).

18. "Monitor World Classroom," distributed under the aegis of the industry's Cable in the Classroom program, was developed and tested in the Boston area prior to the launch of the Monitor Channel through the efforts of this writer, who also set up a project to evaluate the program's effectiveness, undertaken with Dr. Renee Hobbs, then a visiting faculty member at the Harvard School for Education. The vastly improved second-year format and the energetic integration of "Monitor World Classroom" into the Monitor Channel's affiliate sales activities were largely the work of Leah Osterman, a Boston-area specialist in the educational uses of television. The second year's young, racially-mixed hosts, Scott Mercer and Dia Dibble, were an excellent fit with the intended high school audiences. A start had been made with a Spanish-language edition. "Monitor World Classroom" was endorsed by the National Education Association, the American Federation of Teachers, the National School Boards Association, and the National Council of Social Studies.

19. WWOR is a programming service distributed by S.I. Newhouse's Eastern Microwave relay to 13 million scattered households around the United States, Puerto Rico, and the Virgin Islands.

20. "One Norway Street" with host Schuyler Sackett.

21. Jack Hoagland interview; Scott Goodfellow interview; *Monitor Month* (February 1991). The gifted senior producer of *Rodina,* working in Boston, was Tuggelin "Tug" Yourgrau, formerly of WGBH-TV, who also worked at re-shaping other foreign properties for the Monitor Channel, including "The Silk Road" and the Japanese-produced children's serial, "The Mark of the Musketeers."

22. Netty Douglass memo, to all Monitor radio and television staff, "Re: Monitor Broadcast News Standards," March 6, 1991.

The guidelines additionally state: "Monitor broadcasts are not a means to propagate Christian Science. They have no missionary or proselytizing role. Nor do they serve a public relations function for the Church." And further, "The same standards of honesty, fairness, balance, accuracy, completeness, and disinterestedness must apply to our coverage of all issues related to the Christian Science Church itself as to any other issue or story."

23. Personal observation.

24. Uma Pemmaraju was a great favorite with everyone from production staff to management. Mike Sobel, like Malcolm Netburn and Frank McGill at the magazine, found the constraints he was given with regard to ads he could sell acceptable.

Ads and program content alike were surveilled from 1987 to 1992 by a group of self-appointed vigilantes led by Boston-based teacher Glenn Evans, and associated with opposition to the move into television; they reportedly watched WQTV in shifts for violations of their preferences in these matters, and, whenever advertising they felt was offensive was broadcast, saw to it that the station, the Publishing Society, and the Church Directors heard about it.

25. Gail Harris interview.

26. Harry King interviews.

27. Jack Hoagland interview; Netty Douglass interview.

28. Harvey Solomon, "Busy in Boston: Monitor Television Sows Seeds for May Launch of Network," *Cable World* (February 25, 1991); Richard Tedesco, "Monitor's Emerging TV Image," *Cablevision* (February 25, 1991); "Monitor Offers Scholarships in Franchise Area of Ops Launching May 1," *MultiChannel News,* February 28, 1991; "Monitor Seeks Equity Partner," *Cable World* (March 4, 1991); Paul Hemp, "Church Enters Tough Industry with Missionary Zeal," *Boston Globe,* March 24, 1991; Reuters, "Cable Channel Seeks Funds," *New York Times,* March 28, 1991; "Monitor Channel Seeking Investors," *San Diego Union,* March 28, 1991; Richard Walker, "Christian Science Group Seeks Investors for New TV Channel," Reuters, March 29, 1991' Daniel M. Kimmel, "Monitor Empire Looks to Cable as Next Step," *Boston Business Journal* (April 1, 1991); small notices, *Electronic Media* (April 1, 1991) and *Inside Media* (April 3, 1991, and April 8, 1991); Howard Kutz, "Mission or Mistake? TV Splits Church: Subsidized Christian Science Monitor Launching Cable News Channel," *Washington Post,* April 4, 1991; Kim Mitchell, "Monitor Channel Offers Sneak Peek This Week," *MultiChannel News,* April 15, 1991; John Dempsey, "The Monitor Channel Feeling Squeezed at Launch," *Variety,* April 22, 1991; "Monitor Channel Set to Roll: News and Feature Service Begins Several Month Launch," *Broadcasting,* April 29, 1991; short notice in "Media and Marketing" section, *Wall Street Journal,* April 30, 1991; John Dempsey, "Monitor Channel Launch Today," *Variety,* May 1, 1991; "The Christian Science Monitor Comes to TV," *Satellite TV Week;* Harvey Solomon, "Monitor Launches, Expect to Reach 2 Million Homes by Close of June," *Cable World* (May 6, 1991).

29. If numbers given in various records vary, the higher number is always used: $13.5 million in fiscal year 1989, $22.6 million in fiscal year 1990, and $25.9 million in fiscal year 1991.

30. Don Bowersock interview.

31. Don Bowersock interview.

32. Estimated Discovery net dollars to break-even, courtesy former Discovery board member, the late David Glickstein, president, Tendrel Associates. Because none of their programming in their early years involved the expense of original production, the Discovery Channel had reached break-even with a net investment of only $30 million. Near the other end of the spectrum, ABC/Cap Cities' ESPN is said to have spent about $200 million before moving into the black. Estimated CNN net investment to break-even, $133.6 million in current dollars.

CNN's numbers, reconstructed from 1980–1986 annual reports, are given in Table 6.1 with estimates for the following expenses, which were carried for CNN by TBS: the cost of ad sales, cable marketing (estimated at 20 percent of revenues), and transponder fees. See table 6.1.

33. Jack Hoagland interview.

34. The first of these pitched battles had occurred in the mid-1980s, when Hoagland reprinted Irving C. Tomlinson's *Twelve Years with Mary Baker Eddy;* another battle occurred over whether an inexpensive one-volume anthology of Mrs. Eddy's life should be issued to supplement Robert Peel's first-rate but expensive three-volume work.

The central theological issue raised by Bliss Knapp's book, *The Destiny of the Mother Church,* is referred to as a debate over "Mrs. Eddy's place": to wit, was Mary Baker Eddy simply a deeply gifted human being who, after a close and astute reading of the New Testament, had revived Jesus's ancient principle of healing mind and body through spiritual intervention, or was she more specifically like Jesus as he is usually thought of in the Christian tradition—that is, a chosen emissary from a loving God. Bliss Knapp, who counted Monitor editors Roscoe Drummond and Erwin Canham among his many loyal students, was firmly among those who understood Mrs. Eddy to have been

Table 6.1

Cable Network News Start-up Costs

	1980	1981	1982	1983	1984	1985	1986	1987
Reported expenses	23		40	66	70	101	104	96
Revenues	7.2		29*	50	65	86	123	135
Reported operating profit (loss)	(16)	(11)	(16)	(14)	(15)	19	39	45*
Cost of ad sales, cable, marketing	1.4*	5.8*	13.2*	14*	20*	21*	19*	32*
Transponder fees	2*	2*	2*	3*	3*	3*	3*	3*
Full operating profit (loss)	(19.2)*	(18.8)*	(31.2)*	(22)*	(38)*	(5)*	17*	10*

The numbers in brackets are estimates. Capital costs are omitted here.

Estimated net investment to break-even (year 7) = $133.6 million in current dollars.

Estimated net investment to break-even = $186.6 million in 1992 dollars.

Estimated total expenses 1981–1987 = $612.4 million in current dollars.

Estimated total expenses 1981–1987 in 1992 dollars = $859.2 million in 1992 dollars.

Note: Here and elsewhere conversions to constant dollars are made using the U.S. Department of Labor Bureau of Labor Statistics index, obtained courtesy Jesse Thomas, October 13, 1995.

more than merely human. By contrast, to historian Robert Peel and his intellectual circle, the notion that Mrs. Eddy was more than merely human was anathema.

Mrs. Eddy's place is one of four bitterly disputed matters of principle that divide the warring camps. The three other central disputes today turn on archive and publication policies (whether the membership should have access to all of Mrs. Eddy's writings and all of the writings of those who knew her, or only those that are deemed theologically correct), membership policies (whether to let membership shrink to a small "saving remnant" of intellectuals and scholars who will guard Mrs. Eddy's insights, presumably until a more auspicious era, or whether, instead, to seek new members, however un-aggressively, and if so, whether to seek those new members in the Third World), and governance (whether to follow rules set by Mrs. Eddy, specifically the dominant role of a self-perpetuating Church board of directors, or whether to reform).

The board, which backed the attempt to re-position and diversify at the Publishing society from 1982 to 1992, tended to be neutral on the nature of Mrs. Eddy's place; in favor of an open-shelf policy that would gradually make all writings by and about Mrs. Eddy and her work available to the faithful, despite their partly contradictory nature; in favor of reversing the decline in membership if that could be done without aggressive proselytizing, and specifically endorsed welcoming new members from the Third World; and in favor of maintaining church governance as Mrs. Eddy established it, with democratic self-rule at member churches but with enormous power and responsibility vested in the self-perpetuating board of directors at the Mother Church. Personal observation; interviews with Stephen Gottschalk, Jack Hoagland, Harvey Wood; review of written summary above by Earl Foell, Virginia Harris, Richard Nenneman, and John Selover.

35. The Knapp estate trustees and the board reached agreement on June 24, 1991.

36.

Table 6.2

Radio and Television Activities: Report for Twelve Months Ended April 1991 (in millions of dollars)*

	Actual	Budget	Variance
Revenue	$4,439	$7,838	($3,399)
Expense	55,119	43,038	(12,081)
Net cost	50,680	35,200	(15,480)

*May 28 1991.

Expenses in excess of budget include $4.7 million (almost 40 percent of the total variance) was for higher-than-expected Monitor Channel marketing expenses; another $3.8 million (accounting for another 31 percent of the total variance) were costs of overseas coverage, mainly attributable to the Gulf War; and $3.5 (or another 29 percent) went for increased programming costs.

---

37. Don Bowersock enclosure in break-even analysis, "Sources of Funding," December 18, 1990, lists eight alternative sources of funds: contribution from members in response to mailing; use of the Monitor Endowment Fund; use of the Mother Church Endowment Fund; outside investors for Monitor Channel; possible mortgage of short-wave facilities; possible mortgage of Administration and Broadcast buildings; Benevolent Endowment Fund investment in Clearway Street; and the Monitor Endowment

Fund investment in Midtown Hotel property. No recommendation with respect to any of these alternatives was made.

38. By June 1991, Sanden already had either letters of agreement, contracts pending, or signed contracts in hand with nine of the largest twenty-five cable multi-systems operators or MSOs, and with seven of the next twenty-five for carriage in 2.4 million households outside the Greater Boston area; through WQTV, the Monitor Channel reached another 1.3 million cable subscribers. MSOs with early commitments included: ATC, Newhouse, Paragon, Warner, United Artists, Cable American, Coaxial, Columbian International, Greater Media, Hauser, Lenfest, Multivision, Omega, Palmer, Telecable, Tele Media, United Video, and U.S. Cable.

39. Amy Duncan, the newspaper's astute jazz and rock critic, and leader of her own band.

40. Some of the prizes in hand by June 1991 were John Hart's ACE Award for Newscaster of the Year; at the International Film and TV Festival, a bronze medal was awarded to Hart for best anchor, a silver medal to correspondent Net Temko for South African coverage, and a Finalist Certificate for correspondent Martin Gillam for his Special Reports segment on drug enforcement titled, "Colombia's Dirty War"; a National Headliners Award from the Press Club in Atlanta; and three Unity in Media Awards, among others. *Monitor Month* (February and May 1991).

41. "The Filmmaker's Art" list included, among others, *The Grand Illusion, The Discrete Charm of the Bourgeoisie, Open City, My Brilliant Career, 8 1/2, Ashes and Diamonds, The Gold Rush, Ikuru, Woman in the Dunes, Ivan the Terrible, Olympiad, Breathless, Henry V, The Battle of Algiers, Last Year in Marienbad, The River,* and *The Spirit of the Beehive.*

42. Hoagland had kicked off the search for equity partners officially in early 1991, just before launch. Of those in a position to invest, the privately-held Providence Journal Company was among the most attractive for several reasons, including corporate culture, ownership of a number of well-run cable properties, and regional proximity. A few months earlier, in October 1990, the Providence Journal had sold cellular properties in the Southwest to GTE for an estimated $735 million, re-investing an estimated $400 million plus in early 1991 with the purchase of several broadcast TV properties in the Northwest. Approaches were made on the *Monitor*'s behalf both by Bill Clark at Fleet and by Sid Topol, long a friend of Providence Journal's new president, Trygvie Myhren. A visit from the Providence Journal's CFO in June had gone very well indeed.

43. For launch press and other coverage, see note 28.

44. Pete Gatseos' early findings were that the *Monitor*'s ratings were consistently higher than CNBC, FNN, and C-SPAN in the Boston market and on WWOR (October 1990); that an analysis of 112 letters received revealed that half were from women, a quarter from men, and a quarter from children; and that "When all citations are taken together a very clear image of *Monitor* programming emerges that can be broadly described as socially positive" (October 1990). A Simmons' M.B.A. program study he oversaw found that *Monitor* viewers were more upscale than CNN and Headline News viewers and used a greater array of financial services; that they included a significantly higher civic or public affairs constituency; that they favored higher leisure activities such as live theater, reading, and continuing education; and that they traveled more, with particularly high tendency for foreign travel. Also, the fact that Monitor programing had very low commercial clutter—including only seven minutes of advertising per hour instead of the usual fourteen—was of interest to both viewers and some advertisers.

Peter Gatseos interview; Peter Gatseos, "Consumer Demand for Monitor Programming," spring 1991, based in part on Cable Television Advertising and Marketing Association's (CTAM) "Attitude and Usage Study," 1991.

45. Jack Hoagland interview.

Additional sources:

Letter from John Lewis Selover, chairman of the Christian Science board of directors, to Jack Hoagland, April 14, 1989.

Letter from the Christian Science board of directors to Jack Hoagland, June 14, 1990.

Letter from Jack Hoagland, to the Christian Science board of directors, July 16, 1990.

Letter from Stephen Gottschalk to co-workers, March 1, 1990.

Norm Alster, "Netty Douglass's Impossible Task: Racing against Time with Leg Irons on," *Forbes* (September 17, 1990).

Memo from Netty Douglass to all employees, "Re: Response to Article in Forbes Magazine," September 5, 1990.

Memo from Netty Douglass and Jack Hoagland, to radio and television broadcasting staff, "Subject: Taking Our Bearings," September 5, 1990.

Letter from Netty Douglass to James W. Michaels, editor of *Forbes,* September 7, 1990.

Letter from James W. Michaels to Netty Douglass, September 10, 1990.

"The Christian Science Monitor Comes to Television: The Evolution of a Purpose, 1984–1991," Christian Science Publishing Society, 1991.

Richard P. Bond, Thomas P. Griesa, James L. Halferty, "Report of Group Making Inquiry into Finances of the Mother Church," September 16, 1992.

Chapter 7. Clouds

1. Harry King interview; Gail Harris interview; personal observation.

2. Netty Douglass interview; David Cook interview; Danny Wilson interview.

3. Woodstock seminar participants' packet of materials; Sid Topol informal remarks.

4. Cable Operators Survey (commissioned by Gatseos and Associates, executed by Beta Research, Syosset, NY), May 1991. In this survey, the Monitor Channel tied for first place or a little ahead in awareness among new services, in a dead heat with the SciFi Channel, and ahead of Mind Extension University and Court TV. "The Monitor Channel ranked higher than other specific new services on being aggressive promoters of their service." A key which shaped Sanden's tactics: being aggressive in cable sales was reported by the cable operators to be, on balance, a plus, with a significant minority (28 percent) saying aggressive tactics made them more likely to decide to launch a new service.

5. "The Monitor Channel Performance Discount Rate Structure, Effective September 1, 1991: For Period 9/1/91 through 12/31/92," June 28, 1991.

6. Memo from Barbara Bellafiore Sanden to Netty Douglass and Jack Hoagland, "Re: How many eyes are watching?" June 26, 1991; E. Guilfoyle, "The Monitor Channel: Subscriber Actuals vs. Goal: Executive Summary," July 23, 1991.

7. Tim Burditt memo to Sid Topol and Scott Goodfellow, September 19, 1991.

8. Anonymous letter, "Dear Fellow Members of the Mother Church," July 30, 1991; Netty Douglass memo to senior, group, department, and division heads, "Re: Twentieth-Century Biographers Series," August 1, 1991; letter from Beulah M. Roegge,

president of the Board of Education, to Christian Science teachers, "New Items for Your Advance Information," August 2, 1991; Lee Z. Johnson to Librarians of Christian Science Reading Rooms, September 6, 1991; Netty Douglass and Hal M. Friesen to Church members, September 16, 1991.

See also anonymous memo, "To: All Non-Christian Scientists in Monitor TV and Radio Broadcasting, From: Christian Scientists for Honesty, Re: Your role in the purpose of Monitor broadcasting," dated August 12, 1991.

9. Peter F. Drucker, *Managing for Results: Economic Tasks and Risk-Taking Decisions* (New York: Harper and Row, 1964).

10. The Monitor's agreement with the Discovery Channel (dated October 27, 1988) involved the following baseline payments for programming: $1.6 million in year 1, $2.0 million in year 2, $2.4 million in year 3, $2.8 million in year 5, and $3.2 million in year 6.

An October 11, 1990, amendment gave the Publishing Society an additional $100,000 per tenth of a rating point and confirmed that elements of *World Monitor News* programming could be incorporated into other *Monitor* programming, which the Discovery Channel then had the right of first refusal to exhibit. In the fall of 1991, this formula yielded an annual payment of $6.2 million, far more than the Discovery Channel was in the habit of paying for programming, but only about 25 percent of the cost of production. Greg Moyer interview.

11. Personal observation. This activity took place in Monitor MultiMedia, under my direction.

12. *Monitor Month* (November 1991).

13. Positioning statement authored by Sid Topol. An early think-piece is set forth in a memo from Peter Gateos to Topol on "Channel Identity Materials," July 11, 1991.

14. Joan Vennochi, "Money Changes Everything," *Boston Globe,* September 18, 1991.

15. Letter from Jack Hoagland to John S. Driscoll, editor of the *Boston Globe,* September 23, 1991.

16. Joan Vennochi, "Judgment Day," *Boston Globe,* September 25, 1991.

17. Netty Douglass interview.

18. Conversation with Steve Stecklow, staff writer for the *Philadelphia Inquirer.*

19. Jack Hoagland interview.

20. James L. Franklin, "Christian Science Church Defends Book Linked to Bequest," *Boston Globe,* October 13, 1991.

21. Jack Hoagland interview.

22. Terry Ann Knopf, "An Anchor Adrift," *Boston Sunday Globe,* November 10, 1991.

23. Susan Bickelhaupt, "Monitor TV: Hart's 'On Vacation,' " *Boston Globe,* November 12, 1991.

24. Jack Hoagland interview.

25. Personal observation; interviews with Discovery Channel executives Ruth Otte and Greg Moyer.

26. *MultiChannel News,* November 9, 1991.

27. David Cook interview; Ruth Otte interview; Danny Wilson interview.

28. *MultiChannel News,* November 18, 1991.

29. Barbara Bellafiore Sanden memos to staff and correspondence with cable operators; Sanden interview.

30. Barbara Bellafiore Sanden correspondence; Paul Beckelheimer interview.

31. Jack Hoagland interview.

32. Personal observation.

33. Barbara Bellafiore Sanden correspondence; copies of letters of understanding with cable operators; personal observation.

34. Jack Hoagland interview; Stephen Gottschalk interview; Carol Swenson, attorney, interview.

35. *Monitor Month* (December, 1991); Lincoln Bloomfield conversations; personal observation.

36. *Monitor Month* (December 1991); Netty Douglass interview.

37. *Monitor Month* (January 1992).

38. Harry King interview; Lyn Chamberlin interview; personal observation.

39. Harry King interview.

40. Netty Douglass interview; Jack Hoagland interview; Lyn Chamberlin interview.

41. Don Bowersock interviews.

42. Netty Douglass interview; Willis Peligian interview; Lyn Chamberlin interview.

43. Jack Hoagland interviews; Don Bowersock interviews; *Monitor* contract with the Discovery Channel.

44. Jack Hoagland interviews; Don Bowersock interviews; Netty Douglass interview.

45. Don Bowersock, December 5, 1991, handwritten note with four pages of numbers projecting expenses for each of the Publishing Society's media operations forward to the end of the fiscal year.

46. Netty Douglass business diary; Netty Douglass interview.

47. Barbara Bellafiore Sanden memos to Jack Hoagland, December 1991.

48. Netty Douglass business diary; Netty Douglass interview; David Cook interview.

49. Netty Douglass business diary; Netty Douglass interview; Don Bowersock confidential memo to Harvey W. Wood, John Lewis Selover, Richard C. Bergenheim, Olga Chaffee, Virginia S. Harris; copies to Jack Hoagland, Netty Douglass, Tim Burditt, Nan Leatherwood, Harley Gates, Arthur D. Pinkham Jr., "Re: Financial Statement Combining All Television and Radio Activities for the Seven Months Ended November 30, 1991," December 23, 1991.

50. Netty Douglass business diary; Netty Douglass interview; David Cook interview; Lyn Chamberlin interview; Harry King interview; Willis Peligian interview.

51. "The Christian Science Monitor Asset Evaluation," January 15, 1992, covering all media.

52. Netty Douglass business diary; "TCSPS/CSMS Net Results," January 22, 1992, document probably prepared by Don Bowersock, section on "potential sources" (of additional funds).

53. Don Bowersock memo to all employees, February 7, 1992; Douglass had announced a hiring freeze in a January 3, 1992, memo to senior managers.

54. Barbara Bellafiore Sanden interview and files of correspondence; *The Monitor Channel Sales Status Report: Top 100 MSOs,* January 31, 1992.

55. The Monitor's talks with the Providence Journal, initiated by Sid Topol and Fleet executive and Hoagland son-in-law Bill Clark, had got under way the previous June. Several cordial on-site visits by Providence Journal's four top executives followed, with the Chief Financial Officer Jim Stack returning particularly enthusiastic. Jack Hoagland, Netty Douglass interviews; Steve Hamblett and Trygvie Myhren interviews; Bill Clark letter to Trygvie Myhren, June 26, 1991; Jack Hoagland letter to Hamblett, August 13, 1991; draft agreement, January 10, 1992.

Providence Journal Chairman Steve Hamblett was, by his own account, attracted to a Monitor partnership by three elements: above all, by the quality of the enterprise, including the international fare; second, by the prospect of "marrying" print and television at the editorial level; and third, by the fact that the two organizations both had long championed the same sorts of journalistic goals.

56. James L. Franklin, "A Christian Science Dispute: Four Editors Quit Following Publication of Book on Church's Founder," *Boston Globe,* February 26, 1992. The resignations were pointedly not linked to the simultaneous delay in settling the Knapp

bequest, which was reported in a 200–word mention in the Economy section (Joan Vennochi, "Downtown Crossing," February 26, 1992).

57. Stories and word counts from a Nexus search.

58. Stories and word counts from a Nexus search.

59. A number of former *Monitor* staffers say they took it upon themselves to send letters to the editor of the *Globe* protesting the coverage, though none was ever published; this writer did, naively assuming that those making decisions at the *Globe* had not noticed the great value of the work being done at the Monitor's television operations.

Still another explanation offered was rooted in the *Globe*'s—and Tom Winship's—past, in which the fight to defeat the *Monitor* could be seen as a warped reenactment of the *Globe*'s successful crusade in the 1950s and 1960s to bring down the once-mighty *Boston Herald Traveler* by challenging its control over Boston's Channel 5. Back then, the *Globe* (still under Winship's father) put an ace reporter on the case, who came up with proof of corrupt dealings with the FCC, which after fifteen years of legal and bureaucratic delays eventually did cause the station to change hands. In this fight, the *Globe* used its privileged position as a newspaper to undertake aggressive investigative reporting of the wrongful dealings of a business rival; by taking the high moral ground against that flawed adversary, the paper also reaped significant corporate advantage in the process. See J. Anthony Lukas, *Common Ground: A Turbulent Decade in the Lives of Three American Families* (New York: Vintage Books, 1985), especially pages 485–486; Sterling Red Quinlan, *The Hundred Million Dollar Lunch: The Broadcasting Industry's Own Watergate* (Chicago: J. Philip O'Hara, 1974); and Jack Thomas, "Did Boston's 'Herald Traveler' Have To Fail?" *Columbia Journalism Review* (July–August 1972).

60. "Boston Globe Parent Posts 58% Decline in 2nd-Quarter Net," *Wall Street Journal,* July 22, 1991; "Affiliated Publications Will Sell Majority Stake in Publishing Unit," *Wall Street Journal,* November 27, 1991, noting "The sale [of *Billboard* magazine] comes as speculation continues that the venerable New England Daily is being quietly shopped around"; Mitchell Zuckoff, "Affiliated Holder May Seek Changes," *Boston Globe,* November 28, 1991.

61. Affiliated Publications was taken public in 1973 to finance the *Globe*'s relocation to new headquarters and the installation of a state-of-the-art printing plant. In 1988, Affiliated sold an interest in McCaw Cellular Communications for $2.6 billion and distributed the proceeds to shareholders. By 1991, the company had divested itself of all significant properties except the *Globe*. By the beginning of 1991, the *Globe*'s earnings had fallen for three years.

Table 7.1

Affiliated Publications, 1988–1992 (in millions of dollars)

	1988	1989	1990	1991	1992
Revenues	446.5	438.2	416.0	392.8	414.0
Operating income	92.4	79.0	52.1	30.1	50.9
Depreciation	18.2	18.3	19.6	19.6[*] est.	19.6[*]
Amortization	0.4	0.4	0.4	0.4[*] est.	0.4[*]
Net income	16 .3	24.2	(66.9)	14.1	

Source: Except as noted the numbers were taken from Affiliated's 10–K forms and represent millions of dollars.

[*]Figures omitted in 10–K; estimate used is 1990 figure.

In April 1991, the *Globe* started an attrition program to cut 100 white-collar jobs and reduced the space dedicated to news for a newsprint savings of $1 million per year (*Wall Street Journal*, April 26, 1991). The next month, the paper announced it might buy out some management contracts to cut costs further (*Wall Street Journal*, May 3, 1991), and in the same month, Affiliated discontinued its annual report, to save $250,000 (*Wall Street Journal*, May 16, 1991). Affiliated's second quarter revenues fell 58 percent over the same quarter the previous year (*Wall Street Journal*, July 21, 1991), then in the third quarter fell 125 percent and lost $1 million (*Wall Street Journal*, October 18, 1991), ending 1991 with a net loss of $970,000 (*Wall Street Journal*, February 7, 1992). In August, Affiliated's chairman denied rumors published the day before in *Boston Herald* that a buyer was being sought for the *Globe* (John H. Kennedy, "No Sale Discussions, Globe Says: Report of Negotiations Fuels Interest on Wall Street," *Boston Globe*, August 16, 1991).

In November, Affiliated sold its interest in a specialty publishing group, leaving the *Globe* its only major holding, amid rumors heard since the previous summer than the newspaper was being "quietly shopped around" . . . but "analysts say that with *Globe* earnings down sharply, it is unlikely the company could fetch the rumored $1 billion asking price." (*Wall Street Journal*, November 27, 1991). The next day, Affiliated's third-largest shareholder (after the two family trusts), Southeastern Management Inc. of Memphis, announced its intention to seek changes in *Globe* management or the sale of the company (Mitchell Zuckoff, "Affiliated Holder May Seek Changes," *Boston Globe*, November 28, 1991).

See also Michael Fritz, "Boston's accidental demibillionaires," *Forbes* (October 23, 1989); and John Strahinich, "The Tinkering Taylors," *Boston Magazine* (September 1992).

62. "Business, Briefly: Fanning to Fill Globe Director Seat," *Boston Globe*, January 24, 1992.

63. Danny Wilson interview.

Additional sources:

Christian Science board of directors, "Addenda to Bliss Knapp Memo," November 1, 1974.

Netty Douglass, "Synergy That Works," remarks to the Third Annual EPM Entertainment Marketing Conference, Los Angeles, October 28, 1991.

Stephen Gottschalk, "Honesty, Blasphemy and the Destiny of the Mother Church," *The Christian Century*, November 6, 1991.

Bliss Knapp letters to the Christian Science board of directors, January 31, 1947, January 11, 1949, and March 7, 1951.

Mailing Fund, Boston, MA, including "Destiny and Disobedience: A Chronology of the Knapp Controversy" and other documents, mailed June 1993.

Catherine G. Runner, corresponding secretary of the Christian Science board of directors, letter to Mr. Bliss Knapp, February 20, 1948.

Carol Swenson, Senior University Counsel of Stanford University, memo to Stephen Gottschalk, "Re: Eloise M. Knapp and Bella Mabury Trusts," April 13, 1992.

Carol Swenson telephone interview, December 1995.

Chapter 8. Collapse

1. "Treasurer's Financial Narrative, Fiscal Year 1991/92: Nine Months (May 1, 1991–January 31, 1992)," Report 04–B-1, February 27, 1992, distributed to: the Chris-

tian Science board of directors (five members), the finance committee (four members), D. Bowersock, A. Pinkham, Jr., A. Douglass, H. Gaes, J. Gilmore, K. Benedict-Gill.

2. Hoagland and Wood suspected that Franklin's source was a member of the finance committee, perhaps acting through an intermediary, who went on to resign on May 12, aligning himself with the opposition.

3. James L. Franklin, "Christian Science Church Defends Publishing Book Linked to Bequest," *Boston Globe,* October 13, 1991.

4. The Church's use of that portion of its general funds that were designated as a pension reserve to support the Publishing Society's activities in 1992 was, it would seem, redundantly legal. While religious organizations are not required to set up pension plans for employees at all, if they do, as the Mother Church did some sixty years ago, the legal obligation is simply to fulfill the contractual commitment—that is, to pay retirees when payments are due. The law does not require religious organizations to set aside money in "trust" for such a purpose, and the Church has not done so. Such obligations, although voluntarily undertaken, are binding once they are assumed, and the law will intervene if—and only if—at some point these obligations are not honored. Since no payments had ever been missed over the decades, no breach of agreement had occurred.

The Church's borrowing from the pension fund and from two separate smaller trusts was at prime or prime-plus interest in every case.

But did the Church's use of funds in the winter of 1992 put its ability to meet its future obligations to retirees in jeopardy? According to the actuarial norms and legal standards governing such matters in corporate life, it did not.

As part of the reforms of the early 1980s, the Church engaged an independent actuary to track its obligations to retirees year to year. Given fluctuating stock and real estate values, a pension fund was created within the general fund, as an accounting device to track the level of assets needed at any specific time to meet obligations to retirees according to their changing numbers and ages, for ten, twenty, and thirty years into the future. Total future obligations to retirees and the assets needed to meet them were calculated according to the same formula used by corporations whose pension plans were governed by federal law under the Employee Retirement Income Security Act of 1974 (ERISA). Using this formula, assets deemed necessary to meet all future obligations to all retirees would have amounted to $100–$110 million in 1992 dollars, spread out over the next thirty or forty years.

Because of the way these obligations are set up, the Church's retirees have a far broader legal claim on the organization's assets than do the employees of conventional corporations. The Church's liability is not limited to funds in a trust or in any separate account, which, when exhausted, exhaust the legal recourse of retirees seeking to collect benefits, as in the case of a normal corporation. In the Church's case, liability would extend to all its assets and all future income from any source. In February 1992, the Church's total restricted and unrestricted funds were $60–$65 million, its total debt-free real estate holdings were worth about $100 million in 1992 dollars, and its expected income from all sources remained in the neighborhood of $60–$70 million annually.

In sum, under fiscal and legal guidelines governing corporations, which the Church was not required to meet, its ability to meet its obligations to retirees was not in jeopardy during the cash flow crisis of the winter of 1992. Assets sufficient to meet all future obligations were available. (Beyond the February–March crisis and borrowings, costs associated with shutting down the Monitor Channel would be met with further borrowings from the pension fund but, again, without jeopardizing payment of current or future pensions by any legal or normal business standards).

In meeting the 1991–1992 cash crisis, the Church also borrowed from two smaller separate funds: the Endowment Fund for the *Christian Science Monitor,* set up in 1978 under the editorship of John Hughes, and the trust under the will of Mary Baker Eddy, administered by the probate court in New Hampshire. In both cases, borrowings were reviewed in advance by outside counsel.

Conversations with Church attorney, Gary Jones; with outside counsel at Finnegan, Hickey, Dinsmoor, and Johnson; and with the Office of the Massachusetts Attorney General. See also Marc Gertner, ed., *Trustees Handbook: A Basic Text on Labor–Management Employee Benefit Plans,* especially Section 6; "Memorandum: Endowment Fund for the Christian Science Monitor," Legal Department, July 7, 1978, and materials sent to members soliciting contributions; Brian G. Pennix, general counsel, "Memorandum Re: Purchase of Satellite Transponder," (August 21, 1990); letters from George H. Kidder, of Hemenway & Barnes, to Brian G. Pennix, December 14, 1990, and January 18, 1991; letter from Donald Bowersock to retirees, April 22, 1991; "Treasurer's Financial Narrative, Fiscal Year 1991/92: Nine Months (May 1, 1991–January 31, 1992)," February 26, 1992; letter from Donald Bowersock to members, January 1992; memorandum from Donald Bowersock, to all employees, "Subject: Borrowing From Church Funds," March 3, 1992; "Pension Reserve: Estimated Use for Ongoing and Discontinued Operations, Exhibit V," treasurer's office; memorandum from the board of directors to all employees, retirees and members, April 15, 1992; letter from twenty-two members to board of directors, April 18, 1992; letter to retirees from twenty-two members, April 16, 1992; letter to directors and managing treasurer from George H. Cole, Jr., attorney with Jackson, Tufts, Cole, and Black in San Jose, CA, on behalf of eleven members; "A Report to Members from the Office of the Treasurer," annual meeting, June 8, 1992; Richard P. Bond, Judge Thomas P. Griesa, James L. Halferty, "Report of Group Making Inquiry into Finances of the Mother Church," September 16, 1992; "A Report to Members from the Office of the Treasurer on the Year Ended April 30, 1993 (Fiscal 1993)," delivered at annual meeting, June 7, 1993.

5. James L. Franklin, "Christian Science Borrowing Stirs Alarm," *Boston Globe,* March 1, 1992, and "Pension Fund of Church Has Fallen Too Low, Says Member," *Boston Globe,* March 2, 1992.

6. Conversations with personnel at the office of the Massachusetts Attorney General.

7. Ibid.

8. James L. Franklin, "Christian Science Retirees Criticize Use of Pension Fund," *Boston Globe,* March 3, 1992.

9. Philip Bennett, "TV Glitch Puts More Heat on Science Church," *Boston Globe,* March 3, 1992.

10. Philip Bennett and James L. Franklin, "Dissent Marked Broadcasting Attempt from Start," *Boston Globe,* March 10, 1992.

11. Memo "To All Employees of the Publishing Society from the Board of Trustees and Manager, Re: Television Broadcasting of the *Christian Science Monitor,*" March 9, 1992; "Memorandum from The Christian Science Board of Directors To All Employees, March 9, 1992."

12. James L. Franklin, "Church Officials Defend Loan from Pension Plan," *Boston Globe,* March 4, 1992.

13. Steve Hamblett said in an interview that a *Globe* reporter pursued him and other executives relentlessly by phone during this period, asking for reactions to the *Globe*'s articles on the Monitor and inquiring whether Providence Journal intended to proceed with the investment under discussion anyway; John Strahinich in "The Tinkering Taylors," *Boston Magazine,* September 1992, identifies the *Globe* reporter and business writer, Paul Hemp, as a Winship protégé.

14. Margaret Rennie, "Speaking the Truth in Love," letter submitted in obedience to Art. I, Sect. 9, of the *Manual of the Mother Church,* March 1992, in six sections. Section

I criticizes publication of the Knapp book because it "misstates our Leader's teachings." Section II deals with finances, attacking the media investments of the previous decade specifically, and asserting that leadership had been less than completely honest about the lack of fit between projections and results overall. Section III was devoted primarily to criticizing television's editorial content, including specific programs as well as advertising; the difference between homes reached and actual audience size in cable was cited there, as elsewhere, as evidence of the directors' and Jack Hoagland's intention to mislead. Section IV documented leadership's ambivalence toward the failing newspaper and the search for new formulas in the 1980s, again as evidence of bad character on the part of the reformers. Sections V and VI put forward the author's alternative version of Mrs. Eddy's vision.

To a respectful outsider such as this author, the substantive matters raised in this complaint and other opposition materials are apt to balance upon a single procedural point and that is the question of legitimacy: who legitimately decides what is doctrinally correct in this organization? And who legitimately defines and oversees the range of its activities? Other questions are secondary: what Mrs. Eddy really meant, whether she was consistent in all matters at all times, and whether what she said or wrote (however interpreted) can or should be the last word; whether the system of governance Mrs. Eddy set up is sacrosanct, or not wholly adequate; what level of financial risk is comfortable; what the nature of the Church's commitment to journalism is or should be. Again, to this outsider, it seems that these matters are too "hot" for most Church members to confront directly, and so strongly held differences of opinion are displaced, and misplaced, into highly personal attacks on those with whom one has disagreements. To put the procedural and doctrinal disputes dividing the Christian Science movement in perspective, one need only note their similarity to the divisions in other contemporary Christian communities searching—often contentiously—for a workable mix of continuity and change.

15. What follows is based on these sources: Harvey Wood interview; Jack Hoagland interview; Netty Douglass interview; Netty Douglass business journal.

16. James L. Franklin, "Christian Science Membership Sees Crisis of Identity," *Boston Sunday Globe,* March 8, 1992.

17. Don Bowersock interview; Netty Douglass interview; Netty Douglass business journal.

18. Jack Hoagland interview.

19. Harvey Wood interview; Jack Hoagland interview; Netty Douglass interview; Netty Douglass business journal.

20. David Cook's notes.

21. David Cook's notes.

22. Remarks summarized in "Memorandum from the Christian Science Board of Directors To All Employees, March 9, 1992;" Memorandum, "From the Board of Trustees and Manager of the Publishing Society, To: All Employees of the Publishing Society; Re: Television Broadcasting and the Christian Science Monitor," March 9, 1992.

23. James L. Franklin, "Strong Leaders Put Church on Media Path," "Christian Scientists to Sell Network, Reorganize: Reshuffling Replaces Man in Top Posts"; Paul Hemp, "Monitor TV Buyer May Be Tough to Find"; Philip Bennett and James L. Franklin, "Dissent Marked Broadcasting Attempt From Start"; Ed Siegel, "Cable effort took poor aim"; all in *Boston Globe,* March 10, 1992.

24. "The Group," WGBH-TV, March 10, 1992. Participants included James L. Franklin, Terri Ann Knopf, Steven Simurda (a determined critic of the *Monitor's* diversification), Arthur Cohen (a local television producer), and Robert Bergenheim (former Manager of the Publishing Society and former publisher of *Boston Herald,* no longer a Church member himself but father of Church director Richard Bergenheim).

25. John Higgins, financial editor of *MultiChannel News,* quoted in Paul Hemp's "Monitor TV Buyer May Be Tough to Find," *Boston Globe,* March 10, 1992. It was Winship protégé Hemp who badgered Providence Journal management with telephone calls demanding to know whether, given revelations that seemed to point to fiscal mismanagement or worse published in the Globe, they still intended to proceed with the planned investment; John Stahinich, "Not Ready for Prime Time," *Boston Magazine,* July 1992; Steve Hamblett, Trygvie Myhren joint interview.

26. Netty Douglass interview; Tim Burditt interview. Douglass's new plan was reviewed by Fleet and published as "The Monitor Channel: Confidential Information Memorandum," Fleet Associates, March 1992.

27. Interview with Steve Hamblett and Trygvie Myhren.

28. The evidence available suggests that the Monitor Channel would have been able to attract audiences and advertisers in sufficient numbers to allow it eventually to become profitable. Ratings in the Boston market (WQTV) and on WOR (distributed by microwave relay as a partial channel to some 13 million homes) were consistently higher than CNBC, FNN, and C-SPAN. Gatseos and Associates, "Insights on Positioning the Monitor Channel to Consumers," April 8, 1992; Gatseos and Associates, memo summarizing research, February 27, 1992; "A Survey of WQTV Viewer Attitudes: March, April, May 1992," Monitor Television staff; Gatsos and Associates, "Channel Line-up and Content Analysis," January 1990; Gatseos and Associates, "Lowering Costs while Increasing Quality," fall 1991, including analysis of competitive previews in three markets; Gatseos and Associates, "Consumer Demand for Monitor Programming," spring 1991; "Reaching Active Citizens with the Monitor Channel," a presentation of Simmons Market Research Bureau findings in the Boston market, fall 1990.

29. William Bruce Dredge interview; Willis Peligian interview; Netty Douglas interview.

30. James L. Franklin, "Church Members Demand Accounting," March 11, 1992; Frederic M. Biddle, "Can the Monitor Regain Past Glory?" March 13, 1992; James L. Franklin, "Christian Scientists Refuse Entry to Former Editors," "Church Must Borrow, Sources Say: Christian Science Monthly Spending Reported to Be Twice That of Income," and "Many in Church Begin Open Critique of Policy," *Boston Globe,* March 27, 1992.

31. Netty Douglass interviews and business journal; Jack Hoagland interviews.

32. Tim Burditt interview.

33. Netty Douglass interview.

34. James L. Franklin, "Mailings Rap Christian Science's Officials: Teachers Say Church Survival at Stake," April 14, 1992; Tom Coakley, "Staffers bid farewell, as live programming ceases," April 16, 1992; James L. Franklin, "Church Officials Quit Media Posts," April 18, 1992; James L. Franklin, "Auditor's Warning to Church Deleted," April 19, 1992; James L. Franklin, "At the Hub of Church Controversy," April 23, 1992; James L. Franklin, "Church Mulled, Rejected Continuing TV," May 2, 1992; "Church Denies Directors Mulled Reviving Channel," May 4, 1992; James L. Franklin, "Official Says Church Spent $14–$15 M from Fund," May 13, 1992; James L. Franklin, "Citing Unheeded Warnings, Church Official Resigns," May 15, 1992; James L. Franklin, "Church Lawyer Called Fund Use Wrong," May 16, 1992; Daniel Golden, "Can Mary Baker Eddy's Church Heal Itself?" May 17, 1992; James L. Franklin, "Fiscal Needs Lead Church to Seek Sale of TV Station," May 18, 1992; James L. Franklin, "Christian Science Was Set Aside at Monitor Radio, TV," May 26, 1992; James L. Franklin, "Eddy Book's Withdrawal Pondered by Church Heads," May 29, 1992, all stories appeared in the *Boston Globe.*

35. "Fanning to fill *Globe* director seat," *Boston Globe,* January 24, 1992; formal

notice of Fanning's nomination and her ownership of 7,400 shares of A-stock appeared in Affiliated Publications, Inc., "Notice of 1992 Annual Meeting of Stockholders: May 20, 1992," Boston, April 6, 1992. Affiliated annual shareholders' meeting was held on May 21, 1992.

36. Tim Burditt interview; Barbara Sanden interview; Sid Topol conversations.

37. Conversations with Virginia Harris and John Selover.

38. Willis Peligian interview; William Bruce Dredge interview; Sid Topol conversations.

39. William Bruce Dredge interview; Sid Topol, Virginia Harris, and John Selover conversations.

40. James L. Franklin, "Church Said to Get Three Bids for Cable System," June 3, 1992; "Science Church to Cut Workers, Shut Cable TV," June 5, 1992; "Ex-Officials Troubled by Church's Big Spending," June 7, 1992; and "Church to Open Meeting; Christian Science Goal: Talk, Healing," June 8, 1992, all stories appeared in the *Boston Globe*.

41. Personal observation.

42. Shay Studley, "Annual Meeting Fails to Reassure Everyone about Future of Church," June 9, 1992; James L. Franklin, "Church Gives Grim Fiscal News: After Unity Plea, Christian Scientists Hear of TV Costs," June 9, 1992; and "Science Church Not Heeding Call to Address Funds Shortage," June 18, 1992; all articles appeared in the *Boston Globe*.

Chapter 9. Perspective

1. Auletta, *Three Blind Mice;* Boyer, *Who Killed CBS?*; Frank, *Out of Thin Air.*

2. MacNeil/Lehrer, in which Gannett briefly held an interest in the 1970s, was subsequently wholly owned by Robert MacNeil and Jim Lehrer until MacNeil's retirement in 1995; at that time, Liberty Media, a subsidiary of cable giant TCI, purchased two-thirds of the company for an undisclosed sum. Laurence Jarvik, *PBS: Behind the Screen* (Rocklin, CA: Forum, 1997). For a critique of MacNeil/Lehrer's editorial policies, see *Extra!: A Publication of FAIR* (Fairness & Accuracy in Reporting), Special Issue (winter 1990).

3. See John Stranhinich, "Not Ready for Prime Time," *Boston Magazine* (July 1992); Netty Douglass, "Synergy that Works," remarks to the Third Annual EPM Entertainment Marketing Conference, October 28, 1991.

4. Network news budgets are never published, and even privately obtained annual figures give little indication of exactly what is included as part of a given news division's costs, programming product, or revenues. ABC's John Fitzgerald and others were helpful in confirming the general orders of magnitude.

5. Combining six iterations of a working model generated by the Monitor's entrepreneurs and their advisers and amending their assumptions to show annual programming costs of $55 million and total costs of about $85 million (by including marketing, ad sales, transmission costs, and so forth) suggests a net investment to break-even of $360 to $400 million over about seven or eight years. Assuming annual programming costs of $75 million, which seems a more realistic figure, investment to break-even becomes just under $500 million, with break-even in year ten. See chapter 6, note 32 (table 6.1) for CNN's start-up numbers.

Monitor Channel draft plans, October 8, 1990 and November 1, 1990; Tendrel Associates (David Glickstein) high and low estimates, December 24, 1990; Fleet Associates, "The Monitor Channel, Inc.: Confidential Information Memorandum," February 1991; and Fleet Associates, "The Monitor Channel: Confidential Information Memorandum," March 1992.

6. "Sports Illustrated: A 40–Year Perspective," Sports Illustrated Communications, courtesy Dave Mingey, senior publicist; Dean Foust, "What's Black and White and Blue and Yellow—And Less in the Red? A More Serious USA Today Could Get Its first Taste of Profits This Year," *Business Week* (July 12, 1993). The *Atlantic Monthly* is subsidized by businessman Mort Zuckerman and *Harper's* by a foundation established for that purpose.

7. A Donaldson, Lufkin & Jenrette analyst's estimate of Turner's combined news operations (CNN and Headline News Network) in millions of dollars for 1991 was $476 million in revenues, offset by $319 million in operating costs, leaving an operating profit of $158 million.

8. "Murdoch Takes Aim at 'Leftists'," *Business Week* (February 12, 1996).

9. Both men made important points. Sid Topol stressed the fact that to secure maximum cable distribution, the Monitor Channel had to differentiate itself from CNN. Danny Wilson was enthusiastic about creating a strong inventory of documentaries not only because he felt they were worthwhile communications, but also since they could be re-broadcast periodically for two, three, or four years, they were more economical than a steady diet of breaking news in the long run.

The communications industry honored both "World Monitor News" and the Monitor Channel with a long list of major awards. These included an Emmy for Best Public Affairs Series (1991) from the New England Academy of Television Arts and Sciences; Best News Documentary/Special, Best Public Affairs Program, Best News Anchor (Gail Harris) from the International Film and TV Festival of New York (1991); a National Emmy for Outstanding Informational, Cultural or Historical Programming (for stories reported from the former Soviet Union); the Maggie Award (Planned Parenthood Foundation) for "Women with AIDS" (1991); Award for Cable Excellence (ACE), to John Hart as Newscaster of the Year; and many others, including numerous awards for graphics and design.

10. A growing literature is beginning to document some disturbing effects. Two complementary perspectives are furnished by Robert D. Putnam, "The Strange Disappearance of Civic America," *The American Prospect* (winter 1996), and Byron Reeves and Clifford Nass, *The Media Equation: How People Treat Computers, Television and New Media Like Real People and Places* (Stanford: CSLI Publications, Center for the Study of Language and Information, 1996).

Chapter 10. Epilogue Notes

1. Alfred C. Sikes, "Monday Memo: The Eight Blindspots of TV News Have Left Us Poorly Informed," *Broadcasting* (May 11, 1992).

2. Jack Hoagland interview; Mort Sahl interview; Gail Harris interview.

3. *Wall Street Journal,* June 11, 1993.

4. James L. Franklin, "Monitor Channel Is Missed," *Boston Globe,* April 24, 1994.

5. *Boston Globe,* May 9, 1994.

6. Mark Jurkowitz, "Making the Monitor Matter," *Boston Globe,* August 6, 1997.

7. The Providence Journal's cable partners in the Food Channel were Landmark Communications, Scripps-Howard, Continental Cablevision and the Tribune Broadcasting Company. Providence Journal acted as lead investor and managing partner. "Providence Journal Co. Serves Up Food Net," *MultiChannel News,* January 18, 1993; the *Wall Street Journal,* November 23, 1995, September 27, 1996, and September 30, 1996.

8. Stanford University and the Los Angeles County Museum agreed to settle the Knapp bequest out of court in 1993, but Church members in opposition to the Church's

policies, challenging the Knapp trustees' right to settle, kept the case tied up in California until October 1995. The money was disbursed in fiscal year 1996 (see table 10.1 below), with 53 percent, or about $53 million, going to the Church and 23.5 percent each going to Stanford and the Museum.

Those joining the Church with the friend-of-the-court brief in the *Weaver v. Harvey Wood et al.* case challenging Church governance were Americans United for Separation of Church and State; American Jewish Congress; James E. Andrews, Clerk of the General Assembly of the Presbyterian Church (United States); Baptist Joint Committee on Public Affairs; Church of Jesus Christ of Latter-Day Saints; Church of the Nazarene; Christian Legal Society; Episcopal Diocese of Massachusetts, Inc. (by its bishop, the Right Reverend Thomas M. Shaw, S.S.J.E.); Evangelical Lutheran Church in America; General Conference of Seventh-Day Adventists; Massachusetts Council of Churches; National Association of Evangelicals; National Council of the Churches of Christ in the USA; New England Conference of the United Methodist Church; Reorganized Church of Jesus Christ of Latter-Day Saints; Unitarian Universalist Association; United States Catholic Conference; and Worldwide Church of God.

Having twice been denied standing by unanimous decision in the Massachusetts Supreme Judicial Court (Case No. 07156), the Church members mounting this challenge engaged star Harvard Law School litigator Lawrence Tribe in an attempt to get the United States Supreme Court to hear the case. On January 12, 1998, the United States Supreme Court also refused, unanimously and without comment, to hear the case, thus allowing the Massachusetts Supreme Judicial Court's 1997 decision to remain.

Who has been funding these costly legal actions is unclear.

Table 10.1

Church Finances, 1992–1997 (in millions of dollars)

	Income	Expenses*	Funds on Hand**			
			Total	Restricted	Unreserved	Pension Reserve
FY91–92	70	215***	(11)	104	(115)	135
FY92–93	77	77	64	27	111	(84)
FY93–94	75	75	63	45	116	(71)
FY94–95	87	87	64	68	124	(57)
FY95–96	137	137	64	140	135	5
FY96–97	93	93	75****	155	129	26

Source: Numbers for 91–92, 92–93, 93–94 are as reported to annual meetings by John Selover, Church Director and Treasurer; numbers for 95–96 and 96–97 are the same, except that they are converted from new federal reporting requirements back to comparable series by extending the old way of accounting, as per October 14, 1997 telephone conversation with Harley Gates, Church treasurer's office.

*Including capital expenditures.

**"Funds on hand" is used in Church Treasurer's reports to mean more or less liquid assets.

***Figure includes $69 million in anticipated severance payments.

****Includes $7 million in one-time expenses for shutting down MonitoRadio.

Abbreviated Bibliography

Abbot, Willis J. *Watching the World Go By.* Boston: Little, Brown, 1934.

Auletta, Ken. *Three Blind Mice: How the TV Networks Lost Their Way.* New York: Vintage Books, 1991.

Barnouw, Erik. *A Tower of Babel: A History of Broadcasting in the United States to 1933.* New York: Oxford University Press, 1966.

————. *The Golden Web: A History of Broadcasting in the United States, 1933–1953.* New York: Oxford University Press, 1968.

————. *The Image Empire: A History of Broadcasting in the United States from 1953.* New York: Oxford University Press, 1970.

————. *Tube of Plenty: The Evolution of American Television.* 2d rev. ed. New York: Oxford University Press, 1990.

Beasley, Norman. *The Cross and the Crown: The History of Christian Science.* Boston: Little, Brown, 1952.

Bibb, Porter. *Ted Turner's Amazing Story: It Ain't As Easy As It Looks.* New York: Crown, 1993.

Bliss, Edward Jr. *Now the News: The Story of Broadcast Journalism.* New York: Columbia University Press, 1991.

Boyer, Peter J. *Who Killed CBS? The Undoing of America's Number One News Network.* New York: St. Martin's Press, 1988.

Canham, Erwin D. *Commitment to Freedom: The Story of the Christian Science Monitor.* Boston: Houghton Mifflin, 1958.

The Carnegie Commission Report, *A Public Trust: The Landmark Report of the Carnegie Commission on the Future of Broadcasting.* New York: Bantam, 1979.

Clabes, Judith G., ed. *New Guardians of the Press: Selected Profiles of America's Woman Newspaper Editors.* New York: Scholastic Blue Ribbon Group, 1983.

Drucker, Peter F. *Managing for Results: Economic Tasks and Risk-Taking Decisions.* New York: Harper and Row, 1964.

Dunn, Ruben J., and John Morris. *The Crash Put Simply: October, 1987.* New York: Praeger, 1988.

Eddy, Mary Baker. *Science and Health with Key to the Scriptures.* Boston: First Church of Christ, Scientist, 1875.

————. *Miscellaneous Writings, 1883–1896.* Boston: First Church of Christ, Scientist, 1896.

Fallows, James. *Breaking the News: How the Media Undermine American Democracy.* New York: Pantheon Books, 1996.

Frank, Reuven. *Out of Thin Air: The Brief Wonderful Life of Network News.* New York: Simon and Schuster, 1991.

Friendly, Fred W. *Due to Circumstances Beyond Our Control*. New York: Vintage Books, 1967.

Gertner, Marc, Ed. *Trustees Handbook: A Basic Text on Labor-Management Employee Benefit Plans*. 4th ed. Brookfield, WI: International Foundation of Employee Benefit Plans, 1990.

Gottschalk, Stephen. *The Emergence of Christian Science in American Religious Life*. Berkeley: University of California Press, 1973.

Halberstam, David. *The Powers That Be*. New York: Alfred A. Knopf, 1979.

Head, Sydney W., and Christopher H. Sterling. *Broadcasting in America: A Survey of Electronic Media*. 5th ed. Boston: Houghton Mifflin, 1987.

Hilliard, Robert L., and Michael C. Keith. *The Broadcast Century: A Biography of American Broadcasting*. Stoneham, MA: Butterworth Heinemann, 1992.

Jarvik, Laurence. *PBS: Behind the Screen*. Rocklin, CA: Forum, 1997.

Knapp, Bliss. *The Destiny of the Mother Church*. Boston: Christian Science Publishing Society, 1947.

Lukas, J. Anthony. *Common Ground: A Turbulent Decade in the Lives of Three American Families*. New York: Vintage Books, 1985.

Lyndon, Donlyn. *The City Observed: Boston; A Guide to the Architecture of the Hub*. New York: Random House, 1982.

Peel, Robert. *Christian Science: Its Encounter with American Culture*. New York: Henry Holt, 1958.

————. *Health and Medicine in the Christian Science Tradition: Principle, Practice and Challenge*. New York: Crossroads, 1991.

————. *Mary Baker Eddy: The Years of Trial*. Boston: Christian Science Publishing Society, 1971.

Putnam, Robert D. "The Strange Disappearance of Civic America," *The American Prospect* (winter 1996).

Quinlan, Sterling Red. *The Hundred Million Dollar Lunch: The Broadcasting Industry's Own Watergate*. Chicago: J. Philip O'Hara, 1974.

Reeves, Bryon, and Clifford Nass. *The Media Equation: How People Treat Computers, Television and New Media Like Real People and Places*. Stanford: CSLI Publications, Center for the Study of Language and Information, 1996.

Smith, Sally Bedell. *In All His Glory: The Life and Times of William S. Paley: The Legendary Tycoon and His Brilliant Circle*. New York: Touchstone, 1990.

Squires, James D. *Read All About It! The Corporate Takeover of America's Newspapers*. New York: Times Books, 1993.

Sterling, Christopher H. and John M. Kitross. *Stay Tuned: A Concise History of American Broadcasting*. 2d ed. Belmont, CA: Wadsworth, 1990.

Twain, Mark (Samuel L. Clemens). *Christian Science: With Notes Containing Corrections to Date*. New York: Harper and Brothers, 1899.

Underwood, Doug. *When MBAs Rule the Newsroom: How the Marketers and Managers Are Reshaping Today's Media*. New York: Columbia University Press, 1993.

Whittemore, Hank. *CNN: The Inside Story: How a Band of Mavericks Changed the Face of Television News*. Boston: Little, Brown, 1990.

Williams, Christian. *Lead, Follow or Get Out of the Way: The Story of Ted Turner*. New York: Times Books, 1981.

Index

About the Author

Susan Bridge is a Boston-based writer and consultant who has worked on the business side of television programming for fifteen years. She has taught political science at Wesleyan University and has worked in Europe and at the United Nations. She was educated at Wellesley, the Sorbonne, and at Yale.